Discounting, LIBOR, CVA and Funding

Discounting, LIBOR, CVA and Funding

Interest Rate and Credit Pricing

Chris Kenyon and Roland Stamm

First published 2012 by
PALGRAVE MACMILLAN

Palgrave Macmillan in the UK is an imprint of Macmillan Publishers Limited, registered in England, company number 785998, of Houndmills, Basingstoke, Hampshire RG21 6XS.

Palgrave Macmillan in the US is a division of St Martin's Press LLC, 175 Fifth Avenue, New York, NY 10010.

Palgrave Macmillan is the global academic imprint of the above companies and has companies and representatives throughout the world.

Palgrave® and Macmillan® are registered trademarks in the United States, the United Kingdom, Europe and other countries.

ISBN: 978–1–137–26851–8

This book is printed on paper suitable for recycling and made from fully managed and sustained forest sources. Logging, pulping and manufacturing processes are expected to conform to the environmental regulations of the country of origin.

A catalog record for this book is available from the British Library.

A catalog record for this book is available from the Library of Congress.

10 9 8 7 6 5 4 3 2 1
21 20 19 18 17 16 15 14 13 12

Printed and bound in Great Britain by
CPI Antony Rowe, Chippenham and Eastbourne

To Anabel and Leon

To Jeanne

Contents

Tables

Figures

Preface

NYM [Sheathing his sword] I shall have my noble?
PISTOL In cash most justly paid.
NYM [Shaking hands] Well, then, that's the humour of't.
Shakespeare, *Henry V*

One of the most basic yet also most important questions in the financial world is the worth of one currency unit in the future versus one unit now. The answer to this question provides the *discount curve* allowing payments at all future times to be compared and brought back to the present. Obviously, the answer will depend on the credit quality or riskiness of the person or company that promises you to pay you the EUR 1; you might trust a family member more to make good on the promise than a total stranger, or you trust your government more than your bank, and trust a car salesperson even less. Or maybe not.

Ideological debates aside, financial instruments traded on an exchange or through clearing houses are the least risky – from a credit perspective. This is because all participants have to post cash collateral to a margin account, and have to replenish this account on a daily basis if their position's value moves against them. The curve that is used to discount the outstanding future payments of such collateralized trades could therefore be considered a risk-free curve. The definition of a risk-free curve is important because it will be the benchmark against which the credit riskiness of future cash flows will be measured.

London, 17 June 2010
LCH.Clearnet Ltd (LCH.Clearnet), which operates the world's leading interest rate swap (IRS) clearing service, SwapClear, is to begin using the overnight index swap (OIS) rate curves to discount its $218 trillion IRS portfolio.

This quote demonstrates a fundamental change to the discount curve by a major clearing house for a vast quantity of derivatives, $0.2 *quadrillion*. Just as an example, as of November 29, 2010, the discount factor from an EONIA-based curve for December 01, 2020, was 2.75% as opposed to 3.104% from the standard 6 month EURIBOR curve. That's 35 basis points difference (p.a.!). Note that one basis point on a notional of $218 trillion is $21.8 billion.

How is it possible to disagree about such a fundamental building block in finance as the discount curve? What is this curve? What was the market using before? Will it change its mind again? Does this mean that all banks use this (and only this) curve for all purposes? We shall see that the answers to these questions usher in a new beginning for mathematical finance and the pricing of interest rate and credit derivatives.

The no-arbitrage principle ("there is no such thing as a free lunch") was and still is one of the foundations of financial pricing models. This principle is accompanied by two fundamental theorems:

1. A market is arbitrage free if and only if there is an equivalent martingale measure.
2. A market is complete if and only if this equivalent martingale measure is unique.

The famous Black–Scholes–Merton model is a simple result of this; so simple, in fact, that there were several major changes since its inception in 1973:

1. **emergence of the volatility smile** in 1987 with the Wall Street Crash;
2. **implicit disregard for no-arbitrage** with the widespread adoption of stochastic volatility models to fit observed volatility smiles around 1997–2002 (these models are incomplete-market models; e.g., typically the volatility of the volatility cannot be hedged with liquid instruments);
3. **complete abandonment of no-arbitrage** in the structured credit markets with the adoption of copula-based Collateraized Debt Obligation (CDO) pricing around 2001. Also compounded by using CDO pricing models depending on unobservable parameters with **no** tradable market quotes at all, e.g. recovery rates and correlations. This is even before considering stochastic or dynamic models.
4. **liquidity and credit become significant** this is the current state, where LIBOR fixings can no longer be predicted from discount curves, and the market is changing from quotes-on-spreads to quote-by-price (e.g. the ISDA (International Swaps and Derivatives Association) CDS Big Bang in April 2009) for many instruments because institutions cannot agree on which discount curve to use.
5. **Basel III** a direct consequence of the previous point, regulation now has a significant impact on trading – starting even before its implementation date of 1st January, 2013.

We mention one common misunderstanding at this point. The fact that hedging produces unique prices, even under incomplete markets, makes some people think that incompleteness is only a minor distraction. The hedging statement is true but applies only to *attainable* claims (instruments that can be priced by hedging). The problem is that even very simple products, such as European options, may be un-attainable (see chapter 11 of [Shreve (2004)] for a nice exposition and [Cont and Tankov (2003)] for more depth). No-arbitrage then only gives bounds on prices, and these can be too wide to be useful. Although this book is not about incomplete markets, the fact that real markets are generally incomplete is a significant practical limitation.

At the extremes, many of the Black–Scholes–Merton assumptions have always been broken – but before 2007 the general view was that this could be safely ignored. The financial and sovereign debt crises of 2007–2012 did away with the assumption that market players could borrow and lend freely at the riskless rate. Nowadays, the question of where to get the funding from and whether one has to post collateral in order to get it is paramount. The new mantra therefore is **"funding, funding, funding"**.

This text aims to rebuild interest rate product pricing and credit product pricing for the new world in which bankers, and everyone else, now live. Funding and default risk are no longer quiet niches but central to pricing. We shall also see that there is no longer a Law of One Price: depending on what it costs an institution to borrow, or which currency it runs its business in, it will see prices that are different from its peers'. Collateralization, once considered the end of all pricing arguments, has been broken by the simple question "but where do you get the collateral from?" This has been reinforced by the US Dodd–Frank Wall Street Reform and Consumer Protection Act of 2010 which even discourages rehypothecation, i.e. using received collateral from one party as collateral for a second party. We provide the state of the art, in practice, from practicing bankers and theoreticians who have to answer these questions every day.

Readers should be aware that Mathematical Finance in the post-crisis world has changed at every level of complexity. For yield curve building (now discount and LIBOR curves) the complexity is limited as the techniques are relatively straightforward (at least in common cases). When we start to price with the new curves we immediately get into measure changes and FX analogies. When calculating the credit value adjustment (CVA), we find that now even linear instruments, like vanilla swaps, acquire option-like characteristics (a swap with an uncollater-alized counterparty is a sold option on the right to default). Taking one's own credit riskiness into account by calculating the debit value adjustment (DVA) as well, one allows both parties to have options. One redeeming feature of CVA and DVA is that default is not exercised like an American option, i.e. intelligently or economically, to maximise the value of individual derivatives, but simply as a contingent event. Then we see that careful consideration of closeout and funding means that pricing becomes recursive. If all this were not enough, when we look at the firm-level we see effects that involve the whole balance sheet.

Because of the above, the required level of mathematical background varies in this text. For the first six chapters, a good basic knowledge of mathematics is sufficient; the few differential equations shining up here and there can be safely ignored. Chapters 7 through 11, how-ever, require a thorough understanding of interest rate models such as the Hull–White model and LIBOR Market Models as described in [Brigo and Mercurio (2006)], and the mathematics underlying them, at least at the level of [Shreve (2004)].

Here is a brief outline of the book. Chapter 1 is a reminder of the basic terminology and details of the interest rate markets, as well as the "old school" approach of pricing simple interest rate products. Chapter 2 explains how to build a zero/discount curve from market data.

After the introduction to credit instruments and associated terminol-ogy, Chapter 3 presents the most relevant definitions of credit spreads and the instruments associated with them, their market risk, and the connections between them.

Leaving the credit spreads behind, Chapter 4 introduces the prob-lems with the old way of pricing that arose with the credit crisis in 2008. The basis spreads, formerly almost irrelevant phenomena in the inter-est rate markets, became a new source of market risk as well as pricing complexity. Their impact on curve building and pricing is investigated in Chapter 5, which describes what happens in a one-currency world, and Chapter 6 which makes the jump to foreign currencies. To close the topic of basis spreads, Chapter 7 presents what needs to be done for non-linear products, i.e. products that contain optional components.

The next two chapters are concerned with CVA, and its cousins DVA and funding value adjustment (FVA). While Chapter 8 gives an overview of the current state of research in this area, Chapter 9 presents strong evidence that the common view of DVA giving rise to profits if one's own credit quality deteriorates is false when the bank's balance sheet as a whole is considered. Firm-level effects may appear to be only paper or accounting realities, but they have real effects. If your balance sheet says that your equity is below its regulatory threshold then there are firm-level consequences. Furthermore, regulators decided to introduce the CVA volatility capital charge as a direct consequence of CVA losses in the 2008 crisis. The fact that trading realities are not accounting realities creates tensions for trading desks.

Moving on to Basel III, Chapter 10, the cry is not "funding, funding, funding", but **"capital, capital, capital"**. Basel III brings in a host of innovations, the first of which to hit significantly is the capital charge for CVA volatility. Note that Basel III does not require the pricing in of CVA (or DVA or FVA), but *changes* in CVA. The choice facing traders is now whether to pay a capital charge for their position or buy credit protection (e.g. via not very liquid contingent credit default swaps, or CCDS). This is already reshaping the trading business of banks *as it was intended to*. Quants cannot ignore the effect, whether or not they only see it as a change in their funding costs.

Finally, Chapter 11 is on backtesting of risk factor equations (RFEs). Capital charges for trading desks are calculated from counterparty exposure profiles per legally enforceable netting set. Basel III insists that banks may only use one exposure profile for both default charge and the CVA volatility charge. These, traditionally, *have been* related to fundamentally different concepts: historical default versus market-implied credit valuation adjustment (which *must* be calculated using market CDS spreads). Exposure profiles depend on the future development of underlying risk factors (e.g. discount curves, market-implied swaption volatilities, etc.). Basel III explicitly permits calibration of RFEs to either historical data, or market-implied. However these RFEs are calibrated they must pass *historical* backtesting. We present a Basel III inspired framework for this historical backtesting that can be applied however RFEs are calibrated, paying special attention to the case where all available models fail.

A lot of the material in this book is not new. However, there are a few exceptions: details of hedge accounting with respect to multiple curves, in Chapter 6; the derivation of a two-factor short rate model in a discount + spread curve environment within Chapter 7; most of the results for CVA at the firm level in Chapter 9; and the backtesting framework in Chapter 11.

The authors acknowledge the continuing inspiration of the financial and sovereign debt crises of 2007–2012, the front-row seats provided by their employer (in the case of CK, former employer), Hypo Real Estate Group (now nationalized, split up, and rebranded), and the generosity of the German government for more than €100 billion of funding: to the bank – not the authors.

London, April 2012   *Dr Chris Kenyon*
Mainz, April 2012   *Dr Roland Stamm*

Acknowledgments

This work would not have been possible without the contributions and support of the following people: Sarp Kaya Acar, Klaus Böcker, Melanie Ilg, Kalina Natcheva-Acar, Adam Snieg, Ralf Werner, and especially Isabel Stamm. In addition, Chris Kenyon would like to acknowledge the contributions and support of: Ronnie Barnes, Prof Damiano Brigo, Donal Gallagher. Chris Kenyon would also like to thank Fabrizio Anfuso and Prof. Ser-huang Poon for numerous discussions on the practical applications of the material in Chapter 11 which made many details clearer. Contribution and support does not imply, of course, agreement with the expressed opinions of the authors – and any errors remain the responsibility of the authors.

The authors are also grateful to the following professional training conference organizers for invitations to present material from the latter chapters (particularly Chapter 9 and Chapter 11), and to the participants for their feedback:

- Marcus Evans: 2nd Annual CVA and Counterparty Risk, January 2011, London
- RISK Magazine: Measuring and Controlling Model Risk, October 2011, London
- WBS Training: Discounting & Funding: Interest Rates, CVA & Counterparty Risk, November 2011, London
- WBS Training: The CVA Conference: Implementation, Trading, Liquidity, Modelling & Funding, March 2012, London

Disclaimer

The views and opinions expressed in this book are those of the authors and are not those of their employers, either present or former, subsidiaries or affiliate companies ("the Banks"). Accordingly, the Banks do not accept any liability over the content of this book or any claims, losses, or damages arising from the use of, or reliance on, all or any part of this book. Nothing in this book is or should be taken as information regarding, or a description of, any operations or business practice of the Banks. Similarly, nothing in this book should be taken as information regarding any failure or shortcomings within the business, credit or risk or other control, or assessment procedures within the Banks.

Use at your own risk. Not guaranteed fit for any purpose.

1
Back to the Basics

SHYLOCK Three thousand ducats, well.
BASSANIO Ay, sir, for three months.
SHYLOCK For three months, well.
Shakespeare, *The Merchant of Venice*.

This chapter is meant to refresh the reader's memory about the pre-crisis valuation standards. For an excellent introduction to the topic, see, for instance, [Hull (2009)]. As this text is meant to be used in practice, a lot of emphasis is put on the nitty-gritty details that are often ignored in other books.

1.1 Interest rates

1.1.1 LIBOR

Interest is the price someone has to pay for borrowing money. The interest usually depends on the maturity of the loan as well as the creditworthiness of the borrower. The latter is influenced by the borrower's (projected) liquidity situation and her available assets. Creditworthiness is improved if collateral is posted to the lender. This collateral can be a lien in the case of a mortgage, bonds or shares, commodities like precious metals, or even cash.

One particularly important market in the financial world is the money market, where banks lend each other cash or borrow it from the central bank. Maturities in the money market are typically up to one year. Although the rate at which two banks enter into a loan is always negotiated individually and changes arbitrarily over time, there is the concept of an average rate which is fixed once on a daily basis. This Interbank Offer Rate is called EURIBOR in the EUR market, LIBOR for all currencies that are traded on the money market in London, and by some similar name for local rates, like STIBOR for the SEK rate fixed in Stockholm, for instance. We will refer to any of these as LIBOR in what follows. The rates are fixed for many different maturities, starting with overnight (ON), one week, one month, and then monthly up to one year. The most important ones – because they are most often used as basis tenors – are overnight, three months and six months. A lot of interest rates are directly linked to a LIBOR rate. Such loans or bonds are called floating rate loans/bonds or floaters for short, and they pay LIBOR plus a predetermined spread which expresses the credit quality of the borrower. We will come back to the spread later.

For maturities longer than one year, banks as well as other major market participants – like sovereign countries, sub-sovereigns like states, regions, or municipalities and large corporates – have to find other means of raising money. The most liquid way of doing that is by issuing bonds in the capital market which pay a fixed interest rate on a regular basis, e.g. annually or semi-annually.

1.1.2 Day count conventions

Interest rates are always quoted per annum. If an interest period is shorter than a year, the amount due has to be calculated from the rate and the *day count fraction* of the period, which we will denote by $\tau_{s,t}$ for a period starting in s and ending in t throughout the text. This fraction is calculated by using a day count convention and dividing the counted days by the number of days in a year associated with the convention. There are more than a dozen day count conventions, but below are the most important ones, together with an example calculation for the period September 12, 2011 to March 14, 2012:

- 30/360: the number of days in the interest period on the basis of a year of 360 days with twelve 30-day months, divided by 360. Note: all months have a length of 30 days in this convention, even February. This is most commonly used for bonds. The day count fraction is $182/360 = 0.505556$.
- ACT/360: the actual number of days in the interest period, divided by 360. Most commonly used in the money market in EUR and USD, for instance. The day count fraction is $184/360 = 0.51111$.
- ACT/365: the actual number of days in the interest period, divided by 365. Used in the GBP money market. The day count fraction is $184/365 = 0.50411$.
- ACT/ACT (ISDA): the number of days in the interest period that fall into a leap year divided by 366 plus the number of days that

fall outside of a leap year divided by 365. The day count fraction is $110/365 + 74/366 = 0.503556$.

- ACT/ACT (ISMA): 1 divided by the number of coupons paid per year. The day count fraction is 0.5 if it is just one interest period.

As payments for long-term contracts are normally scheduled to happen on a certain date periodically, like the 15th of September every year, payment dates regularly fall on weekends or holidays. As money cannot be exchanged on such dates, a date roll convention describes when to make the payment, either the next or the previous business day (*following* and *preceding*, resp.). A multi-currency trade that pays interest in two or more different currencies that are fixed in yet another country can easily have three or even more calendars attached to it that are needed to predict the correct payment dates.

If a date needs to be rolled, the exact interest amount also depends on whether the roll impacts the period length or not. For bonds, it usually doesn't; in the money market, it usually does.

All these details may seem irrelevant for quick calculations and the computation of long-term risk figures, but they are very important when it comes to the actual handling of trades. They are also relevant when computing the short-term liquidity risk of a position, because the liquidity management of a bank has to know the exact dates of any in- and out-flows.

1.1.3 Accrued interest and spot

If a bond is bought or sold in the middle of an interest period, the seller has to be compensated for the interest that has accrued since the beginning of the period, as the buyer will receive the full coupon at the end of the interest period. Also, daily profit and loss (P&L) calculations include the accrued interest of all outstanding contracts. In both cases, the interest is assumed to accrue linearly over time. There are exceptions to this rule, for instance for zero bonds which accrue interest exponentially on a daily basis. Again, the day count convention is relevant when calculating the accrual; for instance, it happens under 30/360 that the 31st of a month does not accrue interest since a month is assumed to have 30 days.

If the accrual was included in the bond prices in the market, prices would follow a saw-tooth pattern even if market conditions did not change at all. Therefore, bond prices quoted in the market are always *clean prices*, i.e. excluding accrued interest. The price that has to be actually paid on delivery is the *dirty price*.

Most prices that are quoted in the market refer to an exchange in the near future, on the *value date*, depending on the market segment. The business days in between are the *spot period*. For instance, in the EUR market, all money market and derivatives contracts start two business days after they were struck. The exceptions are overnight or tomorrow/next money market trades. For bonds in the EUR market, the spot period is three business days. The date the bonds change owner is called the *settlement date*. The GBP market, on the other hand, has no spot period. Note also that the LIBOR fixings that were mentioned above always refer to a money market deal starting in spot days (except overnight fixings, of course). When dealing with multi-currency trades, like, for instance, cross-currency swaps (see Section 1.3.2), it may happen that the spot convention for a currency is not the standard one.

1.1.4 Zero rates and discounting

The most important tool for pricing future cash flows is the curve of zero rates. It translates into the discount curve, which in turn tells us today's worth of one currency unit at any future time.

A zero bond is a bond that pays no interest but just pays back the notional amount at maturity. Obviously, an investor in this bond will not have to pay the notional amount at inception but some price $P < 1$. So another view of a zero bond is that of a bond with notional P that pays interest $1 - P$ at maturity. This is supported by the so-called pull to par: as time approaches the maturity date of the zero bond, its price moves to 1, despite changes in the interest rate or credit environment. Be aware, though, that these changes do not necessarily make the pull to par a monotonic move. This means that someone selling the bond before maturity wants to have an equivalent of accrued interest as compensation.

The zero rate $r(t)$ for time $t > 0$ is the yield of a zero bond starting today ($t = 0$, no spot period) and ending in t. It is usually assumed that this zero bond compounds interest continuously, i.e. if one currency unit is invested today, it pays out $e^{r(t)t}$ at time t. On the other hand, this tells us that the value of one currency unit at time t is worth $d_t = e^{-r(t)t}$ today (assuming an actual/actual type of day count fraction), the *discount factor* for time t. The discount factor is nothing else but the price of a zero bond paying out 1 at time t. If the compounding is not done continuously, the translation between $r(t)$ and d_t is different, but the concept remains exactly the same. Other standards for compounding are:

linearly: in particular in the money market, where maturities are below one year, the compounding is done linearly. That means that the borrower pays $1 + rt$ at maturity, where $t <= 1$ is the term of the loan (in years) and r is the interest rate.

simply: fixed payments are sometimes simply compounded, which means that the payment at maturity is $(1 + r)^t$.

Now, given a set of cash flows $c(t_i), i = 1, \ldots, n$, we can compute their *present value* as

$$V = \sum_{i=1}^{n} c(t_i) d_{t_i}. \tag{1.1}$$

Given a set of bond prices for bonds of different maturities, it is possible to strip a zero rate curve from these prices. Note, however, that these bonds should all be of the same credit quality and liquidity class. Even then, the resulting curve may look bumpy.

1.2 Interest rate derivatives

1.2.1 FRAs and swaps

From cash instruments we move on to simple interest rate derivatives. A *forward rate agreement*, or FRA for short, is a contract in which two parties agree today $(t = 0)$ on an interest rate $f(t_1, t_2)$ for a period t_1 to t_2 that lies in the future (beyond spot). The payer will pay that interest rate at t_2. If the LIBOR $L(t_1, t_2)$ fixing in t_1 for that period is above $f(t_1, t_2)$, the payer has saved the excess amount; if it is lower, she has lost the difference. It is therefore also common to just exchange the t_1 value of the difference in t_1 without exchanging any notionals. This value is given by $(L(t_1, t_2) - f(t_1, t_2)) d_{t_2}$, where the discount factor d_{t_2} is the one seen at t_1.

The fair rate is the one which makes the contract worth zero at inception. To calculate this from the zero rates, one uses the following replication argument: Borrowing 1 from $t = 0$ to t_1 at $r(t_1)$, repaying and borrowing again $e^{r(t_1)t_1}$ at $f(t_1, t_2)$ is the same as borrowing 1 at $r(t_2)$ from $t = 0$ to t_2. Otherwise, an arbitrageur would go and borrow money in one contract and deposit it in the other without any risk. This makes the assumption that one (or at least large banks) can borrow and deposit at the same rates in arbitrary amounts, and that the risk involved in a derivative (like an FRA) is the same as in a cash position. The argument leads to the following formula for the fair forward rate:

$$e^{r(t_1)t_1} e^{f(t_1, t_2) \tau_{t_1, t_2}} = e^{r(t_2)t_2}.$$

where τ_{t_1,t_2} is the period length between times t_1 and t_2 in years.

Now, the forward periods are usually shorter than one year, which implies that the interest is not continuously but linearly compounding, i.e. the notional plus interest paid at the end of the forward period is $1 + f^{lc}(t_1,t_2)\tau_{t_1,t_2}$. This means that the linearly compounding forward rate is given by

$$f^{lc}(t_1,t_2) = \frac{1}{\tau_{t_1,t_2}} \frac{d_{t_1} - d_{t_2}}{d_{t_2}}, \qquad (1.2)$$

and that is the forward rate we shall use in what follows.

Note that because of Equation (1.2), a bond paying LIBOR with the matching frequency is always worth *par*, i.e. the face value or notional, on each fixing date (this is only true if the bond has the same credit quality as the instruments from which the LIBOR curve was built). The intuitive reason is that it always pays the fair coupon in each period. Mathematically,

$$V = d_s - \sum_{i=1}^{n} f^{lc}(t_{i-1},t_i)\tau_{t_{i-1},t_i}d_{t_i} - d_{t_n} = d_s - \sum_{i=1}^{n}(d_{t_{i-1}} - d_{t_i}) - d_{t_n} = d_s,$$

where s is the settlement date. As the notional of 1 changes hands on the settlement date and not today, we have to discount from s to today by using d_s.

An interest rate swap or swap for short is a contract in which two parties agree to exchange (swap) two sets of cash flows. The simple version, usually referred to as a plain vanilla swap, has party A (the *payer*) paying a fixed rate c, expressed as a per annum interest rate on a given notional, on a regular basis, and party B (the *receiver*) paying LIBOR on a regular basis on the same notional. The standard payment frequency for fixed legs is annually in EUR and GBP, and semi-annually in USD, for instance; for floating legs, it is semi-annually in EUR and GBP, and quarterly in USD. The fixed rate is chosen in such a manner that the contract is worth zero at inception. These fair swap rates or *par rates* are quoted in the market for a manifold of currencies and maturities. They always refer to a swap starting at spot.

To value such a swap, we can discount the fixed flows using Equation (1.1). The floating leg of the swap is priced using Equation (1.2). Thus, the value of the swap from the receiver's point of view is

$$V = c \sum_{i=1}^{n} \tau_{t_{i-1},t_i} d_{t_i} - \sum_{j=1}^{m} \frac{1}{\tau_{t'_{j-1},t'_j}} \frac{d_{t'_{j-1}} - d_{t'_j}}{d_{t'_j}} \tau_{t'_{j-1},t'_j} d_{t'_j}$$

$$= c \sum_{i=1}^{n} \tau_{t_{i-1},t_i} d_{t_i} - \sum_{j=1}^{m} d_{t'_{j-1}} - d_{t'_j}$$

$$= c \sum_{i=1}^{n} \tau_{t_{i-1},t_i} d_{t_i} - (d_{t'_0} - d_{t'_m}). \qquad (1.3)$$

Note that we use different points in time for the floating and the fixed legs of the swap, resp., because the cash flows in general happen at different times and with different frequencies. However, $t'_0 = t_0$ is the starting date of the swap, and $t'_m = t_n$ the last payment date.

The condition that $V = 0$ in Equation (1.3) at inception forces the fair swap rate c to be

$$c = \frac{d_{t'_0} - d_{t'_m}}{\sum_{i=1}^{n} \tau_{t_{i-1},t_i} d_{t_i}}.$$

The expression $A(t_0, t_n) = \sum \tau_{t_{i-1},t_i} d_{t_i}$ in the denominator is called the *annuity factor* (of the fixed leg of the swap).

If we artificially introduce a notional exchange of 1 at the beginning and the end of the swap, we can view the swap as an exchange of two bonds, one paying a fixed rate, the other paying a floating rate. The floating rate bond is worth par at inception. Therefore, if the fixed rate is chosen to make the swap worth zero, the fixed rate bond must be worth par as well, hence the expression par rate for the fair swap rate.

Another interesting and important type of swap is an overnight-indexed swap (OIS). An OIS exchanges the overnight rate (accumulated over quarterly, semiannual, or annual periods) against a fixed rate. The name for OIS varies in different countries: EONIA (EUR overnight interest average) in Euroland, SONIA (Sterling overnight interest average) in the UK, etc.

1.2.2 Caps, floors, and swaptions

There are two types of very basic options in the interest rate world: caps and floors, which are series of options on LIBOR, and swaptions, which are options on swaps.

A caplet is a call option to exchange LIBOR for a future period t_1 to t_2 against the strike rate at the end t_2 of the period. In other words, party A buys from party B the right to receive LIBOR and to pay the predetermined rate K. This will only be exercised if LIBOR is above K, so the payoff at time t_2 is $\max(0, L(t_1) - K)$. A cap is a series of caplets for a number of consecutive periods. A floorlet is a put option with the payoff $\max(0, K - L(t_1)) = -\min(0, L(t_1) - K)$, and a floor is a series of consecutive floorlets. Note that the difference of the payoffs of a caplet and a floorlet for the same period and at the same strike is just the payoff of an FRA, which yields a put-call parity for caplets:

$$V(cl(t_1, t_2, K)) - V(fl(t_1, t_2, K)) = (f(t_1, t_2) - K)\tau_{t_1, t_2} d_{t_2}$$
$$= d_{t_1} - d_{t_2} - K\tau_{t_1, t_2} d_{t_2}.$$

The strike is called *at the money* (ATM) if the put-call parity for that strike is zero, i.e. K is the fair forward rate.

For a cap (resp. floor) the ATM strike is defined in what seems to be a more complicated way because the strike is the same for all periods, whereas the ATM strikes of the individual caplets are different. A cap's strike is ATM if the cap has the same value as the floor with the same strike (which is then also ATM). Note that the difference of a cap and a floor can be viewed as a swap whose fixed and float legs have the same periods; the ATM strike of a cap is the strike that makes this swap worth zero. That is why some textbooks claim that the ATM strike of a cap is the par rate. This is only true if Equation (1.3) is valid; if the sum of the float leg payments collapses, we do not need to distinguish between different tenors.

Caplets are priced using a version of the Black–Scholes formula. Under the right measure, the t_2-forward measure, which is associated with the numeraire of the price of the zero bond maturing in t_2, the process of the forward rate $f(t; t_1, t_2)$ becomes a martingale and is assumed to follow a geometric Brownian motion with constant volatility σ:

$$df(t; t_1, t_2) = \sigma f(t; t_1, t_2) dW^{t_2}(t).$$

This can be solved explicitly to give the price

$$V(t) = d_{t_2}\tau_{t_1,1_2}(f(t; t_1, t_2)\Phi(d_1) - K\Phi(d_2)), \tag{1.4}$$

where

$$d_1 = \frac{\ln(f(t; t_1, t_2)/K) + \sigma^2 \tau_{t,t_1}/2}{\sigma}, \quad d_2 = d_1 - \sigma\tau_{t,t_1},$$

and Φ is the standard normal cumulative distribution function. The value of a cap is then just the sum of the values of its individual caplets.

A (European) swaption is an option to enter into a swap contract at one future date, the *expiry date*. As there are two sides in a swap, there are two variants of swaptions: a payer resp. receiver swaption in which the option owner has the right to enter into a swap paying resp. receiving the strike in return for LIBOR rates. The difference between a payer and a receiver swaption with the same strikes is a forward starting swap. A swaption is ATM if the strike makes the underlying swap fair.

The option holder will exercise a payer swaption if the market swap rate c at expiry is higher than the strike rate K of the option. This means that the payoff of the swaption is

$$\max\left(0, (c-K)\sum_{i=1}^{n}\tau_{t_{i-1},t_i}d_{t_i}\right) = \max(0, (c-K)A(t_0, t_n)).$$

Swaptions are also priced with a Black–Scholes-like formula. Again, under the right measure – this time the one associated with the annuity factor numeraire – the process of the forward swap rate $c(t; t_0, t_n)$ becomes a martingale and is assumed to follow a geometric Brownian motion with constant volatility v:

$$dc(t; t_0, t_n) = vc(t; t_0, t_n)\, dW^A(t).$$

As before, this can be solved explicitly to give the price

$$V(t) = A(t; t_0, t_n)(c(t; t_0, t_n)\Phi(e_1) - K\Phi(e_2)), \tag{1.5}$$

where

$$d_1 = \frac{\ln(c(t; t_0, t_n)/K) + v^2\tau_{t,t_0}/2}{v}, \quad d_2 = d_1 - v\tau_{t,t_0}.$$

A Bermudan swaption is a swaption with several exercise dates (however, you can only exercise once). These are far more complex to value than European swaptions because you get a different swap at each exercise date.

1.2.3 Basis swaps

A basis swap is an exchange of two cash flows, both of which are linked to a LIBOR rate, but of different tenors. A typical example would be a swap that exchanges 3-month EURIBOR against 6-month EURIBOR. By introducing notional exchanges at inception and maturity artificially, it is immediate that the basis swap is nothing else but the exchange of two floating rate notes which are both worth par. In the pre-crisis world, this was almost true; there was a very small spread (in the range of 0.5 to 1.5 basis points) that had to be added to the leg with the shorter tenor to make the swap fair. This used to be small enough to be safely ignored.

1.3 FX and cross-currency trades

1.3.1 FX forwards

In a spot foreign exchange (FX) trade, two parties exchange two amounts in two different currencies, at the spot market rate. If the exchange happens further in the future than just the spot date, it becomes an FX derivative called an FX forward. A simple no-arbitrage argument allows the calculation of the forward FX rate: exchange now and receive interest in the foreign currency later is the same as accumulate interest first and exchange later. Mathematically, for d_t and d_t^f the discount factors in the local and the foreign currency, resp., and $X(0)$ and $X(t)$ the spot and the forward FX rate, resp., we must have:

$$X(0)\frac{1}{d_t^f} = \frac{1}{d_t}X(t) \Leftrightarrow X(t) = X(0)\frac{d_t}{d_t^f}.$$

1.3.2 Cross-currency swaps

A cross-currency swap is a contract in which two parties agree to exchange cash flows in two different currencies. The market standard is to exchange two notionals in two different currencies at the prevailing FX rate (or forward FX rate for a forward starting swap), then pay LIBOR-based interest, and at maturity swap back the notional amounts at the same FX rate. For example, if the spot FX rate between EUR and USD is 1.36, party A might pay 1 EUR and receive 1.36 USD at inception, pay USD LIBOR and receive EURIBOR quarterly, and finally receive 1 EUR in exchange for 1.36 USD at final maturity. Theoretically, the construction just described must be worth zero at inception, because the two parties just exchange floating rate notes in two different currencies, which are therefore worth par in their respective currency, at the prevailing exchange rate. However, even pre-crisis there was a non-zero cross-currency basis which is quoted in the market as basis points per annum that have to be added to one of the swap legs to make the swap fair. This was always a bit of an embarrassment for the text books, and was ignored on the basis that the spread was usually small.

2
Bootstrapping of Zero Curves

Errors are not in the art but in the artificers.
Isaac Newton

This chapter gives a practical introduction to bootstrapping a zero curve from existing market data. It is important to understand that apart from the money market segment, where actual zero rates are quoted, the market only states that certain instruments (forwards and swaps) are fair if the quoted rate is used. It does *not* quote discount factors or zero rates for longer maturities.

To get a zero curve from market data, usually two or three types of market data are used. These are the money market rates up to 12 months and the swap rates, and possibly futures or forward rates. Since the basis effect forces us to strip a curve from tenor-consistent instruments only, we focus on forwards, as these are available in all relevant tenors (at least for major currencies). Furthermore, no convexity adjustment is necessary as is the case for futures, see [Hull (2009)] p. 139. Finally, the fixed roll dates of futures can cause substantial irregularities in the resulting zero curves, especially shortly before a rollover. As an example, consider the EURIBOR curve on September8, 2010. Figure 2.1 shows the forwards generated from two different curves: one built using futures, the other built from forwards. As can be seen, we get negative forwards on the curve built from futures; this (incorrect) effect does not occur on the other curve. It is caused by the rollover effect from futures as the shortest futures contract approaches expiry. Another reason for the problem is the tenor mismatch of the instruments which are used to build the curve. Finally, the tenor of the forwards does not match either of the curve-building instruments. On these last two points, see Chapter 4.

The advantage of using futures is that they are extremely liquid, at least for shorter maturities.

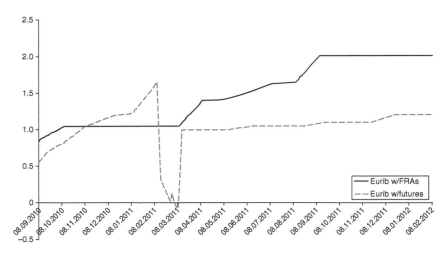

Figure 2.1   1-month forward rates for EURIBOR as of September 8, 2010.

2.1   Money market rates

Money market rates are usually quoted with a basis of Actual/360 or Actual/365, depending on the currency used and the market one is looking at. It is obviously important to know which one is used; a difference of 5 days out of 365 is a relative change of almost 1.4%. In the following text we focus on EURIBOR which is quoted with an A360 basis, so we use this consistently throughout the text without further mention. Now one would expect to start with, e.g., the 1M rate r_{1M} and calculate the discount factor as $\frac{1}{1+r_{1M} \cdot n/360}$, where n is the number of days in the following month. Unfortunately, money market trades, and actually forwards and swaps as well, usually start with a spot lag of two business days, which means that this approach would be neglecting the discounting for these two business days. Note that the spot lag may be different in some markets; in GBP, for instance, the spot lag is 0. The solution is to use overnight and tomorrow/next rates for the first two days and then successively use the money market rates. This means that one uses the overnight rate r_{ON} as described, that is the discount factor for tomorrow $d_{1D} = \frac{1}{1+r_{ON}/360}$, the one for spot is $d_{2D} = d_{1D} \cdot \frac{1}{1+r_{TN}/360}$, and after that you always have $d_t = d_{2D} \cdot \frac{1}{1+r_t \cdot n_t/360}$, where t is 1W, 2W, 1M, etc. and n_t is the number of days until the end of the period.

Once a discount factor is found for a given date, one can calculate zero rates until that date. The zero rates are usually interpreted

Table 2.1 Bootstrapping the money market rates

Maturity	Rate	Days	Discount Factor	Formula	Zero Rate
1D	2.065	1	0.999942642	1/(1+2.065/36000)	2.09362051
2D	2.065	2	0.999885288	1/(1+2.065/36000) × 0.999942642	2.09362051
3D	2.065	5	0.999713254	1/(1+2.065×(5−2)/36000) ×0.999885288	2.093548463
1W	2.065	9	0.999483967	1/(1+2.065×(9−2)/36000) ×0.999885288	2.093340372
2W	2.065	16	0.999082969	1/(1+2.065×(16−2)/36000) ×0.999885288	2.092937856
3W etc.	2.09	23	0.998667745	1/(1+2.09×(23−2)/36000) ×0.999885288	2.115640008

as continuously compounding, i.e., the interest paid after time t is e^{rt}. However, the calculation of a zero rate again needs a decision on which day count convention to use. The standard choice is Actual/365.

The process is shown in Table 2.1.

The use of cash rates in the curve-building process is certainly questionable if the resulting curve is supposed to be used for pricing derivatives, as the cash rates contain the credit risk premium which is superfluous for collateralized derivatives. One might instead consider using OIS rates as the short end instruments of choice as these are considered risk free. However, a separate money market curve is then needed to price actual cash trades.

2.2 Forward rates

Like money market and swap rates, forward rates are quoted with a spot start date in most countries. Forwards can be used to bridge the gap between money market and swap rates, which is usually between 1 and 1.5 years long. Assume we have a forward whose interest rate period starts before but ends after the maturity of the longest money market rate we want to use. For instance, looking at a 6-month EURIBOR curve, we'd use the MM rates up to 6-months, and now use a 6 month forward starting in 1 month to find the 7-month point on the zero curve. In general, we have a forward starting in t_1, for which we have a zero rate r_1, and maturing in t_2, with a forward rate f_{t_1,t_2} from which we want to derive the zero rate r_2. As forwards are quoted as simply compounding, annual interest rates, we have the following formula if r_1 and r_2 are also simply compounding:

$$(1+\tau_{t_0,t_1}r_1)(1+\tau_{t_1,t_2}f_{t_1,t_2}) = 1+\tau_{t_0,t_2}r_2,$$

where $\tau_{s,t}$ denotes the length of the interest period in years. This is easily solved for r_2:

$$r_2 = ((1+\tau_{t_0,t_1}r_1)(1+\tau_{t_1,t_2}f_{t_1,t_2})-1)/\tau_{t_0,t_2}.$$

If the r_i are continuously compounding, the formula for r_2 becomes:

$$r_2 = (\tau_{t_0,t_1}r_1 + \ln(1+\tau_{t_1,t_2}f_{t_1,t_2}))/\tau_{t_0,t_2}.$$

2.3 Swap rates

The swap rates can be considered as par yields because they express the fair value of a fixed rate bond against a floater which is (at least on the fixing date of each period) always worth par, at least, if the tenor of the floater is the same as the tenor of the floating rate leg of the swaps from which the curve is built (for other tenors, the basis spreads come into play: see Section 4.1 and following). This means that the formula to calculate a discount factor is given by

$$1 = \sum_{i=1}^{n-1} c \cdot d_i \cdot \tau_{t_{i-1},t_i} + (c \cdot \tau_{t_{n-1},t_n}+1) \cdot d_n,$$

where the notional is 1, c is the fair swap rate, and d_i is short for d_{t_i}. This leads to the inductive calculation of d_n as

$$d_n = \frac{1-\sum_{i=1}^{n-1} c \cdot d_i \cdot \tau_{t_{i-1},t_i}}{c \cdot \tau_{t_{n-1},t_n}+1}. \tag{2.1}$$

As an example, take the 2Y swap rate on December 8, 2004 which was 2.454. This leads to two coupon payments, one of 2.467633333 in 369 days, one of 2.4471833 in 733 days (because the first period has 362, the second one 359 days in a 30/360 basis, and the swap starts with 2 days' spot lag). This leads to the discount factor

$$d_{733} = \frac{100 - 2.467633333 \cdot 0.977562114}{102.4471833} = 0.952566308.$$

Note that the 1Y discount factor was derived from the 12M money market rate, which is not what one would actually do since the crisis.

2.4 Interpolation issues

Instead of using fair swap rates, one can use other bond prices. However, one should be aware that these have to have the same credit seniority as collateralized swaps in order to prevent credit effects from disturbing the zero curve. An example might be secured funding like a Pfandbrief. Since a given live bond also usually does not sell at par, the formula to calculate the next discount factor has to be adjusted accordingly. Furthermore, the coupons are not necessarily constant, and redemption might be different from 1. This is reflected in the formula below. It is an easy exercise to also incorporate amortizations.

$$\text{dirty price} = \sum_{i=1}^{n-1} r_i \cdot df_i + (r_n + R) \cdot df_n.$$

Note that even bonds from the same issuer do not necessarily give a well-behaved curve. The following factors influence the liquidity of the bond and hence its bid–ask spread as well as its price:

Issuance date: bonds freshly issued create a higher demand than those that have been issued a while ago

Volume: the higher the volume of the issuance, the higher the liquidity

Coupon: the higher the coupon, the higher the demand for a bond (compared to another bond of the same maturity, but with a lower coupon).

Thus, it may happen that bonds of the same maturity and by the same issuer give different discount factors. Of course, all of the above are only valid when the issuer in question is not (seen by the market as being) in distress.

Another problem with using live bonds is that usually their coupon dates do not match the dates for which discount factors are already available. This means that some interpolation has to be done to find matching discount factors. Although there are obviously many possible methods, one of the simplest is described here.

Suppose you want to calculate the discount factor for date t_0 which lies between two dates t_1 and t_2 for which we have the discount factors df_1 and df_2 respectively. Then one does not linearly interpolate the discount factors directly but rather goes through the zero rates and interpolates there:

$$r_i = -\frac{\ln d_i}{t_i}, \, i = 1, 2 \text{ and}$$

$$r_0 = r_1 \frac{t_2 - t_0}{t_2 - t_1} + r_2 \frac{t_0 - t_1}{t_2 - t_1},$$

and $d_0 = e^{-t_0 r_0}$ as usual.

This will yield a zero curve which seems to behave reasonably well, except maybe for the effect of the turn-of-year jump, which is most prominent for money market rates going beyond the 31st of December. However, if a forward curve is plotted from the resulting zero curve, it shows a strong sawtooth pattern, implying that linear interpolation on the zero rates is maybe not such a good idea. One gets much better results by using a monotonic cubic spline interpolation; see also [Ametrano and Bianchetti (2010)] and Section 5.3.

3
A Plethora of Credit Spreads

Credit is a system whereby a person who can not pay gets another person who can not pay to guarantee that he can pay.
Charles Dickens

3.1 Introduction

Ever since lending money was invented, the risk that the borrower might default has been present. For a potential lender (including bond investors) it is very important to know the probability of such an event: first, to determine the extra premium she will require to compensate her for the default risk, and second, to manage her credit risk once the money has been lent. There are two possible ways of determining the default probability:

- One can look at historical default events and try to estimate the borrower's default probability from those. In order to do that, one must have a view on the credit quality of the borrower and a history of defaults for that quality. This is, in short, what rating agencies do: they analyze the borrower's credit quality and label it with a rating, and they publish historical default probabilities for the different rating classes. It is often referred to as estimating *real-world probabilities*, even though it is a purely statistical task.
- One can look at the markets for credit derivatives and analyze the prices that are quoted there. The default probabilities that the market expects are encoded in those prices. Default probabilities derived that way are referred to as *risk-neutral probabilities*. If available, these are the ones that should always be used for pricing purposes.

Market participants often measure an asset's credit quality in terms of credit spreads. A high credit spread implies a low credit quality, or relatively high default probability. The problem is that there are various different concepts of credit spreads being used. In this chapter, we want to investigate the differences and connections between various definitions of credit spreads for bonds, with a strong focus on credit default swap spreads and asset swap spreads as the most common and liquid instruments.

This introductory section contains the definitions and terminology that are valid throughout the text. Then we present the different credit instruments that use a credit spread of some sort to make a connection between the market price for a risky asset and its probability of default. The valuation of credit products depends on knowledge of the distribution of the default probabilities. However, under certain assumptions it is also possible to use market quotes for liquid instruments to derive the risk-neutral default probabilities, i.e. the default probabilities seen by the market. Section 3.7 describes the connections between these definitions, and how to convert one spread into another for the most commonly used versions where possible.

Throughout the text, the probability measure will be the appropriate risk-neutral measure that is based on market observations, and *not* on real-world default probabilities.

A basic set of definitions and notation will remain the same throughout the text:

- c is the coupon of a fixed coupon bond (potentially 0);
- ζ is the (stochastic) time of default of the issuer;
- $\mathbf{P}$ is the (risk-neutral) default probability measure. We also use the symbol $\mathbf{P}$ to denote the distribution function and the survival probabilities: $\mathbf{P}(t) := \mathbf{P}(\zeta <= t)$ and $\mathbf{P}_s(t) := 1 - \mathbf{P}(t) = \mathbf{P}(\zeta > t)$;
- $\tau_{s,t}$ is the time in years between times s and t. To ease notation, we omit the day count basis in the function τ but it should be noted that the time in years between s and t can be different depending on the context in which it appears (e.g. the float vs fixed legs on a swap, which are often on an actual/365 and actual/360 basis, respectively);
- r_t is the risk-free zero rate for a contract maturing in t;
- d_t is the (risk-free) discount factor for time t, i.e. $d_t = e^{-r_t t}$;
- $\bar{d}_t$ is the risky discount factor for time t that includes the default risk of the underlying. In other words, $\bar{d}_t = d_t \mathbf{P}_s(t)$;
- if we consider a series of times $t_0,\ldots,t_N$ and a time $t \in [t_0,t_N]$, then $[t] = \max\{t_i | t_i \le t\}$ is the start time of the period which contains t;
- $n(t) = \{i | t_i = [t]\}$. When we have two separate sets of times $t_1,\ldots,t_n$ and $T_1,\ldots,T_k$, we use $n(T_j) = \max\{t_i | t_i \le T_j\}$ and $N(t_i) = \max\{T_j | T_j \le t_i\}$;

- a_t denotes interest accrual (of an underlying bond) at time t, so $a_t = c\tau_{[t],t}$;
- R_t is the (stochastic) recovery rate, i.e. the fraction of the notional that is paid back in the event of default. If we assume R to be deterministic and constant, we drop the index t. The fraction $1 - R_t$ is the part of the notional that is lost in case of default and is usually referred to as the *loss given default* (LGD).

Unless stated differently, all contracts have a notional of 1 in the local currency.

In what follows, we will often extract default probabilities from market-quoted instruments like CDS and bonds. Note that the resulting default probabilities will differ if the discount curve is changed. Thus, it is important to determine a truly risk-free curve first before starting to strip default probabilities.

We will always apply a hazard rate model in what follows; that is, we model the survival probability as

$$\mathbf{P}_S(t) = \exp\left(-\int_0^t h(\tau)\,d\tau \right). \tag{3.1}$$

Without further assumptions, h can be virtually any integrable function, but very often it will have a very simple form (either constant or piecewise constant). In the hazard rate model, $\mathbf{P}$ has a density function given by $\phi(t) = h(t)\mathbf{P}_S(t)$, and $\mathbf{P}_S(t) = 1 - \int_0^t \phi(\tau)\,d\tau$ because $\mathbf{P}'_S(t) = -\phi(t)$ and $\mathbf{P}_S(0) = 1$. We will always assume the hazard rate and the interest rate processes to be independent unless stated differently.

With this definition, we have the risky discount factor

$$\bar{d}_t = d_t \cdot \mathbf{P}_S(t) = \exp\left(-r_t\,t - \int_0^t h(\tau)\,d\tau \right).$$

For a risky bond with a given default distribution, the risky (dirty) bond price P can be calculated as

$$P = \sum_{i=1}^N c\tau_{t_{i-1},t_i} \bar{d}_{t_i} + \bar{d}_{t_N} + \int_0^{t_N} R_t\,d_t\,\phi(t)\,dt \tag{3.2}$$

$$= \sum_{i=1}^N c\tau_{t_{i-1},t_i} \bar{d}_{t_i} + \bar{d}_{t_N} + \int_0^{t_N} R_t h(t)\bar{d}_t\,dt. \tag{3.3}$$

Throughout the text, we sometimes make simplifying assumptions to make values better comparable, and to understand the basics better. This does mean that the results should not be used for any actual decisions as they are at best approximations of the true results. These simplifications are:

- the hazard rate h is constant over time;
- the interest rate r is constant over time;
- the recovery rate R is constant over time;
- the period lengths τ_{t_{i-1}, t_i} are all the same, τ, so $t_i = \tau i$ (or $t_0 + \tau_{i-1}$ if the first period is irregular);
- the accrual a_t to be paid in case of default is 0.

As an example, consider Equation (3.3). Under these assumptions, it becomes

$$P = c\tau \sum_{i=1}^{N} e^{-(r+h)\tau i} + e^{-(r+h)\tau N} + Rh \int_{0}^{\tau N} e^{-(r+h)t}\, dt$$

$$= c\tau e^{-(r+h)\tau} \frac{1 - e^{-(r+h)\tau N}}{1 - e^{-(r+h)\tau}} + e^{-(r+h)\tau N} + \frac{Rh}{r+h}\left(1 - e^{-(r+h)\tau N}\right)$$

$$\approx c\tau(1 - (r+h)\tau)\frac{(r+h)\tau N}{(r+h)\tau} + 1 - (r+h)\tau N + Rh\frac{(r+h)\tau N}{r+h}$$

$$= c\tau N - (r+h)c\tau^2 N + 1 - (r+h)\tau N + Rh\tau N$$

$$= \tau N(c - r(1+c\tau) + h(R - 1 - c\tau)) + 1, \tag{3.4}$$

where we used the first-order Taylor expansion of the exponential function in the approximation. Note that this becomes less accurate the larger N gets. For a given bond market price, we can imply the hazard rate h from this to be

$$h = \frac{P - 1 + (r(1+c\tau) - c)\tau N}{(R - 1 - c\tau)\tau N}. \tag{3.5}$$

Let us stress again that this is a formula to be used with care as the approximation is very bad for large values of N. Nevertheless, it can help get a first understanding for the relationship between market prices and hazard rates.

3.2 CDS spread

3.2.1 Product description

A Credit Default Swap or CDS is basically an insurance contract on an underlying bond (or name), where one side (the *protection buyer*) pays a periodic fee s (called the *spread* of the CDS), which is expressed as an annualized fraction of the protected amount, to the other party (the protection seller). In exchange, the protection seller is obliged to pay a compensation to the buyer in the case of default. This compensation is the difference between the recovery and the face value amount of the underlying. Often, the outstanding interest accrual of the underlying for the period in which the default happened is also paid by the protection seller.

It should be noted that in many instances, in particular high yield underlyings, the premium is paid at settlement date as an upfront payment.

The protection seller will usually be susceptible to default itself, and the valuation of a CDS should incorporate that default risk (which will reduce the premium to be paid to the protection seller). The same applies to the protection buyer, which will have an increasing effect on the premium. In this chapter, *we ignore the counterparty risk for derivatives transactions*, mainly because we assume that these are done under a collateral agreement where collateral is posted by the party for which the value of the transaction is negative. It should be noted, though, that transactions like this were done with non-banks before the financial crisis (like hedge funds or insurance companies) that were not part of a collateral agreement. Because of this, standardized CDS contracts that are done on an exchange, or at least at a central clearing house, are being considered (see Section 3.2.3).

Assuming that the maturity of the CDS contract is t_N and that the premium is paid at times $t_1, \ldots, t_N$, the value for the protection seller of such a transaction of notional 1 at time 0 is given by

$$V = \sum_{i=1}^{N} s\tau_{t_{i-1},t_i} \bar{d}_{t_i} - \int_0^{t_N} (1 - R_t) d_t \, \phi(t) \, dt. \qquad (3.6)$$

Sometimes the contract also specifies that the protection buyer has to pay the accrual of the spread up to the default date, so in this case the value is given by

$$V = \sum_{i=1}^{N} s\tau_{t_{i-1},t_i} \bar{d}_{t_i} + s \int_0^{t_N} \tau_{[t],t}\, d_t\, \phi(t)\, dt - \int_0^{t_N} (1 - R_t) d_t\, \phi(t)\, dt.$$

If the spread is fair at inception of the contract, i.e. the value of the contract is 0, we must have

$$s_{\text{CDS}} = \frac{\int\limits_0^{t_N} (1 - R_t) d_t\, \phi(t)\, dt}{\sum\limits_{i=1}^{N} \tau_{t_{i-1},t_i}\, \bar{d}_{t_i}}. \tag{3.7}$$

If the outstanding accrual is paid at default, then Equation (3.7) becomes

$$s_{\text{CDS}} = \frac{\int\limits_0^{t_N} (1 - R_t) d_t\, \phi(t)\, dt}{\sum\limits_{i=1}^{N} \tau_{t_{i-1},t_i}\, \bar{d}_{t_i} + \int\limits_0^{t_N} \tau_{[t],t}\, d_t\, \phi(t)\, dt}. \tag{3.8}$$

The value of a running contract whose spread was set to $\bar{s}_{\text{CDS}}$ at inception is

$$V = (\bar{s}_{\text{CDS}} - s_{\text{CDS}}(t_N)) \sum_{i=1}^{N} \tau_{t_{i-1},t_i}\, \bar{d}_{t_i}. \tag{3.9}$$

Note that here $t_0 = 0$ is the day of the valuation. That way, premium interest that has accrued since period start is excluded, and V represents the clean value. The spread $s_{\text{CDS}}(t_N)$ appearing in Equation (3.9) is, of course, the one for the remaining time to maturity.

Equation (3.9) seems to imply that the value of a CDS can be arbitrarily negative (from the protection seller's point of view). However, it should be clear that the value cannot exceed that of the insured notional. The mechanism that enforces this boundary is the survival probability that decreases when the spread increases. Therefore, the risky annuity $\sum_{i=1}^{N} \tau_{t_{i-1},t_i}\, \bar{d}_{t_i}$ goes to zero exponentially with increasing s_{CDS} and hence faster than the linear difference $\bar{s}_{\text{CDS}} - s_{\text{CDS}}$ approaches infinity. The dependence of the risky discount factors from the current spread level has an important influence on the calculation of the market risk associated with CDS spread movements; see Section 3.2.5.

Under the simplifying assumptions in Section 3 and without paying premium accruals up to default, Equation (3.7) becomes

$$s = \frac{(1-R)h \int_0^{t_N} e^{-(r+h)t}\, dt}{\tau \sum_{i=1}^{N} e^{-(r+h)\tau i}}$$

$$= \frac{\frac{(1-R)h}{r+h}\left(1 - e^{-(r+h)\tau N}\right)}{\tau \frac{e^{-(r+h)\tau}\left(1-e^{-(r+h)\tau N}\right)}{1-e^{-(r+h)\tau}}}$$

$$= \frac{(1-R)h}{\tau(r+h)}\left(e^{(r+h)\tau} - 1\right)$$

$$\approx \frac{(1-R)h}{\tau(r+h)}(r+h)\tau$$

$$= h(1-R),$$

which can be solved for h to yield

$$h \approx \frac{s}{(1-R)}, \tag{3.10}$$

a formula commonly used in front office. Note that one can derive the same approximation if one assumes that the spread is paid continuously, which is not far from the truth as the accrued spread is usually paid at default: in the limit $\tau \to 0$, the sum $\tau \sum_{i=1}^{N} e^{-(r+h)\tau i}$ in the denominator of Equation (3.7) becomes the integral $\int_0^{t_N} e^{-(r+h)t}\, dt$ which appears in the numerator. In that approximation, we can even drop the simplification that r is constant.

3.2.2 Bootstrapping hazard rates from CDS spreads

The market does not quote default probabilities directly but by providing a recovery rate and a CDS spread; see also Section 3.2.4. *It is not possible to extract market implied default probabilities from CDS spreads alone.* The most liquid market for synthetic credit risk is the CDS market. On the one hand, CDS spreads for maturities of 1, 5, and 10 years (and sometimes other maturities) are quoted and change on a regular basis (depending on the liquidity of the underlying bond or name). On the other hand, the recovery rate is only updated in the market on a very irregular basis, if at all. Unfortunately, there is no liquid market for a second class of instruments, namely constant recovery CDS (or sometimes called *binary CDS*) which pay a fixed amount on default no matter what the actual recovery rate is. If there were such a liquid instrument, it could be used in combination with CDS to derive recoveries and default probabilities without any further assumptions. Recent initiatives move towards a standardized market which quotes premiums for standardized recoveries; see Section 3.2.3.

In this subsection, we assume that a recovery rate is given and is constant in the maturity variable.

Because we only have a small number of discrete points for which a spread is quoted, some assumption on the shape of the hazard rate function has to be made. The most common one used by the market is that hazard rates are piecewise constant, i.e. for quotes for maturities $T_1, \ldots, T_k$ we have $h(t) = h(T_{N(t)})$ for $t \leq T_k$ and $h(t) = h(T_k)$ for $t \geq T_k$. Thus, $h(t)$ is a step function continuous on the left with steps at the maturities for which there are quotes. This implies that

$$\mathbf{P}_s(t) = \exp\left(-\sum_{i=1}^{N(t)} h(T_i)(T_i - T_{i-1}) - h(T_{N(t)})(t - T_{N(t)})\right) \qquad (3.11)$$

$$= \mathbf{P}_s(T_{N(t)})e^{-h(T_{N(t)})(t - T_{N(t)})}.$$

Under this assumption, we can calculate the hazard rate term structure by a bootstrapping algorithm. If we are given the spread quote s_1 for a CDS maturing in T_1, we know that V in Equation (3.6) is zero, and we have to solve

$$0 = s_1 \sum_{i=1}^{n(T_1)} \tau_{t_{i-1}, t_i} e^{-(r_{t_i} + h(T_1))t_i} - (1 - R)h(T_1) \int_0^{T_1} e^{-(r_t + h(T_1))t} \, dt \qquad (3.12)$$

for $h(T_1)$. Unless the yield curve r_t has been parametrized and can be integrated analytically, this means that the integral will have to be calculated numerically.

The next step is then to assume that we have the first k jump points of the hazard rate term structure (and hence the survival probability). Now a spread quote s_{k+1} for a CDS maturing in T_{k+1} is given. That means that we have to solve the following equation for $h(T_{k+1})$ ($T_0 = 0, n(T_0) = 0$; note that $\mathbf{P}_s(t)$ and $\phi(t)$ are known for $t \leq T_k$):

$$0 = \sum_{j=1}^{k} \left(s_{k+1} \sum_{i=n(T_{j-1})+1}^{n(T_j)} \tau_{t_{i-1}, t_i} dt_i \mathbf{P}_s(t_i) - (1 - R)h(T_j) \int_{T_{j-1}}^{T_j} \mathbf{P}_s(t)e^{-r_t t} \, dt \right)$$

$$+ s_{k+1}\mathbf{P}_s(T_k) \sum_{i=n(T_k)+1}^{n(T_{k+1})} \tau_{t_{i-1},t_i} e^{-r_{t_i}t_i - h(T_{k+1})(t_i - T_k)}$$

$$- (1-R)h(T_{k+1})\mathbf{P}_s(T_k) \int_{T_k}^{T_{k+1}} e^{-r_t t - h(T_{k+1})(t-T_k)}\, dt. \tag{3.13}$$

3.2.3 Standard CDS contracts

In the wake of the financial crisis of 2008, MarkIT introduced standardizations in the most liquid markets ("Big Bang" in March 2009 for North America, also known as *Standard North American Contracts* or *SNAC*, "Small Bang" in July 2009 in Europe, and a standardization for Asia and the Emerging Markets) that aim at creating CDS derivatives contracts that are as good as exchange traded. The instruments quoted in that environment are defined with

- standard payment and maturity dates for the CDS contracts: IMM (International Monetary Market) dates
- full premium payments at the end of the first payment period (implying a rebate accrual payment at trade date) – there are no long stub periods so that cash flows after inception are always defined in the same way
- standard premium spreads, compensated by an upfront payment that is quoted: any contract with the same notional and the same maturity will pay the same premium in a given accrual period, which implies that opposite positions will actually have cash flows that cancel out perfectly
- a protection effective date (which allows back dated protection start).

As an example, consider the standard European corporate CDS contract specification as found on http://cdsmodel.com/cdsmodel:

Definitions

- CDS Dates: 20th of Mar/Jun/Sep/Dec
- Business Day Count: Actual/360
- Business Day Convention: Following

Contract Specification With respect to trade date T:

- Maturity Date: A CDS Date, unadjusted

- Coupon Rate:
  (a) Trading: 25bp, 100bp, 500bp or 1000bp
  (b) Backloading: 25bp, 100bp, 300bp, 500bp, 750bp or 1000bp
- Protection Leg:
  (a) Legal Protection Effective Date: $T - 60$ days for credit events, $T - 90$ days for successions events, unadjusted
  (b) Protection Maturity Date: Maturity Date
  (c) Protection Payoff: Par Minus Recovery
- Premium Leg:
  (a) Payment Frequency: Quarterly
  (b) Daycount Basis: Actual/360
  (c) Pay Accrued On Default: True
  (d) Business Day Calendar: Currency dependent
  (e) Adjusted CDS Dates: CDS Dates, business day adjusted Following
  (f) First Coupon Payment Date: Earliest Adjusted CDS Date after $T + 1$ calendar
  (g) Accrual Begin Date: Latest Adjusted CDS Date on or before $T + 1$ calendar
  (h) Accrual Dates: CDS dates business day adjusted Following except for the last accrual date (Maturity Date) which remains unadjusted
  (i) Accrual Periods: From previous accrual date, inclusive, to the next accrual date, exclusive, *except* for the last accrual period where the accrual end date (Maturity Date) is included
  (j) Payment Dates: CDS dates, business day adjusted Following including the last payment day (Maturity Date)
- Currencies: EUR, GBP, CHF, USD
- Business Calendars: Determined by currency:
  (a) EUR: London and TARGET Settlement Day
  (b) GBP: London
  (c) CHF: London and Zurich
  (d) USD: London and New York.

For examples of how the standard CDS work, see the description on www.cdsmodel.com/assets/cds-model/docs/Standard%20CDS%20Exa mples.pdf.

By introducing standard premium payment dates and standard spreads, it is much easier now to actually close out a CDS position without periods of unhedged risk. The only remaining issue is that the counterparty risk may not be adequately addressed. This risk is usually mitigated by collateral agreements. In addition, one might think of hedging the future exposure by actively trading CVA, see Chapter 8. Another advantage of the standardization is that it is easier to compare the actual cost of insuring a name or bond.

The bootstrapping is analogous to what is described in Section 3.2.2, only that now the up-front payment p_i for maturity T_i is implied to make a new trade fair, i.e. Equation (3.12) and Equation (3.13) become

$$p_1 = s \sum_{i=1}^{n(T_1)} \tau_{t_{i-1},t_i} e^{-(r_{t_i}+h(T_1))t_i} - (1-R)h(T_1) \int_0^{T_1} e^{-(r_t+h(T_1))t} \, dt,$$

$$p_n = \sum_{j=1}^{k} \left(s \sum_{i=n(T_{j-1})+1}^{n(T_j)} \tau_{t_{i-1},t_i} d_{t_i} P_s(t_i) - (1-R)h(T_j) \int_{T_{j-1}}^{T_j} P_s(t) e^{-r_t t} \, dt \right)$$

$$+ sP_s(T_k) \sum_{i=n(T_k)+1}^{n(T_{k+1})} \tau_{t_{i-1},t_i} e^{-r_{t_i} t_i - h(T_{k+1})(t_i - T_k)}$$

$$- (1-R)h(T_{k+1})P_s(T_k) \int_{T_k}^{T_{k+1}} e^{-r_t t - h(T_{k+1})(t - T_k)} \, dt.$$

3.2.4 Floating recovery rates

It is important to bear in mind that the CDS market uses the recovery rate as part of the quoting mechanism. The actual recovery rate is a stochastic variable and only materializes after the default of the underlying name. As a matter of fact, even the recovery that CDS counterparties agree on via auction is not necessarily the realized recovery that the creditors of the defaulted company will receive after the wind down process; the auction is used to shorten the period between default and protection payment. If the protection buyer wants to be sure that the notional is fully recovered (apart from credit risk faced with the protection seller, which is an entirely different matter), she needs to do a CDS on a particular bond with physical delivery.

A name used for transferring credit risk via CDS is usually also an issuer of bonds. The prices of bonds should certainly be an upper bound for the issuer's recovery as perceived by the market. Since bonds of the same seniority will recover the same rate regardless of time to maturity, the bond with the deepest discount can be used as the lowest upper bound.

In reality, the quoted recovery rate is usually a static value, i.e. it remains constant over a longer period of time. Thus, it may happen that the price of an issuer's bond falls beneath the quoted CDS recovery rate for the same issuer. Implying the hazard rate from the bond price and the recovery rate at that point, one sees that the hazard rate (and the implied CDS spread for the bond in question) explodes to infinity. An example of this phenomenon is shown in Figure 3.1 which shows the price development of the Greek bonds GR0133003161 (maturity 2024) and GR0138002689 (maturity 2040), Greece's recovery rate as quoted on MarkIT, and the hazard rate implied from GR0138002689 using Equation (3.4). Note that the recovery rate was changed regularly after April 2010, when the European debt crisis started for the PIIGS (Portugal, Italy, Ireland, Greece, and Spain) countries. Since September 2011, the price of GR0138002689 has been consistently below the recovery rate, although the latter was adjusted several times, which is why the implied hazard rate has disappeared in the clouds.

Thus, in the situation described, the recovery rate needs to be adjusted urgently to make the obvious problem go away. However, some questions an auditor might ask are: When does the recovery need to be updated? Why then? By what percentage does it have to be adjusted, and why by that amount? Obviously, the currently used quoting mechanism leads to an arbitrary hazard rate. Observe, for instance, in Figure 3.1 the sharp increase in recovery from 40% to 55% in April 2010 which led to an upward jump in the hazard rate which is not at all justified by the bond price development. In Figure 3.2, we can see that both the zero spread and the asset swap spread, which will be described in detail in Section 3.5, are more robust and much smoother, and hence a better measure for the credit riskiness of GR0138002689. However, Figure 3.2 also shows that the asset swap spread is limited above while the zero spread can grow arbitrarily high; see Section 3.5.

To sum things up, one has to be extremely careful when using data from the CDS market in the cash bond market. Recovery rates are just a quoting mechanism.

A possible approach is to model the recovery rate as a floating variable. The simplest approach would be to use a percentage of the price of a certain bond rather than a percentage of par. At issuance, the bond may be issued at par, and the recovery rate (as derived by rating or some other mechanism) is a fraction of that. This fraction is then applied to the bond price if it goes down, and to par if it goes above 100. This approach, while addressing the questions above, has the drawback that even an instant before default, there is a difference between the bond price and the recovery rate, which should not be the case as the market is usually not taken by surprise by defaults.

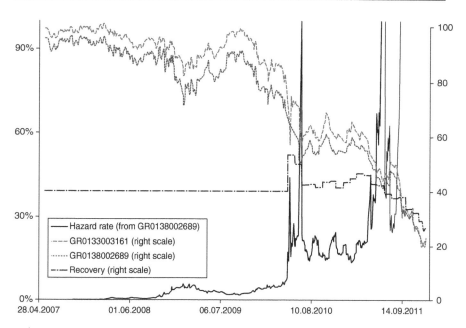

Figure 3.1 The development of the price of GR0133003161 and GR0138002689, Greece's recovery from MarkIT, and the hazard rate implied from the quoted recovery and the price of GR0138002689. Sources: Bloomberg and MarkIT.

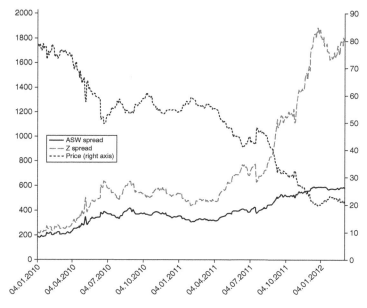

Figure 3.2 The development of the price of GR0138002689, its zero spread, and its asset swap spread, both implied from the price.

Notice that modeling recovery rates as stochastic variables, as in [Ech-Chatbi(2008), Li(2009), Werpachowski(2009), Höcht and Zagst (2009)] does not help for bonds. Stochastic recovery can be made to fit with different tranche prices for CDOs, but with simple bonds like the ones discussed above the expected recovery rate is an *input* so we are no further forward.

Instead of the two extremes for recovery rates (percentage-of-par, percentage-of-price) we suggest using a variable percentage of price via heuristics [Kenyon and Werner (2011)]. To some extent we take a step backwards and consider a dynamic calibration of traditional static CDS models to market data. We start from the usual daily model recalibration and propose heuristics for market-consistent calibration of static data, specifically the recovery rate within static hazard rate models. These heuristics can be extended and generalized in different ways within static stochastic models, i.e. analogies to stochastic hazard rate models. For example, the market-implied recovery rate that is now an output can be the input for a stochastic recovery rate model. Note that this approach is an alternative to RMV (recovery of market value) [Schönbucher (2005)] (chapter 6), and is advantageous in that our static approach works with standard CDS, CDO, etc. pricing. Thus we aim to make practical the recent more expressive models, e.g. [Ech-Chatbi (2008), Li (2009), Werpachowski (2009)]. However, we limit the scope here to market-consistent calibration of static recovery rates.

We first demonstrate theoretical limits on feasible recovery rates. Secondly we propose market-consistent heuristic dynamic updating mechanisms within static CDS models.

3.2.4.1   Theoretical limits on recovery rates

We want to obtain a deterministic hazard rate and a deterministic recovery rate that fits a set of CDS prices (or spreads). We work throughout in terms of CDS prices, and often in terms of 1-CDS prices. This avoids any consideration of bond prices. We do not want to mix bond prices and CDS prices because bonds are funded instruments and CDSs are not. Whilst, conventionally for a risky bond matched to the CDS terms, and at inception, we might expect:

$$\text{Risky bond} + \text{CDS} \stackrel{?}{=} \text{Riskless bond},$$

this is not true in today's markets. The connection between risky bonds, CDS prices, and par is market dependent.

Our starting point, considering only the CDS, from the point of view of the protection buyer, but which is true at any time, is:

CDS price = protection leg NPV − premium leg NPV.

This second equation provides a limit on the recovery rate in a deterministic hazard rate model [Brigo and Mercurio (2006)], since, assuming a static recovery rate:

CDS price =

$$
-\left[c \int_0^T P(0,t)(t - T_{\beta(t)-1}) d_t \mathbf{Q}(\zeta \geq t) + c \sum_{i=a+1}^b P(0, T_i)\alpha_i \mathbf{Q}(\zeta \geq T_i) \right]
$$
$$
+ (1 - R) \int_0^T P(0,t) d_t \mathbf{Q}(\zeta \geq t), \tag{3.14}
$$

where we mostly use the terminology of [Brigo and Mercurio (2006)]. Note especially that R is the recovery rate, c the CDS spread (fee), and α_i the year fraction of the ith protection interval. The CDS runs from a to b with protection payments (absent default) at T_i. $P(0,t)$ is the riskless discount factor to time t from time 0, $\mathbf{Q}$ is the default distribution and ζ the default time. $\beta(t)$ gives the index just before t.

Equation 3.14 implies that recovery rates face a hard constraint:

$R \leq 1 - \text{CDS price}$.

Using a static (aka deterministic) hazard rate model, the time to default is an exponential random variable with parameter λ. If we are considering multiple CDS quotes for different maturities then we can have $\lambda(t)$ (still deterministic). So if ζ is the default time, we have:

$$\zeta \sim \text{Exponential}(\lambda).$$

Now consider when a bond is very close to default. Let us assume at this point that, using the static (aka deterministic) hazard rate model, we have $\lambda = 400\%$. This implies that the expected probability of default within one year is $1 - \exp(-4) = 0.98$ (i.e. 98%). Now, given a price (i.e. NPV) for the CDS we can solve for the recovery rate numerically: see Figure 3.3.

Figure 3.3 shows implied recovery rates close to default for a range of (1-CDS price) values. Lower implied recovery rates are possible in the grey area for higher implied hazard rates. There are **no** feasible hazard rates left of the (exact) diagonal. The $\lambda = 100\%$ (dashed) line is very close to the $\lambda = 400\%$ diagonal full line. The diagonal is the maximum feasible recovery rate.

For example, looking at Figure 3.3 we see that if we observe a (1-CDS price) of 70% (i.e. 0.7 on the horizontal axis) then it is impossible to have a recovery rate of 80% assuming that $\lambda = 400\%$ implies default (or very near default). Hence, if we have an assumed recovery rate of 80% and we observe a (1-CDS price) of 70% we have a broken model. At least, the *assumption* of a recovery rate of 80% is contradicted by *observation*.

3.2.4.2 *Market-consistent heuristics*

The key point is how the recovery rate approaches the envelope of the maximum feasible recovery rate as the observed (1-CDS price) decreases. We propose and analyze a continuous family of B-spline functions that are indexed by the weight given to the corner point, and the position of the lower end point.

The obvious choice for the lower end point position appears to be (0,0), since this is feasible. However, this choice would imply that – when using B-splines – the implied hazard rate would attain extreme values at about half the originally assumed recovery rate. That is, there would be an effective default at half the assumed recovery rate. Thus

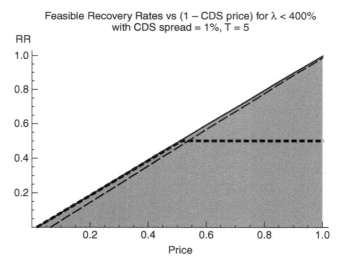

Figure 3.3 Feasible recovery rates. In the grey area $\lambda < 400\%$, the diagonal long-dashed line is for $\lambda = 100\%$; note that these are close together and very close to the exact diagonal. There are no solutions for λ to the left of the (exact) diagonal. The (exact) diagonal is the maximum feasible recovery rate. Hence, for a bond that has an assumed recovery rate of 50% when price is par, the short-dashed line gives the envelope of feasible recovery rates.

some regularization is required, and we propose using the feasible envelope of λ < 400%, which is almost indistinguishable from the exact diagonal in Figure 3.3.

These are shown in Figure 3.4.

These recovery rate families could be adapted to stochastic formulation whereby we introduce an observation equation between the actual recovery rate and the calculated recovery rate. In the stochastic formulations we could then recover the optimal recovery rate via a Kalman filter.

We analyse this family of heuristics according to these criteria:

Hazard Monotonicity: does the hazard rate increase as the price decreases?

Hazard Convexity: is the implied hazard rate convex?

Hazard Linearity: does the hazard rate increase proportionately as the price decreases?

Default Probability Linearity: does the default probability increase proportionately as the price decreases?

Consistent with Constant Recovery Rate: where this is possible, how far do you deviate from a constant assumption?

Simplicity: the i.e. number of estimated (arbitrary) parameters required.

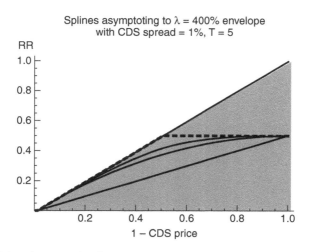

Figure 3.4 Spline functions for the recovery rate. They are generated using the endpoints and the corner by giving different weights to the corner: 0 (straight line); 1 and 2 shown. A weight of ∞ would reproduce the envelope (in practice, 20 is quite close).

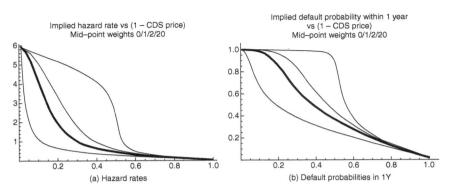

Figure 3.5 Implied hazard rates and implied default probability within one year. Corner weight increases left-to-right, with corner weight of one (1) in bold.

Smoothness: if the recovery rate estimate has jumps this can be awkward practically for hedging and risk calculations.

These criteria are subjective, as are any criteria not determined by objective data. However, they serve as a guide for readers to start from, and to experiment with.

An example of the possible implied hazard rates versus (1-CDS price) curves is shown in Figure 3.5, together with implied default probabilities within one year. Note that an exactly linear increase in hazard rates as (1-CDS price) decreases is *not* feasible. The best that can be done is a roughly linear increase in both hazard and default probability (within one year) for equal corner weights.

3.2.4.3 Results

The family of implied recovery rates indexed by the corner-weight is shown in Table 3.1 according to the criteria we suggested.

Depending on which criteria are judged more important, any of the four corner weights given here can be the optimal choice. Clearly, a constant recovery rate will fail for dramatic market movements such as those seen during recent crises (especially when ratings appear out of sync with market prices).

3.2.4.4 Commentary

Market price movements can be far more dramatic than can be accommodated by just about any choice of constant recovery rates. Practically, this leads to a necessity for recovery rates that can be daily recalibrated so as to be consistent with market observations – even for

Table 3.1 Checking the criteria of implied recovery rates for different values of corner weights

Criteria	Spline corner weight			
	0	1	2	High (20)
Hazard Monotonicity	Yes	Yes	Yes	Yes
Hazard Convexity	Yes	Roughly	Roughly	No
Hazard Linearity	No	No	No	No
Default Probability Linearity	No	Roughly	Roughly	No
Consistency with Constant RR	Poor	Fair	Fair	Good
Simplicity	Yes	Yes	Less	Yes
Smoothness	Less	Yes	Yes	Less

static models. This has led various authors to propose stochastic recovery rate models [Ech-Chatbi (2008), Li (2009), Werpachowski (2009), Höcht and Zagst (2009)]. However, a missing starting point has been the actual determination of the expected recovery rate to start these models off when used with simple bonds.

We have given a simple heuristic to permit market-consistent recovery rates based on two observations: first, the recovery rate must be feasible given either the CDS price or the CDS spread in (at least) a static recovery rate and static hazard rate model; and secondly, that as one-minus-the-CDS price decreases, the chance of default increases (i.e. hazard rates increase). This leads to dynamic recovery rates that are stochastic in time but deterministically linked to the equivalent bond prices. The only requirement is the initial assumption on the recovery rate when the CDS price is zero (i.e. at inception of the CDS contract, where a bond price would be par), the weight to give the corner of the feasible envelope of recovery rates, and a decision on the maximum observable recovery rate prior to actual default. Apart from this starting data no further inputs to the model are required across the whole price range. Whilst assumptions are subjective, they can be consistent across an institution.

Dynamic recovery rates avoid the problem with static assumptions that can be contradicted by market data. They are parsimonious in that they do not require recovery rates to depend on a volatility parameter (although this can be incorporated). This approach works across the whole range of observed prices from very low to high.

This floating recovery approach is complementary to percentage-of-price (RMV [Schönbucher (2005)]), and can be viewed as a time-inconsistent simplification of it. The advantage of our separate, static, approach is that it leaves the CDS, CDO, etc. pricing as standard, e.g. as in [Brigo and Mercurio (2006), Hull and White (2004)].

Future research could apply this feasibility exercise to stochastic recovery rate models [Ech-Chatbi (2008), Li (2009), Werpachowski (2009), Höcht and Zagst (2009)]. In fact, the existence of hard limits for recovery rates needs to be included in these models for added realism.

If asked, we would recommend a spline corner weight choice on grounds of smoother hazard rates, roughly linear default probabilities, and more consistency with a constant default probability. (Note that the linear alternative has the largest, and most immediate, deviation from a constant recovery rate.) In the example above this would be achieved with a corner weight of one.

3.2.5 CDS spread risk

The sensitivity of Equation (3.9) to moves in the spread s_{CDS} is given by

$$\frac{\partial V}{\partial s_{CDS}} = -\sum_{i=1}^{N} \tau_{t_{i-1},t_i} \bar{d}_{t_i} + (\bar{s} - s_{CDS}) \sum_{i=1}^{N} \tau_{t_{i-1},t_i} \frac{\partial \bar{d}_{t_i}}{\partial s_{CDS}}. \tag{3.15}$$

Now Equation (3.10) tells us that $h \approx s_{CDS}/(1-R)$, so if we shift s_{CDS}, which is the CDS spread of the remaining maturity, by one basis point, this will result in an approximate change of

$$\frac{\partial \bar{d}_t}{\partial s_{CDS}} = d_t \frac{\partial \mathbf{P}_s(t)}{\partial s_{CDS}} \approx -d_t \frac{t - T_{N(t)}}{1-R} \mathbf{P}_s(t) = -\bar{d}_t \frac{t - T_{N(t)}}{1-R} \tag{3.16}$$

for all $t > T_{n(T)}$, the last quoted bucket before maturity. Here, we have assumed a piecewise constant hazard rate as in Equation (3.11). In total, we get the approximation

$$\frac{\partial V}{\partial s_{CDS}} \approx -\sum_{i=1}^{N} \tau_{t_{i-1},t_i} \bar{d}_{t_i} - \frac{\bar{s} - s_{CDS}}{1-R} \sum_{\{i|t_i \geq N(t_N)\}} \tau_{t_{i-1},t_i} \bar{d}_{t_i}(t_i - T_{N(t_N)}). \tag{3.17}$$

As this can be done similarly for the other buckets as well, we can estimate the effect of a (very small) parallel shift of the whole CDS spread curve to be

$$\frac{\partial V}{\partial s_{curve}} \approx -\sum_{i=1}^{N} \tau_{t_{i-1},t_i} \bar{d}_{t_i} - \frac{\bar{s} - s_{CDS}}{1-R} \sum_{i=1}^{N} \tau_{t_{i-1},t_i} \bar{d}_{t_i} t_i. \tag{3.18}$$

3.3 Zero spread

The (continuous) *zero spread*, Z spread, or yield spread is a quantity which is added to the risk-free yield curve (or zero curve) in order to correctly price a risky bond. A risk-free bond's dirty price is given by:

$$P_{RF}d_s = \sum_{i=1}^{N} c\tau_{t_{i-1},t_i}\, d_{t_i} + d_{t_N}$$

$$= c \sum_{i=1}^{N} \tau_{t_{i-1},t_i}\, e^{-r_{t_i}t_i} + e^{-r_{t_N}t_N}. \qquad (3.19)$$

The factor d_s is introduced here to make the risk-free price consistent with market practice, which is that the price is paid on settlement date s. We do not explicitly consider the possibility that interest is paid between the valuation and the settlement date; this can be healed by requiring that $t_1 > t_s$. See also Section 3.5.

Given the dirty market price P for a risky bond, the zero spread is the number s_{ZS} such that

$$P = c \sum_{i=1}^{N} \tau_{t_{i-1},t_i}\, e^{-(r_{t_i}+s_{ZS})t_i} + e^{-(r_{t_N}+s_{ZS})t_N}, \qquad (3.20)$$

where P is given as in Equation (3.3). In other words, a constant spread is added to the risk-free curve to arrive at the dirty market price P. This spread has to be implied by some numerical algorithm. However, under the simplifying assumptions in Chapter 3, and using the first-order Taylor expansion of the exponential function, we can explicitly calculate s_{ZS}:

$$P \approx c\tau N - (r+s_{ZS})c\tau^2 N + 1 - (r+s_{ZS})\tau N,$$

which solves to

$$s_{ZS} \approx \frac{1+c\tau N - P}{c\tau^2 \frac{N(N+1)}{2} + \tau N} - r. \qquad (3.21)$$

A higher order of accuracy in the Taylor series of the exponential function leads to a higher accuracy, but also to more complexity in the derivation of s_{ZS} from the bond price. For large N, the above approximation is rather bad. For instance, if $\tau N = 20$, i.e. the maturity is 20 years, and $r+s = 5\%$, then the first-order approximation of $e^{-1} = 0.3679$ is 0. Also, the assumption of a fixed interest rate is at least questionable, but one would think that the repayment suppresses the coupons (if it is not too far in the future).

The Z spread can be found on Bloomberg for vanilla bonds.

A variant of the zero spread is the *simple zero spread* s'_{ZS}, which is defined for simply compounding discount factors rather than continuous ones as in Equation (3.20):

$$P = c \sum_{i=1}^{N} \frac{\tau_{t_{i-1},t_i}}{(1+r'_{t_i}+s'_{ZS})^{t_i}} + \frac{1}{(1+r'_{t_N}+s'_{ZS})^{t_N}}, \tag{3.22}$$

where r'_t is the simple compounded zero rate for time t.

3.3.1 Zero spread risk

The sensitivity of Equation (3.20) to moves in the spread s_{ZS} is given by

$$\frac{\partial P}{\partial s_{ZS}} = -c \sum_{i=1}^{N} \tau_{t_{i-1},t_i} t_i e^{-(r_{t_i}+s_{ZS})t_i} - t_N e^{-(r_{t_N}+s_{ZS})t_N}, \tag{3.23}$$

an expression similar to the one used to define *duration*.

3.4 I spread

The *I spread* of a bond (which can also be found on Bloomberg for vanilla bonds) is basically the difference between the risk-free and the risky yield of the bond: in Equation (3.19), we defined the risk-free price P_{RF} of the bond's cash flows. The *risk-free yield*, or sometimes internal rate of return, is the number y_{RF} which solves the equation

$$P_{RF} = c \sum_{i=1}^{N} \tau_{t_{i-1},t_i} e^{-y_{RF}t_i} + e^{-y_{RF}t_N}.$$

Now the I spread is the number s_I that solves the equation

$$P = c \sum_{i=1}^{N} \tau_{t_{i-1},t_i} e^{-(y_{RF}+s_I)t_i} + e^{-(y_{RF}+s_I)t_N}. \tag{3.24}$$

In other words, s_I is the difference between the internal rates of return for the risk-free and the market price of the bond.

It may be easier to imply s_I if one assumes that the period lengths τ_{t_{i-1},t_i} are constant, which implies $t_i = i\tau$. For $q = e^{-y_{RF}\tau}$ we can write

$$P_{RF} = c\tau \sum_{i=1}^{N} q^i + q^N = c\tau q \frac{1-q^N}{1-q} + q^N.$$

Shuffling the parameters a bit we have to solve the polynomial equation

$$q^{N+1}(1+c\tau) - q^N - q(c\tau + P_{RF}) + P_{RF} = 0,$$

which in general is not possible analytically, but which should require less computing power than solving the equation with the exponentials. Once q is found, $y_{RF} = -\ln(q)/\tau$. Repeat for $y_{RF} + s_I$ and P instead of y_{RF} and P_{RF}, respectively.

The value of the I spread is very similar to that of the Z spread. Only for deep discounts, i.e. high spread levels, do they start to diverge noticeably. The curve used to determine the risk-free value of the bond could be constructed from Treasuries, covered bonds like Pfandbriefs, or from interbank swap rates which might also be considered risk-free because of the collateral agreements that are in place.

As in the case of the Z spread, there is a *simple I spread* defined in the same way for simply compounding zero rates.

3.4.1 I spread risk

The sensitivity of Equation (3.24) to moves in the spread s_{IS} is given by

$$\frac{\partial P}{\partial s_{IS}} = -c\sum_{i=1}^{N} \tau_{t_{i-1},t_i} t_i e^{-(y_{RF}+s_{IS})t_i} - t_N e^{-(y_{RF}+s_{IS})t_N}, \qquad (3.25)$$

where y_{RF} is the risk-free yield of the bond. If we assume that the τ are constant and $t_i = \tau i$, we can simplify this expression. Note that

$$\sum_{i=1}^{N} iq^i = q\sum_{i=1}^{N} iq^{i-1}$$

$$= q\frac{\partial}{\partial q}\left(\sum_{i=1}^{N} q^i\right)$$

$$= q\frac{(N+1)q^N(q-1) - (q^{N+1}-1)}{(q-1)^2}$$

$$= q\frac{Nq^{N+1} - (N+1)q^N + 1}{(q-1)^2}$$

$$= q\frac{q^N(N(q-1)-1)+1}{(q-1)^2}.$$

Replacing q with $e^{-(y_{RF}+s_{IS})\tau}$, we get

$$\frac{\partial P}{\partial s_{IS}} = c\tau^2 e^{-(y_{RF}+s_{IS})\tau} \frac{e^{-(y_{RF}+s_{IS})\tau N} \left(N(e^{-(y_{RF}+s_{IS})\tau}-1)-1\right)+1}{(e^{-(y_{RF}+s_{IS})\tau}-1)^2}$$

$$- N\tau e^{-(y_{RF}+s_{IS})\tau}. \tag{3.26}$$

3.5 Par asset swap spread

3.5.1 Product description

A par asset swap (or asset swap for short) is a perfect interest rate risk hedge for a fixed rate (or structured) bond. On the trade date of the bond, the swap is designed to pay the bond cash flows and receive LIBOR plus the asset swap spread s_{ASW} which is implied to make the combined market value of bond and asset swap 1 (i.e., par, hence the name). This means that the investor pays 1 regardless of what the bond's dirty price P actually is. Note that because the settlement of the asset swap package is in the future (three business days in most markets), the value of the notional exchange on settlement date s needs to be discounted to the trade date with the discount factor d_s.

It should be noted that in the case of default of the underlying bond the swap continues nonetheless. Therefore, default probabilities do not enter the valuation of the swap, only for the bond cash flows. Thus, an asset swap cannot be considered a credit derivative as such, and it does not hedge any credit risk. It is still related to an issuer's credit risk at inception.

We assume here that the funding leg of the asset swap pays the default tenor version of LIBOR, e.g. 6 months in the case of EURIBOR, or 3 months in the case of USD LIBOR. Any non-standard tenor swap can be split into two components, a standard tenor swap and a basis swap. The conversion of the standard tenor asset swap spread into non-standard tenor spreads or even spreads for swaps in different currencies is described in Section 3.5.3. The topic of a discount curve built from OIS instruments will be discussed in Section 5.1.2.

The future cash flows are the following: the investor pays the coupon of the bond to the seller and receives LIBOR plus the asset swap spread in return. This spread s_{ASW} is determined such that the package value is 1, i.e. the bond's premium/discount $1 - P$ equals the swap's value from the investor's point of view:

$$(1-P)d_s = -\sum_{i=1}^{N} c_i \tau_{t_{i-1},t_i}\, d_{t_i} + \sum_{j=1}^{M} (L_{t'_{j-1}} + s_{ASW})\tau_{t'_{j-1},t'_j}\, d_{t'_j}. \tag{3.27}$$

Here $L_{t'_{j-1}}$ is the forward value of LIBOR for the period t'_{j-1}, t'_j. If we assume for the time being that the discount curve is built from the same instruments as the forward curve, we get

$$
L_{t'_{j-1}} = \frac{d_{t'_{j-1}} - d_{t'_j}}{\tau_{t'_{j-1}, t'_j} d_{t'_j}},
$$

which implies

$$
\sum_{j=1}^{M} L_{t'_{j-1}} \tau_{t'_{j-1}, t'_j} d_{t'_j} = \sum_{j=1}^{M} (d_{t'_{j-1}} - d_{t'_j}) = d_{t'_0} - d_{t'_M}.
$$

The t' indicate that the payment dates of the floating side of the swap differ from the ones on the bond side: the standard EUR swap, for example, exchanges a fixed coupon (with 30/360 day count rule and unadjusted payment) annually against a semi-annual floating coupon (with ACT/360 basis and adjusted payment). It should not be confusing to use the same function τ for t and t', although this function not only depends on the start and end points but also on the day count rule of the cash flow in question. Another thing to bear in mind is that t_0 lies in the past if the asset swap is done in the middle of an interest period, whereas t'_0 is one or a few more business days in the future.

As mentioned before, the settlement of the asset swap is, in general, three business days after trade date, whereas the fixing lag of the floating leg is usually two business days. In GBP LIBOR, this is zero days, i.e. t'_0 would be three business days in the future in this case.

This means that the fixed leg of the asset swap pays the full coupon on the first payment date; the floating leg, on the other hand, will have payment periods matching the bond's from maturity *backwards*, leaving a stub period in general. If this stub period is, e.g., one month, the floating leg will pay 1-month LIBOR on the first payment date, which is fixed on trade date plus one business day.

The fact that the asset swap package settles in the future means that Equation (3.27) is valid only if we use the cash flows occurring on or after the future settlement date. This makes a difference if the payment of a bond coupon happens between trade and settlement date, which should then be left out in the sum of the fixed cash flows. Let $P_{RF}d_s$ be the risk-free dirty price of the bond as in Equation (3.19).

Writing $A' = \sum_{j=1}^{M} \tau_{t'_{j-1}, t'_j} d_{t'_j}$ for the *annuity factor*, Equation (3.27) can be solved for s_{ASW} explicitly (still assuming that the discount curve equals the forward curve):

$$s_{\mathrm{ASW}} = \frac{(P_{\mathrm{RF}} - P)d_s - (d_{t_0'} - d_s)}{A'}.$$

(3.28)

Conversely, for a given asset swap spread s_{ASW} and a risk-free dirty price (again, the dirty risk-free price must be calculated without interest payments between trade and settlement date P_{RF}), we can imply the market price P as

$$P = \frac{P_{\mathrm{RF}}d_s - s_{\mathrm{ASW}}A' - (d_{t_0'} - d_s)}{d_s}.$$

(3.29)

Note that this implies that the asset swap spread cannot be arbitrarily high: the price of an asset is certainly floored at 0, so s_{ASW} cannot go above $(P_{\mathrm{RF}}d_s - (d_{t_0'} - d_s))/A'$. As an example, consider a 30-year asset swap spread whose annuity factor is 18.2, and the bond's risk-free price is 91. Then the asset swap spread cannot be higher than $91\%/18.2 = 500$ basis points (ignoring settlement details). As a matter of fact, if the bond's recovery is not 0 but, say, 40%, the ceiling on the spread would be $60\% \times 91/18.2 = 300$ basis points. This maximum possible value for the asset swap spread is in stark contrast to the case of the Z spread, which can take any value greater than zero without bringing the bond price below zero. The reason for this is that the influence of the Z spread is roughly that of the function e^{-szt}, while the asset swap spread reduces the bond price like $C - s_{\mathrm{ASW}}A'$.

If we assume settlement in $t = 0$ or on t_0', Equation (3.28) can be interpreted as

$$s = (P_{\mathrm{RF}} - P)/A'.$$

(3.30)

This means that the asset swap spread is very intuitively given by the difference between risky and risk-free prices, divided by the value of a single basis point on the swap's floating side. Physicists will note that the dimension of this result (basis points) is also correct because the prices are in currency units, and the annuity is currency units per basis point.

If the asset swap spread of a running swap was locked in as $\bar{s}_{\mathrm{ASW}}$, the current value of the asset swap package (i.e. bond plus asset swap) as seen by the investor, i.e. the swap payer, is given by

$$V = \underbrace{Pd_s}_{\text{dirty bond price}} \underbrace{- \sum_{i=1}^{N} c_i \tau_{t_{i-1},t_i}\, d_{t_i}}_{\text{fixed leg}} + \underbrace{\sum_{j=1}^{M} (L_{t'_{j-1}} + \bar{s}_{\text{ASW}}) \tau_{t'_{j-1},t'_j}\, d_{t'_j}}_{\text{float leg}}$$

$$= \bar{s}_{\text{ASW}} A' + \text{something}.$$

On the other hand, we know from the definition of the asset swap spread that

$$d_s = s_{\text{ASW}} A' + \text{same something},$$

which implies that

$$V = (\bar{s}_{\text{ASW}} - s_{\text{ASW}}) A' + d_s, \qquad (3.31)$$

which is (ignoring the fact that d_s is not exactly 1) the book value of the position (namely, 1) plus the value of one basis point times the spread difference between inception and today. Note that s_{ASW} appearing in Equation (3.31) is the spread for the remaining time to maturity of the bond. If we use $1 - d_s \approx 0$, the position's P&L is therefore just

$$\Delta V = (\bar{s}_{\text{ASW}} - s_{\text{ASW}}) A'. \qquad (3.32)$$

Note that Equations (3.27) to (3.32) work for any kind of structured coupon as well, as long as the bond does not amortize and is not callable.

Now let $A = \sum_{j=1}^{N} \tau_{t_{j-1},t_j}\, d_{t_j}$ be the swap's fixed side's annuity. Using the simplification $d_s = 1$ and following [Zhou (2008)], we can reformulate Equation (3.27) for a fixed coupon bond as

$$s_{\text{ASW}} = c - \bar{L} + \frac{1-P}{A'}, \qquad (3.33)$$

where $\bar{L}$ is the average of the LIBOR forwards, weighted by the factors $\tau_{t'_{j-1},t'_j}\, d_{t'_j}$. We have made the approximation $A = A'$, and assumed that the bond sells on a fixing date. This formula shows the asset swap spread to consist of three components: the bond's coupon, the weighted average LIBOR over the swap's life, and the bond's discount scaled by the annuity.

If we drop the assumption that the discount and the forward curves are identical, we cannot use the collapsing property of the floating cash flows. Instead, we observe that the sum of the LIBOR payments (without the spread) is by definition just the fair swap rate s_p for the remaining maturity times the annuity factor A.

This swap rate will most likely have to compensate the first LIBOR period, because the first LIBOR payment will have been fixed already in general. The first fixed period is likely to be shorter than the standard as well. Another thing to note is that the swap will start on the bond settlement date s, not the standard swap spot date.

Since the risk-free price of the bond is $cA + d_{t'_M}$, Equation (3.27) becomes:

$$d_s = Pd_s + (s_\mathrm{p} - c)A + s_\mathrm{ASW}A', \tag{3.34}$$

and

$$V = Pd_s + (s_\mathrm{p} - c)A + \bar{s}_\mathrm{ASW}A',$$

from which Equation (3.31) follows immediately.

Now, because s_p is the par rate, we have $d_s = s_\mathrm{p}A + d_{t_N}$, and the risk-free dirty price of the bond is given by $P_\mathrm{RF}d_s = cA + d_{t_N}$. With this, we can infer from Equation (3.34)

$$\begin{aligned} s_\mathrm{ASW} &= \frac{(1-P)d_s - (s-c)A}{A'} \\ &= \frac{s_\mathrm{p}A + d_{t_N} - Pd_s - s_\mathrm{p}A + cA}{A'} \\ &= \frac{P_\mathrm{RF}d_s - Pd_s}{A'}, \end{aligned}$$

which is the same as Equation (3.30). The reason why the (very small) correction term $d_{t'_0} - d_s$ does not appear is that the distinction between the two dates was "swallowed" by the fact that we defined s_p as a swap rate without specifying when the swap starts.

3.5.2 Inflation-linked asset swaps

An important class of bonds are inflation-linked bonds of the following kind. They pay a fixed coupon c on a notional that is periodically adjusted by the growth of the associated price index. At maturity, they pay back the notional, again adjusted by the price index growth. Formally, if $C(t)$ is the consumer price index (CPI) at time t, the cash flows of the bond are given by $N = 1$ in period 0, $c \times C(t_i)/C(0)$ at time $t_i, i = 1, \ldots, n-1$, and $(1+c) \times C(t_n)/C(0)$ at time t_n. An asset swap done at time $t < t_n$ for such bonds usually swaps the remaining bond cash flows, including the excess notional redemption at time t_n, against LIBOR plus a spread on the fixed time t notional $C(t)/C(0)$. We now want to calculate the P&L at time t of an inflation-linked par asset swap package that was done at time $t = 0$ with a spread of $\bar{s}$, and a notional of 1. We follow one possible convention, namely that the market price of an inflation-linked bond is quoted on the current notional. The other alternative, that the price is quoted on the original notional, is a straightforward exercise.

The value of a new par asset swap package with current spread s at time t – ignoring the settlement details – is given by

$$C(t)N(0) = N(t) = P(t)N(t) + PV_{\text{SWAP}}(s; t).$$

Since the package as a whole was done at par at time 0, the P&L is

$$\Delta PV = P(t)N(t) + PV_{\text{SWAP}}(\bar{s}; t) - 1$$

$$= N(t) - PV_{\text{SWAP}}(s; t) + PV_{\text{SWAP}}(\bar{s}; t) - 1$$

$$= \frac{C(t)}{C(0)} - 1 - \Delta_{\text{fix}} + \Delta_{\text{flt}}.$$

Set $C := C(t)/C(0) - 1$ and $A' = \sum_{j=1}^{m} \tau_j' df_{t_j'}$. We get

$$\Delta_{\text{fix}} = c \sum_{i=1}^{n} \frac{C(t_i)}{C(0)} \tau_i df_i + \left(\frac{C(t_n)}{C(0)} - 1 \right) df_n$$

$$- \left(cN(t) \sum_{i=1}^{n} \frac{C(t_i)}{C(t)} \tau_i df_i + N(t) \left(\frac{C(t_n)}{C(t)} - 1 \right) df_n \right)$$

$$= c \sum_{i=1}^{n} \frac{C(t_i)}{C(0)} \tau_i df_i + \frac{C(t_n) - C(0)}{C(0)} df_n$$

$$- \left(c \sum_{i=1}^{n} \frac{C(t_i)}{C(0)} \tau_i df_i + \frac{C(t_n) - C(t)}{C(0)} df_n \right)$$

$$= C df_n,$$

$$\Delta_{\text{flt}} = \sum_{j=1}^{m} (f_j + \bar{s}) \tau_j' df_{t_j'} - N(t) \sum_{j=1}^{m} (f_j + s) \tau_j' df_{t_j'}$$

$$= -C \sum_{j=1}^{m} f_j \tau_j' df_{t_j'} + \left(s(0) - \frac{C(t)}{C(0)} s(t) \right) A'.$$

Now if we assume that the discount and the forward curve are the same,

$$\frac{C(t)}{C(0)} - 1 - \Delta_{\text{fix}} = C(1 - df_n)$$

$$= C \sum_{j=1}^{m} f_j \tau'_j df_{t'_j},$$

so we see that

$$\Delta PV = \frac{C(t)}{C(0)} - 1 - \Delta_{\text{fix}} + \Delta_{\text{flt}} = \left(s(0) - \frac{C(t)}{C(0)} s(t) \right) A'.$$

Note the similarity to Equation (3.32). It should be clear from the above how to calculate the P&L of other fixed-rate bonds with varying notional.

3.5.3 Implying par asset swap spreads in other currencies

Given a term structure of asset swap spreads for an entity in its domestic currency, is it possible to derive the asset swap spread term structure for that entity in a different currency? The answer is yes, one only has to take into account the cross-currency basis spreads of the two currencies involved. If one or both currencies have a standard swap tenor different from 3 months (which is the standard tenor for cross-currency swaps), the basis spreads of the standard tenor against 3 months also needs to be considered. For a more thorough treatment of basis and cross-currency spreads, see Chapter 5. We present the most general formula below and give an explicit example.

The definition of the par asset swap spread is independent of the currency. So we have to transform the spread on the domestic (standard tenor) float leg to a spread on the standard float leg in the foreign currency. The most important formulae for this are Equation (5.2) and Equation (6.2), which are derived in their respective sections; here we just apply them.

Assume the most general case, where both domestic and foreign currency have a standard tenor of 6 months (e.g. EUR and GBP). That means that we have to do the following calculation. Start with the float leg of the asset swap, 6-month d LIBOR $+s_d^{\text{ASW}}$. This is then transformed into 3-month d LIBOR + something, then into 3-month f LIBOR + something, then 6-month f LIBOR + the foreign asset swap spread.

Recall that a standard cross-currency swap involves a notional exchange at the start and at maturity, so the corresponding discount factors should appear in Equation (3.36). However, the exchange does not influence the spread transformation in the slightest, so we omit it from the equation. The proper transformation is done in Equation (6.1).

While doing this, bear in mind that the notional in currency d has to be transformed into the notional in currency f by using the exchange rate $FX^{d/f}$, and that the values to be shifted from one side of the swap to the other also have to be multiplied with the appropriate exchange rate. In detail,

$$flt_d^{6M} + s_d^{ASW}$$

$$= flt_d^{3M} + s_d^{3/6} + s_d^{ASW} \frac{A_T^{6M,d}}{A_T^{3M,d}} \tag{3.35}$$

$$= flt_f^{3M} + s^{f/USD} + \left(s_d^{3/6} + s_d^{ASW} \frac{A_T^{6M,d}}{A_T^{3M,d}} - s^{d/USD} \right) \frac{A_T^{3M,d}}{A_T^{3M,f}} \tag{3.36}$$

$$= flt_f^{6M} +$$

$$\left(s^{f/USD} - s_f^{3/6} + \left(s_d^{3/6} + s_d^{ASW} \frac{A_T^{6M,d}}{A_T^{3M,d}} - s^{d/USD} \right) \frac{A_T^{3M,d}}{A_T^{3M,f}} \right) \frac{A_T^{3M,f}}{A_T^{6M,f}}. \tag{3.37}$$

Here, we used the following spreads which are quoted in the market:

$s^{f/USD}, s^{d/USD}$: the cross-currency spread of the foreign resp. domestic currency against USD. They are usually quoted such that a swap with a 3-month f LIBOR leg + $s^{f/USD}$ against 3-month USD LIBOR is fair. The only exception is the Mexican Peso (MXN), where the spread is on the USD leg, but this can easily be moved to the standard case via Equation (6.2).

$s_f^{3/6}, s_d^{3/6}$: the spread on the three-month leg of a 3-month vs 6-month swap in currency f resp. d.

Note that this can also be used to determine the asset swap spread in the domestic currency for non-standard tenors; in this case, stop with Equation (3.35). If the foreign currency has a standard tenor of 3 months, stop with Equation (3.36).

Example

Let us take a look at a sample bank's covered bond asset swap spreads (against 6-month EURIBOR) as of September 30, 2009. We would like to

Table 3.2 A sample bank's EUR asset swap spreads
against 6-month EURIBOR, 3 vs 6-month EUR
basis swap spreads, EUR/USD basis swap spreads
(in bp) (September 30, 2009)

Maturity	ASW Spread	EUR 3/6	EUR/USD BS
1 Y	35	22.3	−30.50
2 Y	40	17.5	−26.50
3 Y	40	14.3	−23.75
4 Y	40	12.3	−22.25
5 Y	50	10.8	−21.00
7 Y	60	8.7	−18.50
10 Y	60	6.8	−15.50
15 Y	65	5.0	−7.00
20 Y	65	4.1	0.00
30 Y	65	3.3	4.25

Table 3.3 Annuities of float legs as of September 30,
2009

Maturity	EUR 3M	EUR 6M	USD 3M
1 Y	1.012974832	1.011216669	1.015897216
2 Y	2.000618545	1.995581890	2.009136696
3 Y	2.962994844	2.954421799	2.979383981
4 Y	3.894855315	3.882329904	3.916639267
5 Y	4.793752267	4.777038746	4.817817107
7 Y	6.492301053	6.466869092	6.514318456
10 Y	8.774410116	8.736502308	8.787116290
15 Y	11.94603996	11.88922164	11.96358549
20 Y	14.45271045	14.38151632	14.51022962
30 Y	18.17710300	18.08901009	18.25497713

compute the USD asset swap spreads for that date. The EUR asset swap
term structure and the relevant basis spreads are given by Table 3.2.
The annuities for that date are shown in Table 3.3. The EUR/USD rate
on September 30, 2009 was 1.4643. The cross-currency spread $s^{USD/USD}$
is, of course, 0. Thus we have all the information needed to compute
the USD asset swap spreads, which are displayed in Table 3.4.

3.5.4 Bootstrapping hazard rates from asset swap spreads

In this subsection we want to calculate the hazard rates from quoted
liquid asset swap spreads. The only assumptions we make are that the
survival probabilities are given by Equation (3.11), i.e. that the hazard

Table 3.4 USD asset swap spreads for a
sample bank's covered bonds as of September 30, 2009

Maturity	USD Spread
1 Y	87.49
2 Y	83.54
3 Y	77.51
4 Y	74.01
5 Y	81.22
7 Y	86.67
10 Y	81.92
15 Y	76.58
20 Y	68.51
30 Y	63.46

rates are piecewise constant, and that recovery rates are constant deterministic. We also make the simplification that settlement is at time 0, i.e. $d_s = 1$, so Equation (3.28) becomes

$$
s_{ASW} = \frac{(d_{t_N} - \bar{d}_{t_N}) + c \sum_{i=1}^{N} \tau_{t_{i-1}, t_i} (d_{t_i} - \bar{d}_{t_i}) - \int_0^{t_N} R_t d_t \phi(t) dt}{\sum_{j=1}^{M} \tau_{t'_{j-1}, t'_j} d_{t'_j}}
$$

$$
= \frac{d_{t_N} \mathbf{P}(t_N) + c \sum_{i=1}^{N} \tau_{t_{i-1}, t_i} d_{t_i} \mathbf{P}(t_i) - \int_0^{t_N} R_t d_t \phi(t) dt}{\sum_{j=1}^{M} \tau_{t'_{j-1}, t'_j} d_{t'_j}}, \tag{3.38}
$$

where we used Equation (3.3) to expand P and $t_N = t'_M$.

First, we imply the constant hazard rate from the asset swap spread under the simplifying assumptions in the introduction. Then we can use Equation (3.3) and replace P by the expression for P from Equation (3.27) to get

$$
h = \frac{c\tau \sum_{i=1}^{N} e^{-r\tau i} - 1 + e^{-r\tau N} - s_{ASW}\tau' \sum_{j=1}^{M} e^{-r\tau'j} - c\tau N + r\tau N + rc\tau^2 N}{R\tau N - c\tau^2 N - \tau N}.
$$

$$\tag{3.39}$$

Here, τ' is the length of the periods on the floating side (which as a simplification is assumed to be constant). In most markets, $\tau = 2\tau'$. Note that $\tau' M = \tau N$.

Now for a more realistic approach. To imply the hazard rates from a given set of asset swap spreads for different maturities $T_1, \ldots, T_k$, we start with T_1 and solve Equation (3.38) for $h(t_1)$:

$$s_{\text{ASW}}(T_1) \sum_{j=1}^{n(T_1)} \tau_{t'_{j-1}, t'_j} d_{t'_j} = d_{T_1}(1 - e^{-h(T_1)T_1})$$

$$+ c \sum_{i=1}^{n(T_1)} \tau_{t_{i-1}, t_i} d_{t_i}(1 - e^{-h(T_1)t_i})$$

$$- Rh(T_1) \int_0^{T_1} e^{-r_t t - h(T_1)t} \, dt.$$

As in the case of the bootstrapping from CDS spreads, the integral appearing in the above equation has to be computed numerically unless the interest rate curve has been parameterized in some way that allows analytic evaluation.

Now, assuming we are given hazard rates for times $T_1, \ldots, T_k$ and an asset swap spread $s_{\text{ASW}}(T_{k+1})$, we have to solve

$$s_{\text{ASW}}(T_{k+1}) \sum_{j=1}^{n(T_{k+1})} \tau_{t'_{j-1}, t'_j} d_{t'_j} =$$

$$d_{T_{k+1}} \left(1 - \mathbf{P}_s(T_k)e^{-h(T_{k+1})(T_{k+1} - T_k)}\right)$$

$$+ c \sum_{i=1}^{n(T_k)} \tau_{t_{i-1}, t_i} d_{t_i}(1 - \mathbf{P}_s(t_i))$$

$$+ c \sum_{i=n(T_k)+1}^{n(T_{k+1})} \tau_{t_{i-1}, t_i} d_{t_i} \left(1 - \mathbf{P}_s(T_k)e^{-h(T_{k+1})(T_{k+1} - T_k)}\right)$$

$$- R \sum_{l=1}^{k} h(T_l)\mathbf{P}_s(T_l) \int_{T_{l-1}}^{T_l} e^{-r_t t - h(T_l)(t - T_l)} \, dt$$

$$- Rh(T_{k+1})\mathbf{P}_s(T_{k+1}) \int_{T_k}^{T_{k+1}} e^{-r_t t - h(T_{k+1})(t - T_{k+1})} \, dt$$

for $h(T_{k+1})$.

The problem with this bootstrapping is that the asset swap spreads are quoted for live bonds, so the relevant maturities are usually not integers as in the case of CDS trades for issuers (rather than individual bonds).

3.5.5 Par asset swap spread risk

The sensitivity of Equation (3.31) to moves in the spread s_{ASW} is given by

$$\frac{\partial V}{\partial s_{ASW}} = -A', \tag{3.40}$$

the negative annuity factor of the swap's floating side. For USD bonds, one can directly compare CDS and asset swap spreads because they have the same payment frequency and day count conventions. Since Equation (3.31) does not contain the risky discount factors, there is no further dependence of the asset swap value on the spread (in contrast to the situation in the case of CDS values). For low spreads and relatively short maturities, the sensitivities of asset swaps and CDS are still very close to each other.

3.6 Risky floater spread

If a risky entity issues a floating rate note, it has to pay a premium over LIBOR which is referred to as the risky floater spread. On any given date, the fair premium s_F is determined such that

$$1 = \sum_{j=1}^{M} (L_{t'_{j-1}} + s_F)\tau_{t'_{j-1}, t'_j} d_{t'_j} \mathbf{P}_s(t'_j) + d'_{t_M} \mathbf{P}_s(t'_M) + \int_0^{t_N} R_t\, d_t\, \phi(t)\, dt$$

$$= \sum_{j=1}^{M} (d_{t'_{j-1}} - d_{t'_j} + s_F \tau_{t'_{j-1}, t'_j} d_{t'_j}) \mathbf{P}_s(t'_j) + d'_{t_M} \mathbf{P}_s(t'_M) + \int_0^{t_N} R_t\, d_t\, \phi(t)\, dt,$$

which solves explicitly to

$$s_F = \frac{1 - d'_{t_M} \mathbf{P}_s(t'_M) - \int_0^{t_N} R_t\, d_t\, \phi(t)\, dt - \sum_{j=1}^{M} (d_{t'_{j-1}} - d_{t'_j}) \mathbf{P}_s(t'_j)}{\sum_{j=1}^{M} \tau_{t'_{j-1}, t'_j} d_{t'_j} \mathbf{P}_s(t'_j)} \tag{3.41}$$

Ignoring settlement and fixing gap (i.e. $t'_0 = 0$), we can write $1 = d_{t'_0} P_s(t'_0)$ and simplify Equation (3.41) to

$$
s_F = \frac{\sum\limits_{j=0}^{M-1} d_{t'_j}(P_s(t'_j) - P_s(t'_{j+1})) - \int\limits_0^{t_N} R_t \, d_t \, \phi(t) \, dt}{\sum\limits_{j=1}^{M} \tau_{t'_{j-1}, t'_j} d_{t'_j} P_s(t'_j)}. \tag{3.42}
$$

If the fair spread at inception was $\bar{s}_F$, then the clean value of a risky floater at some later time is given by

$$
V = \sum_{j=1}^{M} (L_{t'_{j-1}} + \bar{s}_F) \tau_{t'_{j-1}, t'_j} \bar{d}_{t'_j} + \bar{d}_{t'_M} + \int_0^{t_N} R_t \, d_t \, \phi(t) \, dt
$$

$$
= (1 + L_{t'_0} \tau_{t'_0, t'_1} \bar{d}_{t'_1}) + (\bar{s}_F - s_F(t_M)) \sum_{j=1}^{M} \tau_{t'_{j-1}, t'_j} \bar{d}_{t'_j}, \tag{3.43}
$$

compared to Equation (3.9) and Equation (3.31). Again, the spread t_M in the formula is the one for the remaining time to maturity. On a fixing date, the term $(1 + L_{t'_0} \tau_{t'_0, t'_1} \bar{d}_{t'_1}) = 1$.

3.6.1 Risky floater spread risk

As in the case of CDS spreads, the risky discount factors occurring in Equation (3.43) are sensitive to changes in the spread themselves, so the sensitivity of Equation (3.43) to moves in the spread s_F is given by

$$
\frac{\partial V}{\partial s_F} = -\sum_{j=1}^{M} \tau_{t'_{j-1}, t'_j} \bar{d}_{t'_j} + (\bar{s} - s_F) \sum_{j=1}^{M} \tau_{t'_{j-1}, t'_j} \frac{\partial \bar{d}_{t'_j}}{\partial s_F}. \tag{3.44}
$$

3.7 Connections between spreads

In this section we try to compare the different measures of credit risk that were introduced in this chapter. One difficulty is certainly that all the concepts presented so far except the CDS spread do not explicitly take default probabilities and recovery rates into account. Take, for instance, the Z spread. In its derivation, the default of the bond is assumed to pay coupons and repay its notional until the end. Certainly the market price of the bond, which is used in the calculation, captures some information about default probability and recovery (see Equation (3.4)), but not in a straight-forward way. And as we have seen in Section 3.2.4, the recovery rate the market assumes for the bond itself is not necessarily compatible with the one it uses for pricing CDS.

To simply take the difference of a bond spread – however defined – and the CDS spread will thus be comparing apples and oranges. Nevertheless, such comparisons are interesting in themselves.

3.7.1 From bond prices to CDS spreads

Since the inception of the credit default swap, the question of the connection between the CDS spread and the credit spread of a bond – which needs to be defined properly – raised an interest both academically as well as practically.

In [Hull *et al.* (2004)], Hull et al. claim a very simple approximate relationship between the yield y of a risky bond, the risk-free yield r, and the CDS spread on the same risky bond:

$$s = y - r,$$

the reason being that the risky bond plus bought protection is basically the same as a risk-free bond. In other words, the CDS spread should be the same as the simple Z spread defined in Section 3.3. However, this only holds under a lot of simplifying assumptions which are at best questionable (see [Hull *et al.* (2004)], pp. 10ff). In particular, the assumption that market participants can borrow at the risk-free rate is certainly not true (and wasn't even before the credit crisis). Furthermore, the assumption that an arbitrageur is able to short the underlying bond is only true if he can borrow the bond in question from some other investor. This is certainly the case for repo-eligible bonds (e.g. Treasuries and other government bonds), but is a lot more difficult for less liquid bonds or small issuances. However, there is a funding cost attached to borrowing a bond that may reduce if not negate any potential arbitrage gains.

In addition, it is not clear what the risk-free curve is. Even in 2004, it was not the government bond curve, which contains too much information that is not credit related, like regulatory requirements to hold government bonds, tax issues, risk-weighted assets (at the time of writing it is still better from a capital perspective for an insurance company to hold a Eurozone bond from, say, Greece or Ireland than to hold a AAA corporate bond), etc.

Nevertheless, [Hull *et al.* (2004)] find that by and large, the relation holds well. Other authors come to the same conclusion for pre-crisis times; see the overview in [Bai and Collin-Dufresne (2011)], p. 2. In

Table 3.5 Goldman Sachs CDS spreads as of January 25, 2012. Source: Bloomberg

Maturity	CDS Spread
6 M	196.48
1 Y	206.94
2 Y	223.93
3 Y	234.78
4 Y	240.20
5 Y	239.70
7 Y	248.77
10 Y	248.06

2007, the basis (CDS spread − bond credit spread) declined to negative values never seen before, to −250 basis points on average for investment grade bonds and to −650 basis points for high-yield bonds. An arbitrageur should have jumped on this immediately, buying the bond and buying CDS protection on it. In the past, even basis values much closer to zero triggered such basis trades, bringing the basis quickly back up to zero. Why did it not happen this time? First of all, the buying of the bonds needs to be funded. Secured funding via repo will be less feasible the lower the credit quality and liquidity of the bond is, and haircuts will also be high. Also, one of the manifestations of the crisis in the years 2007–2009 was a drying up of the repo market. Unsecured funding was also very hard (and expensive) to come by. Finally, the CDS contract was suddenly considered credit risky as well, even when collateralized. In total, the high negative basis did not present an arbitrage opportunity but expressed the overall liquidity squeeze, the increased cost of funding, and the counterparty credit risk of derivatives transactions.

As an example, look at Table 3.5 and Table 3.6, which display CDS spreads resp. Asset Swap spread and Z spread data for Goldman Sachs unsecured bonds as of January 25, 2012.

Without any interpolation efforts, just picking the bond closest to the respective CDS maturity, we get a picture as shown in Figure 3.6 below.

The two bases have roughly the same shape; the main difference is that the CDS–ASW basis changes its sign more markedly from the short end to the long end of the curve.

For a detailed account of the CDS–Bond basis, see for instance [Elizalde (2009)].

Table 3.6 Goldman Sachs Asset Swap and Z spreads as of January 25, 2012. Source: Bloomberg

Coupon	Maturity	ASW Spread	Bid Z Spread
3.625	01/08/2012	157.43	200.29
5.7	01/09/2012	185.58	227.05
5.45	01/11/2012	40.05	80.85
5.25	01/04/2013	141.08	177.75
4.75	15/07/2013	191.75	226.72
5.25	15/10/2013	194.30	226.30
5.15	15/01/2014	196.23	226.57
6	01/05/2014	211.69	238.39
5	01/10/2014	237.83	267.28
5.5	15/11/2014	261.25	289.24
5.125	15/01/2015	274.48	304.27
3.7	01/08/2015	264.75	299.92
5.35	15/01/2016	312.23	339.87
3.625	07/02/2016	288.76	326.61
5.75	01/10/2016	303.93	329.39
6.25	01/09/2017	318.97	341.47
5.95	18/01/2018	351.26	379.79
6.15	01/04/2018	370.16	397.85
7.5	15/02/2019	397.65	409.11
5.375	15/03/2020	331.13	363.89
6	15/06/2020	354.43	381.92
5.25	27/07/2021	305.49	333.09
5	15/08/2022	268.75	298.57

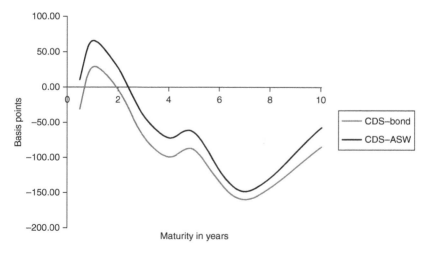

Figure 3.6 The CDS–Bond and CDS–ASW basis for Goldman Sachs as of January 25, 2012.

Table 3.7 German government CDS spreads vs asset swap spreads as of November 30, 2011. Source: Bloomberg

Maturity	CDS Spread	Asset Swap Spread	Basis
2 Y	69.8	−106.0	175.8
3 Y	82.9	−100.4	183.3
5 Y	110.0	−79.1	189.1
7 Y	119.2	−64.0	183.2
10 Y	128.3	−43.8	172.1
15 Y	130.5	−18.3	148.8
20 Y	130.4	7.3	123.1
30 Y	130.7	7.1	123.6

3.7.2 The asset swap – CDS basis

Under the assumption that banks can borrow and lend money at LIBOR, CDS spreads (assuming physical delivery of the bond in case of default in exchange for the face value) and asset swap spreads should be identical. Assume that bank X bought a par asset swap with a spread s_A, so that in effect it owns a floater that pays LIBOR + s_A. To make this investment risk-free, X buys protection on the issuer of the bond, and pays a CDS spread of s_C. To fund the investment, X borrows at LIBOR. In total, X now has a risk-free cash flow of LIBOR $+s_A-$ LIBOR $-s_C = s_A - s_C$ until the issuer defaults. If the issuer defaults, X repays the funds from the protection amount. The no-arbitrage principle forces s_A and s_C to be identical.

In reality, CDS and asset swap spreads do not agree. The difference $s_C - s_A$ is called the *CDS–ASW basis*. As an example, look at the basis for Goldman Sachs in Figure 3.6 above, or the comparison for German government bonds as of November 30, 2011 in Table 3.7, which shows a substantial basis between −150 and −190 basis points for up to 15 years.

The first observation to make is that the asset swap spreads are negative. This can never happen for the CDS spread as this is basically a premium for an insurance policy, which cannot be negative. The reason is that the credit quality of bonds with a negative asset swap spread is viewed as better than your average bank's. Why people would even buy protection on Germany from a bank is a different question. Conversely, we saw that Equation (3.28) implies an upper bound for the asset swap spread which is given by the risk-free price divided by the value of a basis point on the floating leg (ignoring settlement details), whereas the CDS spread can theoretically be almost arbitrarily high.

If default was expected tomorrow and recovery was expected to be 0, the (annualized) CDS spread would be $365 \cdot 10,000 = 3,650,000$ basis points.

Another observation is that CDS are usually written on names rather than individual bonds. In that case, the protection buyer can deliver any bond of the issuer in question after the issuer defaulted (given that its seniority is the same as agreed). Furthermore, CDS contracts very often define events as defaults which are very technical, and after which the issuer might still be able to pay its coupons or even repay its debt. For these additional risks, the protection seller will want an extra premium.

It should also be noted that the CDS spread can be moved around by adjusting the recovery rate if one assumes a given hazard rate; compare Section 3.2.4.

The basis may also be increased if the CDS is written on a specific bond rather than an issuer's name. If the bond in question trades below par, a bond investor has less notional at risk than a seller of protection (who has to insure the full face value). The opposite is true if a bond trades at a premium.

Most importantly, the assumption that banks can lend and borrow at LIBOR is wrong, and an investor's funding spread over LIBOR would have to be added to the CDS spread to compensate for that. (The different day count conventions and payment frequencies for CDS premia and asset swaps would also require accounting for.) Therefore, the CDS basis should be around the average funding level for banks, rather than 0.

Even if there is a basis between CDS and asset swap spreads, the theoretical equality of the two implies that the sensitivities of a bond's value to either spread's movement should be roughly the same, unless the basis itself moves while one of the spreads remains unchanged. However, Section 3.2.5 and Section 3.5.5 show that this is only the case for issuers with a relatively low default risk, which implies that there is a more fundamental difference between asset swap and CDS spreads.

For a detailed account of the CDS–ASW basis, see for instance [Choudhry (2006)].

4
Introduction to Basis Spreads

Basis Virtutum Constantia.
[Constancy is the foundation of virtue]

The financial crisis starting in 2008 has created a phenomenon that was not observable before (or only on such a small scale as to be negligible): there is now a substantial spread between floaters of different tenors or currencies. Examples are 3-month EURIBOR versus 6-month EURIBOR, or 3-month USD LIBOR versus 3-month EURIBOR. As with the emergence of the smile in the volatility quotes for equity options after the market meltdown in 1987, it is not expected that this phenomenon will disappear. Thus, as happened with options and the volatility smile, to price any swap that is not quoted in the market, a model is required. This is true even for such a simple instrument as a non-standard maturity for a standard-tenor swap. There are a wide range of different approaches in the literature and in the market based on combinations of risk, funding, and replication. No simple approach is wholly satisfactory for reasons that will become clear (mostly to do with funding arguments) but there are useful methods that we will describe.

Before going further we remind the reader what the different bases are empirically:

intra-currency basis: for example, if we build a single curve from 3-month USD LIBOR swaps that we use for discounting and for calculating the 3-month floating rates; then we will find that "6-month" floating rates calculated from this single curve will not agree with the market. There exist USD 3-month to 6-month basis swaps which specify how much must be added to a the three-month side to make the swap fair.

cross-currency basis: the most liquid cross-currency basis swaps are USD 3 month to foreign 3 month, and specify the spread that must be added to the non-USD side so that the trade is fair (except for Mexican pesos, where the convention is the other way around). Notice that notionals are exchanged at the start and end of the swap (unlike standard fixed-for-floating intra-currency swaps), and that the ratio between the notionals is set by the spot FX rate. The notionals exchanged at the start and at the end are the same.

4.1 Something is rotten in the state of pricing

What is the evidence for the charge?

4.1.1 Forwards

The pricing of a forward rate agreement (FRA) is supposedly very simple, as we saw in Chapter 1: one calculates the forward rate by using Equation (1.2). That looks simple enough, let's try it for real numbers. As of August 2, 2010, the 3 and 6 month EURIBOR rates were given by $r_3 = 0.85\%$ and $r_6 = 1.08\%$, respectively, leading to a theoretical forward rate $r_{3,6} = 1.3121\%$. The mid-market forward rate, however, was 0.985% – an error of 33%! Obviously, the world the textbook formulas describe has changed. The discrepancy was most pronounced after the collapse of Lehman, where the differences reached levels that were inconceivable before.

The one thing that changed during the crisis was that the market realized that banks contributing to LIBOR can default (even though LIBOR will survive that), and that money markets can dry up. Therefore, the replication of a derivative (and a collateralized one at that, i.e. with as little default risk as possible) with defaultable deposits and loans is just not correct. In the first three months of the outlined replication, the bank we invested our money in might default, or liquidity might just dry up entirely. At the same time, our derivative would be safe due to daily margin calls. In the second three months up to maturity of the FRA, we ourselves might go bust; again, the FRA counterparty would be safe because of the collateral posted. The difference between the theoretical and the actual forward can therefore be seen as the extra premium one has to pay or be paid if one wants to exchange actual money with another bank. Actual money exchanges – by definition – cannot be made as riskless as collateralized derivatives.

The key point is that a FRA is a collateralized, i.e. (almost) risk free, derivative of a risky quantity: LIBOR. It is unreasonable to expect that a single curve can express both a collateralized risk level and the level of risk expressed by LIBOR. Equally, we do not (now) expect one LIBOR tenor to contain the same (compounded) level of risk as any other LIBOR tenor. This leads to basis swaps.

4.1.2 Basis swaps

Another instance of the textbook valuations breaking down is the handling of basis swaps. The standard no-arbitrage replication argument implies that a basis swap is fair if neither party pays an additional spread on top of its interest installments. In fairness to the textbooks, it was already noted that there was a *basis swap spread* to be paid on one side of such a swap to make it fair, but it was also said that such a spread was small enough as to be negligible. Nowadays, this is no longer true. The basis spreads exploded during the crisis, and never came back to the almost zero levels from before. It is expected that this phenomenon will stay for good, just as the volatility smile never went away after the stock market crashes of 1987. Another way of expressing the basis spread is to say that the fixed rate of a fair swap with short tenors (e.g. 1 or 3 months) on the floating side is (sometimes much) lower than that of a swap with long tenors (e.g. 6 or 12 months), given that all other trade details remain the same.

It is clear that if LIBOR banks are deemed risky, then the longer the maturity of the loan they made, the more likely it is that the lender will not get her money back. It is also more likely that another liquidity crisis will strike in the meantime. Therefore, the longer the maturity of a loan, the higher the credit/liquidity premium that has to be paid on top of the risk-free rate (we'll see what the market deems to be a good proxy for that in the next section). Therefore, in addition to the "normal" positive slope of the risk-free yield curve, the LIBOR curve contains extra premia which grow with the maturity; this remains true if the risk-free yield curve is inverse. Conversely, if someone does a basis swap exchanging short vs long tenors, the two legs are usually linked to LIBOR and therefore contain the credit/liquidity premia, despite the fact that the swap is a derivative which is collateralized and can therefore be considered risk free. Hence, the party paying the shorter tenor has to reimburse the party paying the longer tenor in order to make the swap fair again. This is done via the basis swap spread.

4.1.3 Overnight indexed swaps

Finally, one further anomaly that is connected to the forward replication problem is the gap between the overnight indexed swap (OIS) and the LIBOR/EURIBOR swap rates. The gap between OIS and standard swaps observed before the crisis was close enough to zero as to be negligible; in the third quarter of 2008, they exploded to unprecedented levels. The overnight rate to which the floating leg of an OIS is linked can be viewed as the one involving the least possible credit risk; the longer you have to wait for the amount to come back, the higher the possibility that the counterpart may default or does not get the funding to pay back its debt. This view also affects the way the credit risk of derivatives between banks is mitigated. This is usually done by *collateral agreements* (Credit Support Annex, CSA). All trade types specified in the agreement are first netted by present value, and then the party whose net portfolio value is negative has to post collateral (either cash or securities) to the other party. If cash is posted, the collateral receiver has to pay the overnight rate on the collateral amount.

4.2 Origins

LIBOR includes risk. That's it. It just happens that, today, we have (almost) risk-free ways to calculate what it is. It does not mean that LIBOR doesn't have risk simply because we can calculate it.

The most problematic areas in pricing today are how to include multiple currencies and how to deal with the interaction of collateralization and funding. All the simple answers have limitations that derive precisely from funding. Remember that although deposit rates are observable on Bloomberg, actually attempting to execute at significant volume will immediately encounter the question "and who's asking?" Collateralization once appeared the answer to all pricing problems until it met the question "and where do you get the collateral from?" This immediately leads to discussions between Treasury, Collateral Management, and Trading. In effect, the historical separation may be useful operationally, but not for pricing. A fully collateralized trade must also be fully hedged to be free of pricing complexities, i.e. the need to obtain collateral to post when the trade is out of the money.

4.2.1 Collateralization and fixings

A fixing is the official value of a floating rate that is published once or twice a day. The official value may be based on a panel of banks (e.g. EURIBOR, LIBOR, etc.) or it may be calculated from actual transactions.

Consider collateralized swap trades; these are almost all exchange cleared, e.g. on LCH. The "almost all" is because some cross-currency basis swaps are in the process of moving to exchange clearing (early 2012). This is a vital point because it means that we can observe prices that are (at least for these standard instruments) essentially risk free.

"Essentially risk free" means that we have only overnight moves to con-
tend with and gap risk, i.e. the time from when a counterparty defaults
to when we can replace the (standard) trade with another counterparty
(also via central clearing). In a later chapter we consider the case when
trades are not collateralized, i.e. when there is explicit credit risk to
one or both parties.

Now, going back to the issue of risk, if these swaps are all collateralized and cleared via a central exchange, then why is there any basis at
all since there is (almost) no risk? We shall assume for the moment that
the swaps are fully hedged, or equivalently that the banks involved can
borrow at the rate paid on collateral. There is no risk for the swaps, true,
but swaps are derivatives which reference floating rates (i.e. loan rates)
and these floating rates contain risk. Risks are different for different
loan lengths. Notice that the loans that are referred to by the swaps
cannot – by definition – be collateralized *because they are loans*. The
floating rates of swaps are riskless estimates, of market expectations, of
the risk contained in lending for specified periods as reported through
particular mechanisms. Take, for example, the definition of EURIBOR:

> Euribor® is the rate at which Euro interbank term deposits are
> offered by one prime bank to another prime bank within the EMU
> zone, and is published at 11:00 a.m. (CET) for spot value (T+2).

Empirically it does not matter which banks are the prime banks or
even, since the numbers are (trimmed means of) self-reported beliefs
about other banks, whether they are telling the truth. All that matters is that swaps are derivatives of these numbers. An estimate as to
the degree of truthfulness can be obtained by comparing deposit rates
with EURIBOR or LIBOR fixings. Deposit rates will change intra-day,
whereas fixings are at a fixed time and the banks providing the deposit
rates are not the same as those in the panel, but even so an impres-
sion can be formed. However, as mentioned this has no bearing on
prices that reference the EURIBOR or LIBOR rates since these are the
observables, however constructed.

As an aside, at the end of 2011 there were 44 members of the EURI-
BOR panel, including AIB Group (an Irish bank), Dexia Bank (a Belgian
bank that was in the process of being split up) as well as German Lan-
desbanks, Spanish banks and Italian banks. According to EURIBOR, all
these banks were in good standing. In addition, at the same time EU
banks were depositing record sums overnight with the ECB rather than
with each other, e.g. EUR445.7B (December 29–30, 2011) at 0.25%
rather than to each other at the higher Eonia rate of 0.399%. (Of

course, it is much more expensive to borrow from the ECB overnight.) Whilst there are end-of-year effects for 30th December–1st January, the amounts and rates were similar for the preceeding week.

From a funding point of view, the key point is that collateral posted to another bank usually pays the OIS rate in the respective currency. This is set from the CSA between the two banks. Again, it does not matter where OIS comes from but only that cash is actually paid based on it. There is still a remaining complication that often the CSA between banks permits a choice of collateral currency, e.g. EUR, USD, GBP, (possibly CHF), for Western banks, and including JPY for banks operating in Asia.

4.3 Modeling approaches

Since the previous textbook approaches do not match observed prices, something must be done. Given the quantity of money at stake (think of the LCH quote in the introduction of the book), every significant bank has done *something* to match the market. The problem is, however, deep and complex. Simple solutions are approximations, but can still be useful.

4.3.1 Practicalities

It is becoming market consensus that since collateral pays OIS, the right curve to discount *collateralized* derivatives must be the OIS curve in the currency of the derivatives. This consensus involves several assumptions:

- derivative portfolios are fully hedged (i.e. no external funding requirements) within each currency;
- collateral is posted in cash and in the currency of the derivative;
- collateral received from one counterparty can be posted to another counterparty (rehypothecation), or an equivalent.

In credit there is the concept of the cheapest-to-deliver bond; in collateral there is an equivalent concept of the best-paying collateral. For example, why post dollars overnight as collateral if euros give you more yield overnight? Thus the carry trade moves to collateral.

This consensus still leaves open the question of how to discount any trade involving more than one currency. It also leaves open the question of how to discount the non-hedged part of any trade. The degree to which this matters can be surmised by reflecting on the extent to which non-complete-market models are used, such as those involving stochastic volatility. This is even before we consider missing market data, e.g. volatilities for non-standard tenors, correlations between almost anything, etc.

The market consensus above is supported by [Piterbarg (2010)]. If a bank can borrow and lend at the same riskless rate, then this rate is the correct one, from a replication point of view, to discount with. Although this statement appears theoretically abstract it is actually relevant. Consider a bank whose derivative portfolio is fully hedged and fully collateralized. In this case there is no credit risk. There is also no market risk. This means that any cash that needs to be posted will be made available by hedges. For non-prop trading desks this is the aspiration. Depending on the market, and the traders, it can be approached. The difference between aspiration and actuality is one that Product Control, Model Validation, and desk heads have to keep a very careful eye on. Anecdotally, pre-crisis, there were some credit desks that claimed that their CDOs were (mostly) hedged.

The paragraph above illustrates a typical problem, which is that although some sections of a bank may have excellent reasons for a given discount curve, this is only a local analysis. Most banks have more businesses than their derivative desks. Thus from a funding point of view we should use different discount curves (or an equivalent) for differently funded trades. Alternatively, a uniform blended discount curve could be used.

All of this implies a second problem: replication costs for different banks do not have to be the same if they have different funding costs. This was pointed out by [Morini and Prampolini (2011), Fries (2010)]. Market price also does not have to be the same as the (replication) cost for different participants. Although this statement is at odds with pre-crisis mathematical finance texts, it is absolutely no surprise to any trader.

We should also mention that pricing funding costs of non-fully-hedged trades using the risk-neutral measure can be questioned. After all, since they are not hedged their funding volumes will be paid in the real (aka historical) measure even if the rates are linked to LIBOR.

4.3.2 Simple approaches

Given the complexities of pricing, including all the funding possibilities available to a bank, and all the trades [Pallavicini *et al.* (2011)], simple approaches currently dominate practice.

Bianchetti's approach in [Bianchetti (2010)] is to consider the basis spread as a kind of exchange rate between two different indices, and to use a quanto adjustment to handle this in pricing. The disadvantage is that all corrections become model-dependent, even for plain vanilla derivatives like FRA or interest rate swaps.

Another way to attack the problem is to define different interest curves for different instruments. An overview of the different approaches to that is given in [Gallagher and O'Keeffe (2009)]. The so-called homogeneous curves implementation assigns one curve for forward building and discounting to each tenor, so a 3-month swap would be priced off a special 3-month curve, etc. The disadvantage here is that the same cash flow might be discounted differently only because it occurs in a different instrument. For consistent pricing, one has to define one discount curve per currency and then define individual forward curves for each tenor. One would think that the natural discount curve in a given currency would be that currency's default tenor curve, e.g. 6 months in EUR, 3-months in USD.

There is a tendency in the market, e.g. LCH, to use curves built from overnight interest rate swaps (OIS) as the standard discount curve in each currency. We call this the Local Discount Curve approach. Two variants are described in [Mercurio (2009)]. Piterbarg's calculations [Piterbarg (2010)] support this within single currencies when a bank can borrow and lend at the same riskless rate (e.g. fully hedged and collateralized portfolios). This may indeed be valid for the LCH, but we wonder how widely it applies to the LCH clearing members. To price cross-currency basis swaps correctly, the local discount curves have to be adjusted by special factors in cross-currency trades. Again, this introduces different discount factors for the same cash flow, just because it is coming from a special instrument. If the funding and collateral currencies are considered on a per-instrument basis this is justified. To some extent this may be forced by collateral requirements from a clearing house. However, in early 2012, cross-currency basis swaps were not on central clearing.

An approach that produces consistent global discount curves across currencies and basis effects is described in [Tuckman and Hom (2003)], and expanded on in [Gallagher and O'Keeffe (2009)]. We call this the Global Discount Curve approach. It works as follows: first, one defines a reference currency, and calculates the discount and the forward curves in that currency just as before in the [Mercurio (2009)] method. Then one derives the discount and forward curves in another currency by using the available basis spread information in that currency and in the cross-currency market. That means that one will never agree the curves in the second currency with a counterparty calculating values using that currency as a reference, but *all* cash flows in any given currency will be discounted the same way no matter in which instrument they occur.

The key difference between the Local and Global discount curve approaches is the weight that they place on cross-currency basis swaps (CCBS). In the Global approach CCBS are the key to obtaining foreign currency and hence determine the appropriate discount curve for that currency. In the Local approach they simply reflect the use of a non-local collateral currency for at least one of the counterparties.

Both the Local and Global discount approaches are based on fully collateralized and fully hedged trades. Pricing non-hedged trades (even collateralized) requires funding considerations. Pricing non-hedged, non-collateralized trades requires both funding and credit considerations (i.e. CVA, DVA, and FVA). Note that although the acronyms are separate, the calculations need not be (and in some cases cannot be separated).

The next two chapters explore the pricing of simple, linear interest rate derivatives under basis spread risk. Chapter 7 then looks at how to price non-linear products like caps and swaptions. While there are formulas for pricing these in [Mercurio (2009)], it is necessary to obtain volatility data for these products, which are not readily available in the market.

5
Local Discount Curves

Pauca sed matura
[Few, but ripe]
Motto of Carl Friedrich Gauss

For an introduction to the bootstrapping of a zero curve, see Chapter 2. We assume in this chapter that a discount curve is available which can be used to discount any future cash flow.

The main idea in the implementation of basis spread-adjusted curves is the shuffling of the basis spread from one leg to another. In all cases, this is quite straightforward and only involves the value of a base point on the legs of the swaps in question, and possibly the FX rate in the case of cross-currency trades. The most general result is Equation (6.2); all the other formulas can be derived from it by setting the FX rate to 1 and/or setting one of the cross-currency spreads to 0.

A word on notation: in what follows, a lot of basis spreads are used. To distinguish them, we use a superscript to denote the two tenors (or currencies) for which they are valid, e.g. $s^{3/6}$ is the fair basis spread for a 3-month vs 6-month basis swap in one currency, where the spread is applied to the 3-month leg. There will also be a spread $s^{6/3}$ which is applied to the 6-month leg. For cross-currency swaps, the spreads are denoted like $s^{EUR/USD}$, which means this is the fair spread on the EUR leg on a USD/EUR basis swap. To stress the tenor of the EUR leg, we also sometimes write $s^{3EUR/USD}$, etc.

5.1 Basis swaps in one currency

This section describes the construction of a set of forward-generating curves together with a single discounting curve that is applied to any projected or deterministic cash flow in the future. Section 5.1.1 focuses on a discount curve built from instruments having the standard tenor, whereas Section 5.1.2 explains the details when using an OIS discount curve.

5.1.1 Standard tenor discount curve

The market quotes basis swaps via the (annualized) basis spread. This spread is always applied to the leg with the shorter tenor. There are quotes for ON/3, 3/6, 1/3, 1/6, 3/12 and 6/12 swaps (tenor/tenor in months, ON = overnight). For example, if the quote for a 6/12 swap for 4 years maturity is 3.9 bp, this means that a swap paying 6-month EURIBOR + 3.9 bp against 12-month EURIBOR flat is fair at inception. There is another interpretation of the quoted spreads, namely that the number quoted is the difference of the par yields of two swaps, exchanging annual fixed payments against floating with the respective tenors. Compare with Equation (5.1) and Equation (5.4). We will use this interpretation of the basis spread as the difference of swap rates in Chapter 7.

Some valuation systems allow the definition of curves as spread curves over other curves. This means that in the case of a default 6-month tenor curve called EURIB, we define a EUR1M curve which uses the 1/6 spreads as spread over the default curve. This works in such a way that the swap from the example would be priced correctly with 0. The same holds in the 3/6 case. However, in the 6/12 case the spread is quoted on the 6-month leg, so we will have to move the spread to the 12-month leg in that case. This is done as follows. Every forward will have a tenor k associated with it, where k can be 6 or 12. Let $f_i^k = f_i^k(t)$ be the forward rate based on a k-tenor curve at time t for the period t_{i-1}^k to t_i^k. We denote the times assigned to different tenors with a superscript of that tenor so that the periods cannot be confused. To ease notation, we will write from here on

$$\tau_{i,j}^k := \tau_{t_i^k, t_j^k}.$$

Let d_i^k denote the discount factor for time t_i^k. For maturity T, let $n^k(T)$ denote the number of periods between t_0 and T (which is the integer next to $12/k \times T$). Finally, define the *annuity factor* of a *variable* swap leg of tenor k as

$$A_T^k := \sum_{i=1}^{n^k(T)} \tau_{i-1,i}^k d_i^k.$$

Now the spread $s^{6/12}$ is the spread that makes the following equation hold:

$$\sum_{j=1}^{n^{12}(T)} f_j^{12} \tau_{j-1,j}^{12} d_j^{12} = \sum_{i=1}^{n^6(T)} (f_i^6 + s_T^{6/12}) \tau_{i-1,i}^6 d_i^6$$

$$= \sum_{i=1}^{n^6(T)} f_i^6 \tau_{i-1,i}^6 d_i^6 + s^{6/12} A_T^6. \tag{5.1}$$

Bringing $s^{6/12} A_T^6$ to the left-hand side and computing it as a spread $s^{12/6}$, we find

$$s_T^{12/6} = -s_T^{6/12} \frac{A_T^6}{A_T^{12}}. \tag{5.2}$$

The same calculation has to be done, for instance, for the USD LIBOR curve to move the spread on the 3-month leg of 3/6 and 3/12 month swaps to the long tenor leg.

The above calculations can be used as well to derive the basis swap spread from the two swap rates S_T^k and S_T^l which correspond to the two tenors involved in the swap. If we define the *swap rate annuity factor* as

$$A_T^f := \sum_{i=1}^{n^f(T)} \tau_{i-1,i}^f d_i^f,$$

where f is the frequency of a standard fixed-rate leg, we see that

$$S_T^k = \frac{\sum_{j=1}^{n^k(T)} f_j^k \tau_{j-1,j}^k d_j^k}{A_T^f}, \tag{5.3}$$

so the swap rate of tenor k is a martingale under the measure associated with the numeraire A_T^f regardless of the tenor k, and the same is true for the difference of two such swap rates. The definition of A_T^f uses the tenor on the *fixed* leg of a swap, which is, at least in EUR, the same – 12 months – regardless of the tenor on the floating side. Note that the day count convention differs from that of a 12-month floating leg, so the two annuities will be slightly different in that case.

Now we can divide Equation (5.1) (with general frequencies k and l instead of 6 and 12) by A_T^f to get

$$s_T^{k/l} = (S_T^l - S_T^k) \frac{A_T^f}{A_T^k}. \tag{5.4}$$

where the basis spread is assumed to be added to the leg of frequency
k. The difference from the interpretation of the basis swap as the difference of the two swap rates (without the adjustment factor) hinted
at above is very small.

5.1.2 OIS discount curve

Most derivatives, at least those traded between banks, are collateralized. A *collateral agreement* is a contract under which the values of all
derivatives of certain classes with one counterparty are netted, and
the remaining value is secured by the party with a negative net value
by posting collateral to the other party, either as cash or in the form
of securities. The party receiving the cash pays the overnight rate as
interest on it. Nowadays, collateral calls are made on a daily revaluation basis provided the value change reaches a specified threshold.
There is usually a certain lag, called the *margin period of risk*, between
the revaluation and the actual collateral exchange for the value date.
This lag is due to disputes, time spent to send money, and other minor
factors. The development of a collateralized portfolio within the margin period of risk poses the residual credit risk and should not be
ignored. Especially in times of high market stress, e.g. after the default
of Lehman Brothers, values can move substantially in a short time.
However, collateralized derivatives can still be considered less risky
or even risk-free and should be discounted with a curve that reflects
that.

Even before the crisis, there was a discussion about what curve
best represented the risk-free discount curve; see for instance
[Lando (2004)]. In an environment where the government has the
power to print money, the obvious candidate would be a curve built
from government bonds. However, there are liquidity effects that make
newly issued bonds behave differently than more mature ones, or regulatory requirements may distort the bond prices. In addition, in the
Euro zone, no single government has the power to print Euro money;
the current sovereign debt crisis in Europe is in part a result of that
(apart from the fact that several European countries simply have too
much debt).

The next candidate is a curve built from repo rates. There we have
the problem that the market is only liquid up to maturities of 1–2
years, and, in addition, the repo market can completely dry up, too,
as happened in late 2008.

The third candidate is a curve built from overnight instruments.
Overnight Index Swaps (OIS) are trades that swap fixed rate payments

against accumulated overnight fixings on an annual or semiannual basis, or once at maturity if that is less than the standard period length. OIS are traded with maturities starting at 1 week up to 30 years; liquid quotes of these maturities are available in USD, EUR, GBP, CHF, and JPY. Spreads against other tenors are available for up to 30 years as well.

There is a strong tendency in the market, triggered by the big investment banks, to use an OIS curve to price (cash) collateralized derivatives transactions; see [Whittall (2010)] and also the quote on page xvii. The OIS curve is the right curve to discount collateralized deals because cash collateral accrues the overnight rate as interest. As an example, look at a standard EUR swap whose last fixing on the floating leg (linked to 6-month EURIBOR) has just happened. Assume the fixed leg pays 5%, and that the last EURIBOR fixing was 0.952%. Let the notional of the swap be 100 million EUR. This means that the net payment due at the end of the period is $5 - 0.476 = 4.524$ million EUR. To go easy on the computations in the text, the floating resp. fixed period is assumed to be 0.5 resp. 1 year long. The actual year fractions may be slightly different. As the fixing just happened, the value of the net payment is $4,524,000/(1 + 0.476\%) = 4,502,567.78$ EUR if we discount using the standard 6-month curve. However, let's assume that the 6-month OIS rate is, say, 0.483% (p.a.). This means that the expectation of the market is that the collateral of $4,502,567.78$ will be worth $4,513,441.48$ EUR in 6 months' time, which is less than the assumed value of $4,524,000$ EUR. If the discounting happened at the OIS rate, this discrepancy would disappear. The OIS and EURIBOR rates above are actual examples from the same day (April 7, 2010). The difference between the two was even higher during the credit crisis.

The same argument can be used for derivatives with uncertain cash flows. A more formal argument is presented in [Fujii *et al.* (2010)], which we recount here. Assume that collateralization happens continuously without delays caused by disputes, minimum amounts, thresholds, etc. If the standard interest rate is denoted by r, the rate to be paid on collateral (i.e. the OIS rate) by c, h is the value of a specific derivative, a is the size of the derivative position, and V is the collateral that has to be pledged, we have the following stochastic differential equation:

$$dV(s) = (r(s) - c(s))V(s)ds + a(s)dh(s).$$

This can be explicitly solved to

$$V(T) = \exp\left(\int_0^s (r(u) - c(u))\,du\right) V(0)$$

$$+ \int_0^T \exp\left(\int_s^T (r(u) - c(u))\,du\right) a(s)\,dh(s).$$

Now at the start we have $V(0) = h(0)$ because the derivative is perfectly collateralized, and if we choose $a(s) = \exp\left(\int_t^s (r(u) - c(u))\,du\right)$, we get

$$V(T) = \exp\left(\int_0^T (r(u) - c(u))\,du\right) V(0)$$

$$+ \exp\left(\int_0^T (r(u) - c(u))\,du\right) \int_0^T dh(s)$$

$$= \exp\left(\int_0^T (r(u) - c(u))\,du\right) h(T).$$

Discounting to time 0 we get

$$h(0) = \mathbb{E}_0\left(\exp\left(-\int_0^T r(u)\,du\right) \exp\left(\int_0^T (r(u) - c(u))\,du\right) h(T)\right)$$

$$= \mathbb{E}_0\left(\exp\left(-\int_0^T c(u)\,du\right) h(T)\right),$$

where $\mathbb{E}_0(\cdot)$ is expectation conditional on the information available at time $s = 0$.

It should be noted that the OIS rates are much lower than the LIBOR rates. As a result, the future cash flows will have a higher NPV, which means that the party owing collateral under LIBOR discounting will probably owe even more after switching to OIS discounting. This should be considered in liquidity projections.

There is another advantage in using an OIS curve: it is almost completely built from derivative instruments, as opposed to the standard approach where one has to use cash instruments, at least up to the length of the tenor of the curve-building instruments. As the tenor of OIS is overnight, the only cash market rate is the overnight rate, which is the least risky cash rate of them all.

At a first glance, there seems to be a difference between OIS instruments and "normal" swaps, because the OIS pay compounded interest annually (or as a zero coupon for maturities less than one year), in particular, when we want to move spreads from the OIS side to the other. However, if we use a discount curve built from OIS, then first compounding the daily fixings to the end of a payment period and then discounting to the valuation date amounts to the same present value as daily payments that are individually discounted to the valuation date first and then summed up. This is because the discounting and the forward curve are the same, so the fundamental equation

$$f_{t_1,t_2} = \frac{1}{\tau_{1,2}}\left(\frac{d_1}{d_2} - 1\right) \tag{5.5}$$

holds, in other words,

$$f_{t_1,t_2}\tau_{1,2}(1 + f_{t_2,t_3}\tau_{2,3})d_3 = f_{t_1,t_2}\tau_{1,2}d_2.$$

The bottom line of this is: OIS/3m basis swaps are quoted with the spread on the OIS leg, so if we want to move the basis spread from the OIS leg to the 3-month leg, we can apply the analogue of Equation (5.2) to this situation:

$$s^{3/\text{OIS}} = -s^{\text{OIS}/3}\frac{A_T^{\text{OIS}}}{A_T^3}, \tag{5.6}$$

where $A^{\text{OIS}} = \sum_{i=1}^{n^{\text{OIS}}(T)} \tau_{i-1,i}d_i$ and $n^{\text{OIS}}(T)$ is the number of overnight fixings in the period.

Now, to get the fair OIS basis spread for tenor $k = 6, 12$, we split the swap OIS vs k months + $s^{k/\text{OIS}}$ in two, namely an OIS vs 3 months + $s^{3/\text{OIS}}$ swap and a 3 months + $s^{3/\text{OIS}}$ vs k months + $s^{k/\text{OIS}}$. On the latter, we move $s^{3/\text{OIS}}$ to the k-month leg, so we have a fair swap exchanging 3-month flat vs k-month + $s^{k/\text{OIS}} - s^{3/\text{OIS}}A_T^3/A_T^k$. The only way that this is fair is that the spread on the k-month leg equals $s^{k/3}$, so

$$
\begin{aligned}
s^{k/\text{OIS}} &= s^{k/3} + s^{3/\text{OIS}}\frac{A_T^3}{A_T^k} \\
&= -s^{3/k}\frac{A_T^3}{A_T^k} - s^{\text{OIS}/3}\frac{A_T^{\text{OIS}}}{A_T^3}\frac{A_T^3}{A_T^k} \\
&= -\frac{s^{\text{OIS}/3}A_T^{\text{OIS}} + s^{3/k}A_T^3}{A_T^k}.
\end{aligned}
$$

For $k = 1$, the basis spread $s^{1/3}$ against 3 months is already on the 1-month leg, so we get

$$s^{1/\text{OIS}} = s^{1/3} - s^{\text{OIS}/3}\frac{A_T^{\text{OIS}}}{A_T^1}. \tag{5.7}$$

5.2 Building the forward curve

Once one has defined a standard curve used for discounting (and for pricing instruments that have the same tenor as the ones used for building that curve), one has to define the curves to be used for calculating forwards. We will illustrate this with the 3-month EURIBOR curve, where the standard curve is the 6-month EURIBOR curve. We assume we already have the 6-month discount curve and the spreads on the 3-month leg of 3/6 basis swaps for various tenors. These spreads are only available for some discrete points like annual maturities between 1 and 10 years, then 12, 15, 20, 25, 30 years. As the forwards to be generated have maturities shorter than one year (except for the 12-month curve), this means that we have to make assumptions on the behavior of the spread between the quoted points. We interpret zero rates as continuous rates, i.e. the connection between the zero rate r_t for time t and the discount factor d_t is $d_t = \exp(-r_t t)$.

Now we start to bootstrap the forward curve from the default curve and the basis swap spreads. Let l be the standard tenor, $k \neq l$ the tenor for which a curve has to be built. Starting with the 1-year quote, we are looking for spreads $s_i^k, i = 1, \ldots, n^k(1)$ such that the forwards f_i^k generated from the curve associated with $d_i' = \exp(-(r_i + s_i^k)t_i)$ make a basis swap k months + $s^{k/l}$ vs l months fair, where the forwards are defined as in Equation (5.5):

$$
\begin{aligned}
d_0 - d_T &= \sum_{i=1}^{n^l(T)} f_i^l \tau_{i-1,i}^l d_i^l \\
&= \sum_{j=1}^{n^k(T)} (f_j^k + s^{k/l}) \tau_{j-1,j}^k d_j^k \\
&= s^{k/l} A_T^k + \sum_{j=1}^{n^k(T)} \frac{1}{\tau_{j-1,j}^k} \left(\frac{d_{j-1}'}{d_j'^k} - 1 \right) \tau_{j-1,j}^k d_j^k \\
&= s^{k/l} A_T^k + \sum_{j=1}^{n^k(T)} \left(\exp(-(r_{j-1} + s_{j-1}^k)t_{j-1}^k + s_j^k t_j^k) - \exp(-r_j t_j^k) \right).
\end{aligned} \tag{5.8}
$$

As we have no information about the instantaneous basis spread, we assume that the spread is constant up until 1 year. That means, we have to solve

$$
d_0 - d_1 - s^{k/l} A_1^k = \sum_{j=1}^{n^k(1)} \left(\exp(-r_{j-1} t_{j-1}^k - s^k \tau_{j-1,j}^k) - \exp(-r_{t_j^k} t_j^k) \right) \tag{5.9}
$$

for s^k. For higher maturities we follow an inductive process by assuming that the spreads s^k_j have been determined up to $j = n^k(T) - l$, and we want to find the ones for $j = n^k(T) - l + 1, \ldots, n^k(T)$. We have to solve

$$d_0 - d_T - s^{k/l} A^k_T =$$

$$\sum_{j=1}^{n^k(T)-l} \left(\exp(-(r_{j-1} + s^k_{j-1})t^k_{j-1} + s^k_j t^k_j) - \exp(-r_j t^k_j) \right)$$

$$+ \sum_{j=n^k(T)-l+1}^{n^k(T)} \left(\exp(-(r_{j-1} + s^k_{j-1})t^k_{j-1} + s^k_j t^k_j) - \exp(-r_j t^k_j) \right).$$

$$(5.10)$$

Recall that we only have one additional number, the quoted spread $s^{k/l}$, at time $t_{n^k(T)}$. Therefore, one has to either parameterize the spread curve and optimize the parameters to best fit the given data, or to make simplifying assumptions on the shape of the spread term structure. The simplest way to do this is to assume again that the missing $s^k_{t_j}$ are constant, but this is not an approach commonly used.

Another possibility which results in slightly more complex calculations is the assumption that the s^k_j between $s^k_{n^k(T)-l}$ and $s^k_{n^k(T)}$ lie on a straight line which may have a slope $\neq 0$. In other words, we have to find $s^k_{n^k(T)}$ such that for $j = n^k(T) - l + 1, \ldots, n^k(T)$

$$s^k_{t^k_j} = s^k_{n^k(T)-l} + \frac{s^k_{n^k(T)} - s^k_{n^k(T)-l}}{\tau^k_{n^k(T)-l,n^k(T)}} \tau^k_{j,n^k(T)-l}$$

$$= s^k_{n^k(T)-l} \frac{\tau^k_{j,n^k(T)}}{\tau^k_{n^k(T)-l,n^k(T)}} + s^k_{n^k(T)} \frac{\tau^k_{n^k(T)-l,j}}{\tau^k_{n^k(T)-l,n^k(T)}}$$

is satisfied.

Using this piecewise linear approach, we can expand the expression involving spreads in Equation (5.10) with a little algebra as follows:

$$s^k_j t^k_j - s^k_{j-1} t^k_{j-1} = s^k_{n^k(T)-l} \frac{t^k_{n^k(T)} \tau^k_{j-1,j} + ((t^k_j)^2 - (t^k_{j-1})^2)}{\tau^k_{n^k(T)-l,n^k(T)}}$$

$$+ s^k_{n^k(T)} \frac{t^k_{n^k(T)-l} \tau^k_{j-1,j} + ((t^k_{j-1})^2 - (t^k_j)^2)}{\tau^k_{n^k(T)-l,n^k(T)}}.$$

However, using a linear interpolation can lead to unwanted behavior on the forward curve, as the following example shows.

5.3 Example

In this section we want to provide an example of the importance of the chosen interpolation method. Table 5.1 shows the market data from November 21, 2011. On the left are the quotes for EURIBOR instruments (cash up to 6 months, 6-month forwards up to 18 months, swap rates), EONIA swap rates in the middle, and USD LIBOR swap rates on the right.

The resulting zero curves are shown in Figure 5.1 and in Table 5.2. Note that the EURIBOR curve is stripped using linear interpolation, whereas the EONIA curve is stripped using splines. The EURIBOR curve shows a marked spike where the cash instruments are replaced by derivatives.

Table 5.3 shows the spreads that make the quoted 3-month EURIBOR swap fair when discounting with the EURIBOR resp. EONIA zero curve. They are interpreted as the spread one has to add to the 3-month leg (in both cases) in order to make the price of the corresponding basis swap 0.

Figure 5.2 shows the resulting curves which are used to generate the 3-month forwards relative to the corresponding disocunt curve. E3M resp. EO3M is the forward-generating curve associated with EURIBOR resp. EONIA. Apart from the spike at the short end of the E3M curve (which it inherits from the EURIBOR curve, i.e. is caused by the switch from cash to derivative instruments), there does not appear to be much of a difference between the two curves. However, Figure 5.3 shows that the actual forwards generated from these curves are significantly different and look a lot more stable on the EO3M curve. This is mainly due to the two different interpolation methods.

5.4 Cross-currency basis swaps

In principle, the method from the previous section to move spreads from one swap leg to another can be applied to cross-currency swaps. However, there are some details that differ. Cross-currency basis swaps are again quoted via spreads. There is a base currency (usually USD) and the foreign currency, and the spread quoted for such a swap is to be applied on the foreign currency leg. The only exception is the Mexican Peso (MXN), where the spread needs to be applied on the USD

Table 5.1 Market-quoted EURIBOR, EONIA, USD LIBOR, and FedFund rates as of November 21, 2011 (left to right)

Term	Forward End	EURIBOR	EONIA	USD LIBOR	FedFund
1D		0.650	0.650	0.25000	0.27500
2D		0.650	0.650	0.25000	0.25000
3D			0.675		
1W		0.850	0.703	0.32000	0.08600
2W		0.940	0.691	0.40500	0.08850
3W		1.025	0.680	0.44000	0.08750
1M		1.140	0.646	0.47500	0.09100
2M		1.275	0.586	0.61000	0.09500
3M		1.430	0.543	0.73005	0.10200
4M		1.490	0.519		0.10600
5M		1.570	0.510		0.11000
6M		1.680	0.502		0.11300
3M	6M			0.77950	
6M	9M			0.83500	
9M	12M			0.83650	
12M	15M			0.83000	
7M			0.498		0.11500
8M			0.497		0.11700
9M			0.495		0.11800
10M			0.494		0.12000
11M			0.496		0.12200
12M			0.497		0.12400
15M			0.509		0.12800
18M			0.529		0.13500
21M			0.557		0.14500
1M	7M	1.624			
2M	8M	1.565			
3M	9M	1.524			
4M	10M	1.487			
5M	11M	1.465			
6M	12M	1.444			
12M	18M	1.433			
2Y		1.555	0.592	0.79650	0.16000
3Y		1.669	0.796	0.89550	0.28700
4Y		1.845	1.037	1.09450	0.52250
5Y		2.028	1.275	1.33150	0.79400
6Y		2.194	1.486	1.55850	
7Y		2.326	1.665	1.75150	1.27000
8Y		2.433	1.812	1.90750	
9Y		2.526	1.943	2.03550	
10Y		2.607	2.043	2.14350	1.7410
11Y		2.682	2.141		
12Y		2.752	2.232	2.31850	1.94400
15Y		2.891	2.432	2.47850	2.15000
20Y		2.899	2.483	2.58550	2.29500
25Y		2.824	2.443	2.63350	2.37000
30Y		2.741	2.384	2.66450	2.41600
40Y		2.736	2.418	2.67000	
50Y		2.766	2.452	2.63500	2.41600

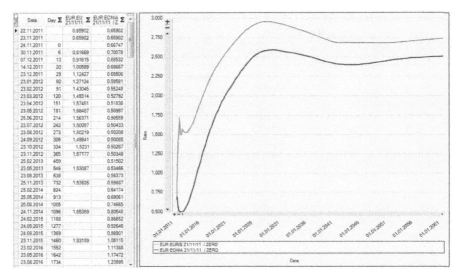

Date	Day Σ	EUR EU 21/11/11 Σ	EUR EONIA 21/11/11 /Σ
22.11.2011		0.65902	0.65902
23.11.2011		0.65902	0.65902
24.11.2011	0		0.66747
30.11.2011	6	0.81669	0.70078
07.12.2011	13	0.91615	0.69532
14.12.2011	20	1.00589	0.68967
23.12.2011	29	1.12427	0.65506
23.01.2012	60	1.27124	0.59581
23.02.2012	91	1.43045	0.55248
23.03.2012	120	1.49314	0.52792
23.04.2012	151	1.57451	0.51838
23.05.2012	181	1.66487	0.50997
25.06.2012	214	1.56371	0.50559
23.07.2012	242	1.50097	0.50433
23.08.2012	273	1.50219	0.50268
24.09.2012	306	1.49841	0.50085
23.10.2012	334	1.5231	0.50267
23.11.2012	365	1.57177	0.50348
25.02.2013	459		0.51502
23.05.2013	546	1.53087	0.53466
23.08.2013	638		0.56373
25.11.2013	732	1.53826	0.59887
25.02.2014	824		0.64174
25.05.2014	913		0.69061
25.08.2014	1005		0.74665
24.11.2014	1096	1.65359	0.80548
24.02.2015	1188		0.86652
24.05.2015	1277		0.92646
24.08.2015	1369		0.98901
23.11.2015	1460	1.93159	1.05115
23.02.2016	1552		1.11388
23.05.2016	1642		1.17472
23.08.2016	1734		1.23595

Figure 5.1   Zero curves generated from EURIBOR and EONIA instrument quotes.

leg. On how to move the spread to the MXN leg, see Chapter 6, and in particular Equation (6.2). There are also some currencies in Eastern European countries (e.g. HUF and CZK) which are only quoted against EUR.

The cross-currency spread is used for pricing by attaching it to the *discount curve* rather than the forward curve. The spread is always quoted against USD, so there is no pricing adjustment needed for USD legs. In the example of a USD/EUR cross-currency swap, we'd have to build the forwards on the EUR leg with the curve associated with the tenor of the leg, and discount the cash flows with the spread-adjusted discount curve. It is important to note that the swaps to which the quotes refer have a 3-month tenor on both legs, and this is where another calculation has to be done for currencies which have a default tenor different from 3 months (like EUR, which has a 6 month default tenor). This computation is done as follows. Assume we have a USD 3m vs EUR 6m swap. In what follows, we assume that all involved swaps have a notional exchange at inception and maturity, because that is the standard for cross-currency swaps. The notional in the reference currency EUR is supposed to be 1. The fact that the spread is only applied to the interest payments means that the formulas don't change because the instruments we use to derive them are fair by market definition. We do not consider notional cash adjustments on either leg of the swap here, although that is also a fairly common type of cross-currency swap. We

Table 5.2 Zero curves for EURIBOR, EONIA, USD LIBOR, and FedFund as of November 21, 2011 (left to right)

[Date]	EURIBOR	EONIA	USD LIBOR	FedFund
22.11.2011	0.65902	0.65902	0.25347	0.278818
23.11.2011	0.65902	0.65902	0.25347	0.266145
30.11.2011	0.81669	0.70078	0.30866	0.126961
07.12.2011	0.91615	0.69532	0.39095	0.111780
14.12.2011	1.00589	0.68667	0.42931	0.104142
23.12.2011	1.12427	0.65506	0.46725	0.103128
23.01.2012	1.27124	0.59591	0.60658	0.101703
23.02.2012	1.43045	0.55248	0.72915	0.106866
23.05.2012	1.68487	0.50997	0.75870	0.110033
23.08.2012	1.50219	0.50208	0.78770	0.120647
23.11.2012	1.57177	0.50348	0.80258	0.126407
25.11.2013	1.53826	0.59887	0.79236	0.162554
24.11.2014	1.65359	0.80548	0.89245	0.290797
23.11.2015	1.83159	1.05115	1.09383	0.530044
23.11.2016	2.01702	1.29572	1.33508	0.806739
23.11.2018	2.32491	1.70194	1.77099	1.301388
25.11.2019	2.43680	1.85712	1.93550	
23.11.2020	2.53428	1.99696	2.07113	
23.11.2021	2.62071	2.10414	2.18719	1.802946
23.11.2026	2.93038	2.53458	2.55366	2.252291
24.11.2031	2.91759	2.57371	2.66558	2.408112
24.11.2036	2.80392	2.50302	2.71120	2.487016
25.11.2041	2.68365	2.41127	2.74099	2.534866
23.11.2061	2.73798	2.50933	2.64540	2.488567

want to determine the spread s^{total} which renders the swap fair. To that end, we split the swap into two fair swaps, a standard cross-currency swap 3m USD vs 3m EUR + $s^{3\text{EUR/USD}}$, and a EUR basis swap EUR 3m + $s^{3\text{EUR/USD}}$ vs EUR 6m + s^{total}. Moving $s^{3\text{EUR/USD}}$ from the 3 to the 6-month leg, we get a fair swap 3m flat vs 6m + $s^{\text{total}} - s^{3\text{EUR/USD}} A_T^3/A_T^6$. Therefore, we must have

$$s^{6/3} = -s^{3/6}\frac{A_T^3}{A_T^6} = s^{\text{total}} - s^{3\text{EUR/USD}}\frac{A_T^3}{A_T^6},$$

which means that

$$s^{\text{total}} = \left(s^{3\text{EUR/USD}} - s^{3/6}\right)\frac{A_T^3}{A_T^6}. \tag{5.11}$$

There is a source for a small error in Equation (5.11). The theoretical derivation is sound as it only uses instruments which are fair by market

Table 5.3 Market-quoted 3 vs 6 month basis spreads (left) and converted EONIA vs 3 month basis spreads (November 21, 2011)

Term	3 vs 6 Spread	EONIA vs 3 Spread
1Y	30.150	−77.9747
2Y	25.200	−68.9793
3Y	21.850	−63.1267
4Y	19.650	−58.5319
5Y	18.000	−54.2915
6Y	16.700	−50.8394
7Y	15.700	−46.9506
8Y	14.650	−43.8494
9Y	13.900	−40.6089
10Y	13.025	−39.4670
11Y	12.350	−37.4586
12Y	11.750	−36.1450
15Y	10.800	−30.7948
20Y	9.100	−28.1888
25Y	8.050	−25.8427
30Y	7.300	−24.3291
40Y	6.300	−21.4537
50Y	5.700	−21.5941

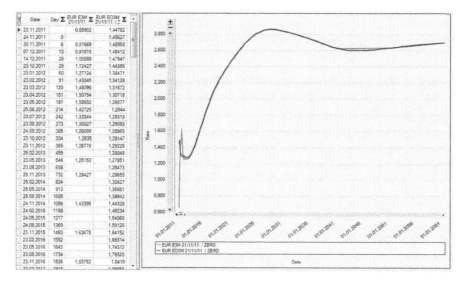

Figure 5.2 3-month forward-generating curves calculated from spreads over EURIBOR and EONIA zero curves.

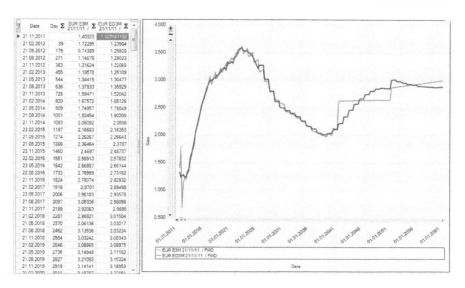

Figure 5.3 3-month forwards calculated from the E3M and EO3M curves.

definition. Yet the practical implementation discounts the EUR leg of the cross-currency swaps differently than in the single currency case. Therefore, the two 3-month legs do *not* cancel each other out. The error is of the order of the quotient A_T^{XCCY}/A_T^3 of the annuities calculated off the cross-currency adjusted EUR discount curve and the 3-month EURIBOR curve, respectively. In practice, this error remains below 0.1 basis points and can be ignored. It is healed completely when using the global discount curve concept discussed in the next chapter because then there is only one discount curve per currency.

6
Global Discount Curve

Truth is ever to be found in simplicity, and not in the multiplicity and confusion of things.
Isaac Newton

With the advent of OIS discounting, the pricing of cross-currency products has also changed. In the past, one was not too concerned to have one discount curve per currency for single currency products, and a separate one per currency to use when pricing cross-currency swaps and such. Given that the latter are collateralized just like the former, it does not make sense to use different discount curves. This means that one has to define all curves in a currency f different from the funding (or domestic) currency d in a way that incorporates market quotes for both single currency instruments and cross-currency swaps to the domestic currency simultaneously. For a simplified approach see [Fujii *et al.* (2010)].

6.1 Curve construction

We assume we have the domestic discount curve completely stripped as well as the forward-generating curve for 3-month forwards, as described in Chapter 2 and Chapter 5. There are also quotes for OIS basis swaps, at least for some currency pairs like USD vs EUR, USD vs GBP, and USD vs JPY. Using these curves instead does not really change the following exposition very much it should only be noted that when 3 months are mentioned below, this should be replaced with overnight. We now want to create a foreign discount curve which renders the quoted standard cross-currency products (FX forwards and cross-currency swaps) fair. One further piece of information we need is the foreign discount factor from today on the spot date, which is 2 working days in most countries. This we take from the foreign money market.

Note that the curve we construct here will have a standard tenor of 3 months due to the conventions in the cross-currency swap market. If the standard tenor of currency f is 6 months, use the techniques described in Chapter 5 to build the discount curve as a 6-month curve by also including the 3/6 month basis spread on the foreign swap leg. The annuities appearing in what follows then have to be adjusted accordingly.

For quoted FX forwards, the derivation is very straightforward. We know the spot FX rate $X_s^{d/f}$, the domestic resp. foreign spot discount factor d_s^d resp. d_s^f, and the quoted FX forward $X_T^{d/f}$ for time T. Then

$$X_s^{d/f} = \frac{d_T^d}{d_s^d} X_T^{d/f} \frac{d_s^f}{d_T^f}, \text{ or}$$

$$d_T^f = \frac{d_T^d}{d_s^d} \frac{X_T^{d/f}}{X_s^{d/f}} d_s^f.$$

Next, we consider the cross-currency swap market between the domestic and foreign currency. A very important feature of a standard cross-currency swap is that it has a notional exchange (of predetermined notionals in the two currencies which are related by the spot FX rate) at the beginning and at the end of the swap. The notional on each leg remains fixed until maturity. To use that for extracting curve information, we have to know how to move the cross-currency spread from the f leg to the d leg. Note that in a cross-currency swap where neither currency is USD, one has to add the respective spread to each floating leg because cross-currency swaps are usually quoted against USD. Therefore, we have a spread on the d and the f leg, where either can be zero as well, for instance when $f = $ USD. Consider the value of the swap

f LIBOR 3m $\longleftrightarrow$ d LIBOR 3m
floating   floating
$+s^{f/\text{USD}}$ $+s^{d/\text{USD}}$
notional 1 f notional $X^{d/f}$ d

where, as before, $X^{d/f}$ is the value of one unit of the foreign currency expressed in the domestic currency. Now if $X^{f/d}$ is the value of one unit of the domestic currency expressed in the foreign currency, the swap's value is

$$
0 = X^{f/d} \left(-X^{d/f} \left(d_s^d + \sum_{i=1}^{n^3(T)} (f_i^{3d} + s_T^{d/\text{USD}}) \tau_{i-1,i}^d d_i^d + d_T^d \right) \right)
$$

$$
+ d_s^f - \sum_{j=1}^{n^3(T)} (f_j^{3f} + s_T^{f/\text{USD}}) \tau_{j-1,j}^f d_j^f - d_T^f
$$

$$
= -d_s^d + \sum_{i=1}^{n^3(T)} f_i^{3d} \tau_{i-1,i}^d d_i^d + s_T^{d/\text{USD}} A_T^{3d} + d_T^d
$$

$$
+ d_s^f - \sum_{j=1}^{n^3(T)} f_j^{3f} \tau_{j-1,j}^f d_j^f - s_T^{f/\text{USD}} A_T^{3f} - d_T^f
$$

$$
= -d_s^d + \sum_{i=1}^{n^3(T)} f_i^{3d} \tau_{i-1,i}^d d_i^d + d_T^d + s_T^{d/\text{USD}} A_T^{3d} - s_T^{f/\text{USD}} A_T^{3f}
$$

$$
+ d_s^f - \sum_{j=1}^{n^3(T)} f_j^{3f} \tau_{j-1,j}^f d_j^f - d_T^f. \tag{6.1}
$$

This means that the fair spread on the domestic currency leg is given by

$$
s^{d/f} = s_T^{d/\text{USD}} \frac{A_T^{3d}}{A_T^{3f}} - s_T^{f/\text{USD}}. \tag{6.2}
$$

We would like to argue now that in Equation (6.1),

$$
-d_s^d + \sum_{i=1}^{n^3(T)} f_i^{3d} \tau_{i-1,i}^d d_i^d + d_T^d = 0,
$$

as this is the cash flow of a floater. This is true if the discount curve is built from 3-month instruments, so one can skip directly to Equation (6.3) in that case and set $s^{3/6d}$ to 0. If, however, the tenor of the discounting curve is different from 3 months, we have to incorporate the corresponding basis spread in order to make the expression above 0. This is shown here for the example of a 6-month discounting curve, which is probably the other standard case:

$$\sum_{i=1}^{n^3(T)} (f_i^{3d} + s^{3/6d})\tau_{i-1,i}^d d_i^d = \sum_{j=1}^{n^6(T)} f_i^{6d}\tau_{j-1,j}^{6,d} d_j^{6,d} \quad \text{or}$$

$$\sum_{i=1}^{n^3(T)} f_i^{3d}\tau_{i-1,i}^d d_i^d = \sum_{j=1}^{n^6(T)} f_i^{6d}\tau_{j-1,j}^{6,d} d_j^{6,d} - s^{3/6d}A_T^{3d}.$$

From this, Equation (6.1) becomes

$$\sum_{j=1}^{n^3(T)} f_j^{3f}\tau_{j-1,j}^f d_j^f = s^{3/6d}A_T^{3d} + s_T^{f/\text{USD}}A_T^{3f} - s_T^{d/\text{USD}}A_T^{3d} - d_s^f + d_T^f. \quad (6.3)$$

At this point we assume that the foreign standard tenor is 3 months. It should be straight-forward to incorporate the 3/6 basis spread in the foreign market should this not be the case; it would just add another spread component times the right annuity factor to Equation (6.3).

To make the new curve consistent with the foreign swap market, we have to consider the second equation that needs to be satisfied:

$$c\sum_{i=1}^{m} \tau_{i-1,i}^f d_i^f = \sum_{j=1}^{n^3(T)} f_j^{3f}\tau_{j-1,j}^f d_j^f. \quad (6.4)$$

Plugging Equation (6.4) into Equation (6.3), we end up with

$$c\sum_{i=1}^{m} \tau_{i-1,i}^f d_i^f = s^{3/6d}A_T^{3d} + s_T^{f/\text{USD}}A_T^{3f} - s_T^{d/\text{USD}}A_T^{3d} - d_s^f + d_T^f. \quad (6.5)$$

If there is only one discount factor missing – d_T^f – then we're done, because from Equation (6.5) we get

$$d_T^f = \frac{-c\sum_{i=1}^{m-1} \tau_{i-1,i}^f d_i^f - s^{3/6d}A_T^{3d} - s_T^{f/\text{USD}}A_T^{3f} + s_T^{d/\text{USD}}A_T^{3d} + d_s^f}{1 - c\tau_{n^f(T)-1,n^f(T)}^f}.$$

$$(6.6)$$

If, however, there are several discount factors missing, we proceed as in Equation (5.10) by assuming that we already have the discount factors for all times t_j with $j = 1, \ldots, n^f(T) - l$ and we want to find them up to the next reference point, i.e. for times $t_j, j = n^f(T) - l + 1, \ldots, n^f(T)$.

Writing discount factors in terms of foreign zero rates, we see that Equation (6.5) can be written as

$$
\sum_{j=n^3(T)-l+1}^{n^3(T)} f_j^{3f} \tau_{j-1,j}^{f} e^{-r_j^f t_j^f} - e^{-r_{nf(T)}^f t_{nf(T)}^f} = \tag{6.7}
$$

$$
s^{3/6d} A_T^{3d} + s_T^{f/\text{USD}} A_T^{3f} - s_T^{d/\text{USD}} A_T^{3d} - d_s^f - \sum_{j=1}^{n^3(T)-l} f_j^{3f} \tau_{j-1,j}^{f} e^{-r_j^f t_j^f}.
$$

We make the assumption again that the zero rates are linear between two points of reference (i.e. times for which spreads are quoted). This means that the following holds for $j = n^f(T) - l + 1, \ldots, n^f(T) - 1$:

$$
r_j^f = r_{nf(T)}^f \frac{\tau_{nf(T)-l,j}^f}{\tau_{nf(T)-l,nf(T)}^f} + r_{nf(T)-l}^f \frac{\tau_{j,nf(T)}^f}{\tau_{nf(T)-l,nf(T)}^f}.
$$

Equation (6.7) can thus be rewritten as

$$
\sum_{j=n^3(T)-l+1}^{n^3(T)} f_j^{3f} \tau_{j-1,j}^{f} \exp\left(-\frac{r_{nf(T)-l}^f \tau_{nf(T),j}^f}{\tau_{nf(T)-l,nf(T)}^f} - \frac{r_{nf(T)}^f \tau_{nf(T)-l,j}^f}{\tau_{nf(T)-l,nf(T)}^f} \right)
$$

$$
- \exp\left(-r_{nf(T)}^f t_{nf(T)}^f \right) =
$$

$$
s^{3/6d} A_T^{3d} + s_T^{f/\text{USD}} A_T^{3f} - s_T^{d/\text{USD}} A_T^{3d} - d_s^f - \sum_{j=1}^{n^3(T)-l} f_j^{3f} \tau_{j-1,j}^{f} e^{-r_j^f t_j^f},
$$

which has to be solved for $r_{nf(T)}^f$.

As was described in Chapter 2 and Section 5.3, it may be necessary to use a more sophisticated interpolation method, like a spline interpolation, which will obviously make the stripping process more complex.

A few comments are in order. First, it should be noted that the discount curve thus constructed will be different from a foreign discount curve created directly from liquid currency f instruments, which can be problematic if one is comparing valuations with a counterparty which is funding itself in currency f; the difference between the curves is given roughly by the cross-currency spread. This problem might occur, for instance, when a EUR-based bank interacts with a USD-based bank. If both banks follow the global discount curve approach with their respective funding currency as base currency, they will not agree on the valuation. This shows that each bank should consider its counterparty's funding cost or the collateral currency when pricing trades; the same argument as in Section 5.1.2 shows that a derivative that is collateralized in the domestic currency has to be priced off a global discounting curve that is constructed as above. This can lead to a very confusing situation when dealing with many different counterparties from different currency environments. Compare [Fries (2010)] and [Fujii *et al.* (2010)].

Secondly, any trade priced off a foreign curve constructed with the global approach will show sensitivities not only against shifts of the foreign swap rates but also against shifts of the various basis spreads involved: the cross-currency swap rates of both domestic and foreign currency against USD, as well as potentially the basis swap spread in both currencies if either the domestic or the foreign standard tenor is different from 3 months (e.g. GBP). However, this makes sense if the collateral for the foreign currency trades is paid (and hence funded) in the domestic currency. Consider a bank B that has two subsidiaries D and F which are based in the domestic and foreign countries, respectively, and which fund themselves in currencies d and f, resp. If both subsidiaries have identical swaps in currency f with another bank C in the foreign country, the swap values calculated by D and F will differ, because D will use the global curve for pricing, whereas F will use its local curve. This shows how strongly the funding influences the pricing. There is a strong trend in the market to adjust collateral agreement contracts (CSAs) to a single currency, which is usually the funding/domestic currency of one of the counterparties.

Thirdly, when an OIS curve is used in the domestic/funding currency, and there are OIS cross-currency basis spreads for the domestic and foreign currencies, then the equation $\sum f_j \tau d_j + d_T = 1$ holds in USD. However, then it is necessary to build the appropriate forward curves based on the global discount curve in the foreign currency as well, but this is completely analogous to what's described in Section 5.2.

6.2 Example

In this section we present an example of the construction and usage of a global discount curve. We assume that the domestic/funding currency is EUR, that all derivatives are collateralized, and that we want to have a set of curves with which to price USD swaps and EUR/USD crosscurrency swaps. We will build the following set of curves:

Table 6.1 Market-quoted FedFund vs EONIA
basis spreads, and implied EONIA vs FedFund
spreads (November 21, 2011)

Term	Quoted FedFund vs EONIA Spread	Implied EONIA vs FedFund Spread
1Y	−74.50	74.6689
2Y	−69.25	69.4892
3Y	−62.25	62.4719
4Y	−56.75	56.9267
5Y	−53.00	53.1416
7Y	−45.50	45.5979
10Y	−33.50	33.5544
15Y	−22.75	22.7370
20Y	−17.50	17.4442
30Y	−10.50	10.5358

(1) a EUR overnight curve based on EONIA swap quotes – for this, we use the EONIA swap data from Table 5.1
(2) a EUR forward curve to generate 3-month EURIBOR forwards such that 3-month swap quotes are priced as 0 – for this, we use the EONIA vs 3-month spreads from Table 5.3
(3) a USD discount curve which renders quoted EUR/USD cross-currency swaps which exchange EONIA vs the FedFund rate fair – the EONIA/FedFund spreads are shown in Table 6.1. That table also shows the implied spreads (as described in Equation (6.2)) that have to be applied to the USD side of a FedFund–EONIA cross-currency swap.
(4) a USD forward curve to generate 3-month LIBOR forwards such that 3-month swap quotes are priced as 0 – the 3-month swap rates are also shown in Table 5.1.

Figure 6.1 shows the resulting curves: the standard LIBOR instrument curve, the FedFund (OIS) curve, and the global discount curve which is basically given by FedFund + FedFund–EONIA basis spread. Note that the LIBOR and the global curve are very close to each other; the reason for that is that the FedFund–3-month LIBOR basis spread is very similar to the FedFund–EONIA spread. To price a EUR-collateralized USD interest rate swap, one would have to build another curve over the global curve, the one which is used for generating the 3-month LIBOR forwards in order to make a quoted swap fair. Alternatively, one can use the LIBOR curve for that, which gives a very good approximation.

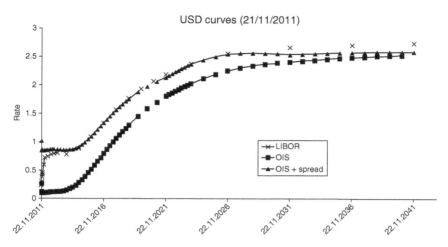

Figure 6.1   USD LIBOR, FedFund (OIS), and global discount curves.

6.3   Impact on hedge accounting

A substantial number of interest rate derivatives is used for pure hedging purposes, and a lot of those as so-called *micro hedges*. This means that some underlying's cash flows are exactly replicated by one side of a swap but with opposite sign, while the other side pays a floating rate (typically LIBOR of a standard tenor like 1 month, 3 months, or 6 months) plus a spread. Such an underlying can be a loan or a bond, either an asset or a liability. Very often, such hedge packages are entered into in the form of par asset swaps; see Section 3.5. For such micro hedge packages, the international accounting standards (IAS) as well as the US GAAP (Generally Accepted Accounting Principles) allow a special treatment known as *hedge accounting*; see [IASB (2010)] and [FASB (2009)].

The advantage of hedge accounting is that a derivative that is a proven hedge does not have to be recognized in the P&L as usual but can be attributed to the underlying. This is useful if the underlying itself is recognized at book value (e.g. if it is in a Loans and Receivables book). In order to be eligible for hedge accounting, the bank has to prove that the hedge is *effective*, which means that the value changes of the hedged item and of the hedging derivative *due to changes in the hedged risk factors* are highly correlated and have a regression between 80% and 125%. This means that if a swap is supposed to hedge a bond's interest rate risk, the fair value change of the bond and its swap due to changes in the interest curve have to be analyzed historically. As an example, consider a fixed rate bond paying $c = 5\%$ for 5 years that is bought at par as part of a par asset swap. The (collateralized) swap pays 5% on its fixed leg, and EURIBOR plus a spread on its floating leg. The relationship between the bond's market values and the swap's will in general not be effective in the above sense because the bond has a credit risk component which the swap does not have. If the credit spread of the bond increases while the interest rate levels remain the same, the swap will not move while the bond value goes down. Therefore, the bank will only designate the interest rate risk, and for hedge accounting purposes ignore the credit spread movement of the bond. As a result, to prove the effectiveness of the hedge, the bond's and the swap's cash flows have to be discounted with the same curve, regardless of the credit quality of the bond.

In the old pricing world, the only source of remaining interest rate risk of this setup is the spread on the floating leg of the swap, because the spread is like a fixed coupon and is thus susceptible to interest rate risk. The hedge ineffectiveness at time $t_0 = t < t'_1, t_1$ can therefore be quantified as the bond clean value minus the book value minus the clean swap value minus the clean value of the spread (taking the clean values means that interest accrual from before t is ignored, i.e. the current period runs from t to t_1 although it started in t_{-1}, and the length of the first period is τ_{t_0,t'_1}):

$$I = c \sum_{i=1}^{n} \tau_{t_{i-1},t_i} df_{t_i} + df_{t_n} - 1 - s \sum_{j=1}^{m} \tau_{t'_{j-1},t'_j} df_{t'_j}$$

$$- \left(c \sum_{i=1}^{n} \tau_{t_{i-1},t_i} df_{t_i} - (L(t_{-1}) + s)\tau_{t_0,t'_1} df_{t'_1} \right.$$

$$\left. - \sum_{j=2}^{m} (f(t, t'_{j-1}, t'_j) + s)\tau_{t'_{j-1},t'_j} df_{t'_j} \right)$$

$$= df_{t_n} - 1 + L(t_{-1})\tau_{t_0,t'_1} df_{t'_1} + \sum_{j=2}^{m} f(t, t'_{j-1}, t'_j)\tau_{t'_{j-1},t'_j} df_{t'_j}$$

$$= -\frac{1 - df_{t'_1}}{\tau_{t_0,t'_1} df_{t'_1}} \tau_{t_0,t'_1} df_{t'_1} - \sum_{j=2}^{m} f(t, t'_{j-1}, t'_j)\tau_{t'_{j-1},t'_j} df_{t'_j}$$

$$+ L(t_{-1})\tau_{t_0,t'_1} df_{t'_1} + \sum_{j=2}^{m} f(t, t'_{j-1}, t'_j)\tau_{t'_{j-1},t'_j} df_{t'_j} \tag{6.8}$$

$$= \left(L(t_{-1}) - \frac{1 - df_{t_1'}}{\tau_{t_0,t_1'} df_{t_1'}} \right) \tau_{t_0,t_1'} df_{t_1'},$$

where t_{-1} is the fixing date of the current period, $L(t_{-1})$ is the fixing for the (floating) period t_0 to t_1', and Equation (6.8) is a consequence of the fundamental Equation (1.2). In other words, the hedge ineffectiveness is given by the difference of the current period's fixing and the forward rate for the time between today and the end of the current period.

That it is correct to subtract the value of the spread on the swap's floating leg before calculating the hedge ineffectiveness is generally accepted. The reason is that the spread is not part of the interest rate hedge as such but rather represents the margin and credit spread of the bond at the time of inception; see for instance [Schubert (2011)]. [Schubert (2011)] has these components as part of the bond coupons, but it is customary in par asset swaps to have them on the swap; compare Section 3.5.

Now we assume that the bank has decided to price all its (collateralized) derivatives on an OIS discounting curve, e.g. EONIA. From the discussion above it is clear that all hedged items also have to be discounted with EONIA lest the hedge relationships become ineffective. This should be taken into account when planning an OIS discounting project. Looking at the above example again, we have to change Equation (6.8) by adjusting the discount factors to df^{OIS}, and by using forwards f^{6M} instead of the forwards f from the discount curve (here we assume a swap that has a 6 month tenor on the floating leg). Note that as long as the discount and the forward curve are the same, we can still apply Equation (1.2) to calculate

$$df_{t_n}^{OIS} - 1 = - \sum_{j=1}^{m} f^{OIS}(t, t_{j-1}', t_j') \tau_{t_{j-1}',t_j'} df_{t_j'}^{OIS}$$

$$= - \sum_{j=1}^{m} (f^{6M}(t, t_{j-1}', t_j') + s^{OIS/6M}) \tau_{t_{j-1}',t_j'} df_{t_j'}^{OIS}, \qquad (6.9)$$

where the second equality follows from the definition of the basis spread $s^{OIS/6M}$. N.B. Because the first period is, in general, shorter in Equation (6.9), the forward rate for the first period does not have the same tenor as the others. Theoretically, it would therefore need a separate spread. If such a spread is available, it is straightforward to adjust Equation (6.10) accordingly.

Thus, Equation (6.8) becomes

$$
\begin{aligned}
I &= c \sum_{i=1}^{n} \tau_{t_{i-1},t_i} df_{t_i}^{\text{OIS}} + df_{t_n}^{\text{OIS}} - 1 - s \sum_{j=1}^{m} \tau_{t'_{j-1},t'_j} df_{t'_j}^{\text{OIS}} \\
&\quad - \left(c \sum_{i=1}^{n} \tau_{t_{i-1},t_i} df_{t_i}^{\text{OIS}} - (L(t_{-1}) + s) \tau_{t_0,t'_1} df_{t'_1}^{\text{OIS}} \right. \\
&\quad \left. - \sum_{j=2}^{m} (f^{6M}(t, t'_{j-1}, t'_j) + s) \tau_{t'_{j-1},t'_j} df_{t'_j}^{\text{OIS}} \right) \qquad (6.10) \\
&= df_{t_n}^{\text{OIS}} - 1 + L(t_{-1}) \tau_{t_0,t'_1} df_{t'_1} + \sum_{j=2}^{m} f^{6M}(t, t'_{j-1}, t'_j) \tau_{t'_{j-1},t'_j} df_{t'_j}^{\text{OIS}} \\
&= -\frac{1 - df_{t'_1}^{6M}}{\tau_{t,t'_1} df_{t'_1}^{6M}} \tau_{t,t'_1} df_{t'_1}^{\text{OIS}} - s^{\text{OIS}/6M} \sum_{j=1}^{m} \tau_{t'_{j-1},t'_j} df_{t'_j}^{\text{OIS}} + L(t_{-1}) \tau_{t_0,t'_1} df_{t'_1}^{\text{OIS}} \\
&= \left(L(t_{-1}) - \frac{1 - df_{t'_1}^{6M}}{\tau_{t_0,t'_1} df_{t'_1}^{6M}} \right) \tau_{t_0,t'_1} df_{t'_1}^{\text{OIS}} - s^{\text{OIS}/6M} \sum_{j=1}^{m} \tau_{t'_{j-1},t'_j} df_{t'_j}^{\text{OIS}}.
\end{aligned}
$$

This shows that in the new pricing world, there is a new source of ineffectiveness, namely the basis spread between the discounting curve and the forwarding curve. The hedge itself does not economically change at all; the cash flows of the underlying remain perfectly matched by the swap. Nevertheless, the strict requirements of IAS 39 make it necessary to handle the change with care.

One would expect that the argument for removing the spread on either the bond's coupons or on the swap's floating side from the ineffectiveness calculation translates for the basis risk as well, as this part of the swap is not used for hedging the bond. This seems to be more problematic, however. Agreement with the auditor is necessary on this, and the industry is still looking for a standard on this. We expect at least one major player to come out soon with an opinion on the topic.

7
Non-Linear Products

That this subject has hitherto been surrounded by mysterious obscurity is to be attributed to an ill-adapted notation.
Carl Friedrich Gauss on imaginary numbers

7.1 Introduction

What do we mean by price? Classically this means the replication cost of a trade under the unique risk-neutral measure. When a market is incomplete, as is the case for stochastic volatility for example, then there are many available risk-neutral measures and we cannot price uniquely by hedging. The hedging bounds are generally simply too wide to have any utility at all. In this case most non-specialist texts simply ignore the problem. Using a risk-neutral measure is useful in that it means that your prices cannot be arbitraged, but if the bounds are tens of percent this is little reassurance. The reader should be worried at this point and remain worried.

There are two useful meanings for the word price in this context.

liquidation price: this is the price seen in the market today for the instrument. It is (with a bid–ask spread) the price that can be used for sale or purchase of the instrument.

replication price: this is what it will cost the bank to construct the instrument, either long or short (usually different) *and hold it to maturity*. Holding it to maturity means that funding must potentially be paid up to maturity.

We have three basic cases for pricing that affect the appropriate discount curve under the usual simplifying assumptions:

collateralized and hedged: use the discount curve derived from the rate that the collateral pays.

collateralized only: different discount curves for in-the-money (ITM) and out-of-the-money (OTM). Note that ITM and OTM is at the counterparty netting set level, not at the individual trade level.

uncollateralized: use discount curve from funding (assuming that this is balanced to allow borrowing and lending at same rate), and price in credit charges and benefits (CVA, etc.; see the next chapter for details). When trades are uncollateralized then it does not matter from a funding point of view whether they are hedged or not since the hedge will not contribute to funding.

The usual simplifying assumptions are:

single currency: all trades involve only one currency.

single collateral currency: collateral is in the same currency as the trades.

cash collateral: all collateral is cash.

rehypothecation: collateral received can be used however the receiver wants.

Pricing non-linear instruments involves models. The usual classification still holds, i.e.:

- Short rate, e.g. Hull–White.
- Markov Functional, usually one-factor.
- Instantaneous Forward Rate, aka HJM. Typically used mechanically for constructing short-rate models that are otherwise difficult to derive.
- Tenor Forward Rate, e.g. LMM (Libor Market Models) aka BGM, LSR (Libor Swap Rate).

Markov Functional and LMM-type models are the easiest to adapt to volatility smiles, but there is renewed interest in short-rate smile models given the proliferation of CVA desks using American Monte Carlo.

Here we will give examples of short rate and tenor forward rate multi-curve models. The basic multi-curve decision is whether to follow an FX analogy or a spread method. Note that the FX analogy strongly implies that we model both currencies (the riskless and the risky) as underlyings. On the other hand, the spread version strongly suggests modeling the risky price as a spread over riskless. This makes sense as we would always expect this spread to be positive, and apart from known and minor historical glitches, this has been the case up to the present (early 2012) throughout the crises.

7.2 Short rate

The FX analogy here follows [Kenyon (2010b)], which derives most closely from [Kijima *et al.* (2009)] on the short-rate side and [Bianchetti (2010)] for the FX analogy. The spread method for short-rate pricing is new and derives most closely from [Mercurio (2010)]. Note that the FX analogy, because of how it is set up (i.e. the FX dynamics end up vanishing), can equally be considered a commodity approach where there are two underlyings: a discount curve, and a f_Δ commodity curve. We are inspired for the spread approach by [Kijima *et al.* (2009)] and extend their work by providing analytic swaption prices (they priced via a Gram–Charlier expansion on the bond price distribution). The aim in both cases is to price swaptions as the basic building block for rates, since a cap is just a series of short swaptions.

In both the FX analogy and the spread method we use affine short rate models and make clear what can be achieved analytically and how. Given the basic manipulations, readers will be able to generalize as well. Since it is possible to price a G2++ Swaption pseudo-analytically, it is not a particular surprise that we can do the same in the multi-curve case where there are two factors.

We provide direct pseudo-analytic swaption pricing formulae within a short-rate setup including the basis between overnight-collateralized instruments (e.g. 6M EONIA) and non-collateralized fixings (e.g. 6M EURIBOR). We use a discounting curve to represent riskless investment and a separate curve for market expectations of non-collateralized fixings. We call this second curve the libor curve. Our approach differs from [Kijima *et al.* (2009)] in that they use discounting and basis curves whereas we use discounting and libor curves. We follow [Bianchetti (2010)] in using an explicit FX argument to deal with potential arbitrage considerations. Our approach can also be generalized as more data becomes available, especially with respect to EONIA-type swaptions (currently missing from the market). Thus we propose a short-rate solution for the observed basis enabling modeling of standard instruments and calibration to swaptions.

7.2.1 FX analogy

The FX analogy for EONIA/EURIBOR modeling, as in [Kijima *et al.* (2009) Bianchetti(2010)], is motivated by the fact that fixed-for-floating swaps have characteristics of quantos: they observe EURIBOR fixings, i.e. based on deposits of a specific tenor, so observe risky+funded, and pay exactly that number in a collateral-ized+unfunded setting (i.e. riskless), which is why replication argue-ments involving both types of instruments do not work anymore. Of course, when swaps go off-market they require funding in as much as they are out of the money, and that they are not part of an asset-swap package, etc. Furthermore, risky and riskless assets are not inter-changeable in the market. The same (uncollateralized) asset will have a different price from entities with different risk levels, thus there is some analogy to an exchange rate between risk levels (or qualities in the language of [Kijima *et al.* (2009)]). The general approach of quoting a spread to price bonds from different issuers serves the same purpose. [Kijima *et al.* (2009)] use a pricing kernel approach to change units (from risky to riskless), whereas [Bianchetti (2010)] uses an FX rate to change units. We regard risky+funded as analogous to one currency, and collateralized+unfunded as analogous to another currency. Note that whilst individual risky entities do default, EURIBOR fixings are not strongly dependent on the default of any single entity. Market practice supports this view that different investment qualities exist in the separation of funded/collateralized (or risky/riskless) worlds. We do not attempt to model the drivers of this separation; we start from the observable EONIA and EURIBOR instruments and derivatives.

Each different EURIBOR tenor fixing, e.g. 1 month, 3 months, 6 months, represents a different level of risk (including liquidity risk). Thus we have a separate libor curve for each tenor Δ, which we label f_Δ to make the source tenor explicit. (In forward-rate models, each differ-ent tenor forward is a different product.) We have a single discounting curve (EONIA). Unlike pre-crisis short-rate modeling, different levels of risk are now priced significantly differently and are not interchange-able. Thus each libor curve is specific to the tenor from which it was constructed. Whilst we could calculate a 1-month rate from a 6-month tenor LIBOR curve, this will not be the same as the 1-month fixing, because it represents a different level of risk. Thus a short-rate approach in the post-crisis world provides tenor fixings at different future times, but not the fixings from different tenors (at least not with the level of risk of the different tenor). This is inherent in the post-crisis market: LIBOR curves multiply whether in short-rate or forward-rate models. Thus the new post-crisis world causes fundamental changes to short-rate modeling – previously, short-rate models could provide future floating rates for any tenor, now a different LIBOR curve is required for each tenor.

A short-rate setup, for the observed basis between discounting and fixing, is potentially useful for a variety of problems, e.g. CVA (credit valuation adjustment); it offers a complementary approach to forward-rate modeling [Brigo *et al.* (2009), Brigo and Masetti (2006)]. In addition, the credit world in general has a strong connection to short-rate modeling because default can happen at any time, not just at tenor-multiple maturities. [Brigo and Mercurio (2006)] expands on this point and concludes that the forward rate approach will be less dominant in the credit space (see chapter 23). As they state, a short rate approach combines naturally with intensity-based hazard rate modeling. Thus this section complements existing forward-rate multi-curve setups (HJM and BGM) [Bianchetti (2010), Henrard (2009), Mercurio (2009), Mercurio (2010), Ametrano and Bianchetti (2010), Pallavicini and Tarenghi (2010)] and extends [Kijima *et al.* (2009)].

7.2.1.1 Model

We put ourselves in the European context by using EURIBOR and EONIA. The equations are general and this naming is only for convenience.

Discount Curve We use a riskless curve as our discount curve. For a concrete example we take Eonia as the riskless discount curve. We aim to price standard fixed income instruments (e.g. swaps, swaptions) subject to collateral agreements, thus the yield curve for similarly collateralized instruments is appropriate for discounting *whatever fixings they reference*.

LIBOR Curve We calibrate a second curve, or "LIBOR curve" to reproduce fixings and market expected fixings (when used together with the discount curve). Note that each different fixing tenor Δ leads to a different libor curve f_Δ. For a concrete example consider the 6-month EURIBOR fixing and market-quoted standard EUR swaps. This follows the concept in [Ametrano and Bianchetti (2010), Kijima *et al.* (2009)] of having a discount curve and a separate curve that, together with the discount curve, reproduce market expectations of fixings and instruments based on them, e.g. forwards and swaps.

N.B. A FRA (Forward Rate Agreement) payment is not the same as a swap payment for the same fixing, because a FRA is paid in advance (discounted with the fixing by definition), whereas a standard swap fixing is paid in arrears.

We use a short-rate model for the discounting curve D, and for the LIBOR curve f_Δ, with short rates $r_D(t)$ and $r_{f_\Delta}(t)$ respectively; we need *d* later for an index, hence the use of *D* for the discounting curve. Note that the level of risk that the LIBOR curve represents is explicitly referenced in Δ. Although the short rates are both denominated in the same currency, say EUR, they represent theoretically different investment qualities (risks), as in [Kijima *et al.* (2009)], thus there is an exchange rate between them. This setup also mirrors that of [Bianchetti (2010)] to preserve no-arbitrage between alternative investment opportunities.

Similarly to [Kijima *et al.* (2009)], the second (fixing) curve f_Δ represents an investment opportunity in as much as market-Δ-fixing-tenor-risk-curve bonds are available. Whilst it may be difficult in practice to find a provider with the appropriate level of risk for a given tenor, this does not affect the consistency of the derivation. All modeling abstracts from reality – for example, no riskless (or overnight-risk-level) bonds exist because even previously safe sovereign government bonds (e.g. US, UK, Germany) have recently exhibited significant yield volatility.

7.2.1.2 Standard instruments

The setup for standard instruments (swaps and swaptions) is very similar to [Kijima *et al.* (2009), Bianchetti (2010), Ametrano and Bianchetti (2010), Mercurio (2009)]; our innovations are in the next section where we show how to price them within a specific short rate setup.

7.2.1.3 Definitions

We define each of our base items here: short rates r_D, r_{f_Δ}; bank accounts $B_l(t)$ $(l = D, f_\Delta)$; and discount factors $P_l(t, T)$. $\mathcal{F}_t$ is the usual filtration at *t*.

- r_D is the instantaneous rate of return of a riskless investment.
- r_{f_Δ} is the instantaneous rate of return of a risky investment with risk level corresponding to LIBOR with tenor Δ.
- $B_l(t) = \exp(\int_0^t r_l(s)ds)$ is a bank account with level of risk $l = D, f_\Delta$.
- $P_l(t, T) = \mathbb{E}_l[B_l(t)/B_l(T)|\mathcal{F}_t]$ is a zero coupon bond with level of risk $l = D, f_\Delta$.

7.2.1.4 Swaps

Swaps in this dual curve setup are similar to differential floating for fixed swaps (aka floating for fixed quanto swaps) in [Brigo and Mercurio (2006)] (p. 623). To price swaps we need to define the simply compounded (LIBOR curve) interest rate that the swaps fix on, $L_k(t)$, at T_{k-1} for the interest rate from T_{k-1} to T_k, i.e. tenor τ^{fix}. Note that f_Δ refers to tenor Δ or τ^{fix} (either can be clearer in context).

We define this rate in terms of the LIBOR curve with tenor Δ:

$$L_k(t) := \frac{1}{\tau^{\text{flt}}} \left(\frac{P_{f_\Delta}(t, T_{k-1})}{P_{f_\Delta}(t, T_k)} - 1 \right).$$

Using the terminology of [Mercurio (2009)] and the equations above, we have for the the floating leg of a swap:

$$\mathbf{FL}(t : T_a, \ldots, T_b) = \sum_{k=a+1}^{b} \mathbf{FL}(t : T_{k-1}, T_k) = \sum_{k=a+1}^{b} \tau_k P_D(t, T_k) L_k(t).$$

N.B. Since separate curves are used for discounting and fixing there is no reason for a floating leg together with repayment of par at the end to price at par. A riskless floating rate bond should price to par, but that bond would not get EURIBOR coupons but EONIA coupons (see the earlier chapters on spreads and curve building for more details). This has previously been pointed out by [Mercurio (2009), Kijima *et al.* (2009)].

From these definitions we can bootstrap both discounting and LIBOR curves from, in Euroland, an EONIA discount curve (built conventionally) and EURIBOR deposits and swaps. Equivalently, we could make use of EONIA/EURIBOR basis swap quotes. Note that we will need the dynamics of $r_*(t)$, where $*$ is either D or f_Δ, under the T-forward measure, i.e. using the zero coupon D-quality (riskless) bond with maturity T, for swaption pricing.

Figure 7.1 shows the discount curve (EONIA) and the LIBOR curve bootstrapped from EURIBOR swaps and 6M deposit. Note that a conventional EURIBOR curve (not shown) would be very close to the LIBOR curve. By conventional we mean one bootstrapped from swaps alone, i.e. done without reference to a riskless discount curve.

7.2.1.5 Swaptions

For a European swaption strike K and maturity T, directly following on from the formulae for a swap above, we have:

$$\mathbf{ES}[\omega, T, K, a, b, c, d]$$

$$= P_D(0, T) \mathbb{E}_D^T \left\{ \left[\omega \left(\sum_{i=a+1}^{b} \tau_i^{\text{flt}} P_D(T, T_i) L_i(T) - \sum_{i=c+1}^{d} \tau_i K P_D(T, T_i) \right) \right]^+ \right\}$$

where $\omega = 1$ for a payer swaption (and -1 for a receiver swaption), and the $a, b, c, d, \tau_i^{\text{flt}}, \tau_i$ take care of the different tenors and payment

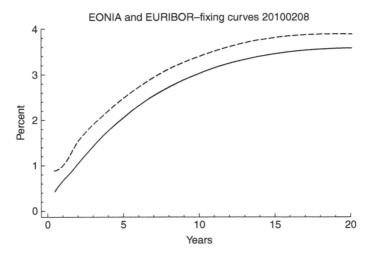

Figure 7.1 Discounting (lower) and fixing (upper) curves. Note that a conventional EURIBOR curve (not shown) would be very close to the EURIBOR fixing curve.

frequencies of the two sides (τ without a superscript is used for the fixed tenor).

Note that because the floating leg does not price to par we must include the specification of the floating coupons. These floating coupons are the market expectation of the relevant fixings $L_i(T)$.

7.2.1.6 Short-rate pricing

We present semi-analytic pricing (i.e. simulation and formulae) for swaptions under general affine short-rate models, and pseudo-analytic (i.e. integration and formulae) pricing in the Gaussian case.

For full analytic tractability we use a 1-factor Hull–White type model for the discount curve (e.g. EONIA), expressed as a G1++ type model (analogous to the terminology in [Brigo and Mercurio (2006)]) for the discounting short rate $r_D(t)$ under the riskless bank-account numeraire for D:

$$r_D(t) = x(t) + \varphi_D(t), \quad r_D(0) = r_{D,0}$$
$$dx(t) = -a_D x(t)dt + \sigma_D dW_1(t). \tag{7.1}$$

We also use a one-factor model for the libor curve, i.e. to fit the market-expected fixings, and we label this short rate $r_{f_\Delta}(t)$ under the Δ-tenor-level risk bank-account numeraire for f_Δ.

$$r_{f_\Delta}(t) = y(t) + \varphi_{f_\Delta}(t), \quad r_{f_\Delta}(0) = r_{f_\Delta,0}$$
$$dy(t) = -a_{f_\Delta}y(t)dt + \sigma_{f_\Delta}dW_2(t). \tag{7.2}$$

where $(W_1(t), W_2(t))$ is a two-dimensional Brownian motion with instantaneous correlation ρ. We also have a quality exchange rate (aka risk exchange rate) X with process under $\mathbf{Q}_{f_\Delta}$ for the quantity of f_Δ-quality (or risk level) investment required to obtain one unit of D-quality investment:

$$dX(t) = (r_{f_\Delta}(t) - r_D(t))X(t)dt + \nu X(t)dW_X(t),$$

where we assume W_X has zero correlation with $W_1(t)$ and with $W_2(t)$. This assumption implies that Equation 7.2 is unchanged under the measure change from $\mathbf{Q}_{f_\Delta}$ to $\mathbf{Q}_D$.

This is a very parsimonious representation relative to two G2++ models. It is, however, sufficient since we only wish to calibrate to EONIA discount rates and EURIBOR swaptions. N.B. neither EONIA caps/floors nor swaptions are liquid at present (early 2012). It is tempting to use 3m swaptions and 6m swaptions to get implied EURIBOR swaption volatility; however, there is a significant difference in their liquidity so this is problematic.

7.2.1.7 *Swaption pricing*

For a European swaption strike K and maturity T we have for any one-factor affine short-rate model (i.e. bond prices available as $A()e^{B()}$):

$$\mathbf{ES}[\omega, T, K, a, b, c, d]$$
$$= P_D(0,T)\,\mathbb{E}^T \left\{ \left[\omega \left(\sum_{i=a+1}^{b} \tau_i^{\text{fix}} P_D(T, T_i) L_i(T) \right. \right. \right.$$
$$\left. \left. \left. - \sum_{i=c+1}^{d} \tau_i K P_D(T, T_i) \right) \right]^+ \right\}$$

$$= P_D(0,T) \mathbb{E}^T \left\{ \left[\omega \left(\sum_{i=a+1}^{b} P_D(T,T_i) \left(\frac{P_{f_\Delta}(T,T_{i-1})}{P_{f_\Delta}(T,T_i)} - 1 \right) \right. \right. \right.$$

$$\left. \left. \left. - \sum_{i=c+1}^{d} \tau_i K P_D(T,T_i) \right) \right]^+ \right\}$$

$$= P_D(0,T) \int_{\mathbb{R}^2} \left\{ \left[\omega \left(\sum_{i=a+1}^{b} A_D(T,T_i) e^{-B_D(T,T_i)x} \right. \right. \right.$$

$$\left. \times \left(\frac{A_{f_\Delta}(T,T_{i-1})}{A_{f_\Delta}(T,T_i)} e^{(-B_{f_\Delta}(T,T_{i-1})+B_{f_\Delta}(T,T_i))y} - 1 \right) \right.$$

$$\left. \left. \left. - \sum_{i=c+1}^{d} \tau_i K A_D(T,T_i) e^{-B_D(T,T_i)x} \right) \right]^+ \right\} f(x,y) dx dy, \qquad (7.3)$$

where $A_*, B_*, * = D, f_\Delta$ are the affine factors for the riskless and f_Δ quality bond prices in their respective units of account. Note that up to this point the equations apply to any affine short-rate model. However, to go further analytically we require the joint distribution of x and y under the T-forward measure, i.e. $f(x,y)$ above. This is available for Gaussian models but not for Cox-Ingersoll-Ross-type specification. This formula could be applied in a CIR-type specification by combining simulation up to T with the affine bond formulae used above.

We require Equations 7.2 and 7.1 in the T_D-forward measure (i.e. zero coupon bond from the discounting curve D as the numeraire). Using standard change-of-numeraire machinery we obtain:

$$dx(t) = \left[-a_D x(t) - \frac{\sigma_D^2}{a_D}(1 - e^{-a_D(T-t)}) \right] dt + \sigma_D dW_1^T$$

$$dy(t) = \left[-a_{f_\Delta} y(t) - \rho \frac{\sigma_{f_\Delta} \sigma_D}{a_D}(1 - e^{-a_D(T-t)}) \right] dt + \sigma_{f_\Delta} dW_2^T.$$

This is because the Radon–Nikodym derivative dQ_D^T/dQ_D uses the zero coupon discounting bond, hence only x is involved in the measure change (not y as well).

These have explicit solutions:

$$x(t) = x(s)e^{-a_D(t-s)} - M_x^T(s,t) + \sigma_D \int_s^t e^{-a_D(t-u)} dW_1^T(u)$$

$$y(t) = y(s)e^{-a_{f_\Delta}(t-s)} - M_y^T(s,t) + \sigma_{f_\Delta} \int_s^t e^{-a_{f_\Delta}(t-u)} dW_2^T(u),$$

where

$$M_x^T(s,t) = \int_s^t \left[\frac{\sigma_D^2}{a_D}(1 - e^{-a_D(T-u)}) \right] e^{-a_D(t-u)} du$$

$$M_y^T(s,t) = \int_s^t \left[\rho \frac{\sigma_{f_\Delta}\sigma_D}{a_D}(1 - e^{-a_D(T-u)}) \right] e^{-a_{f_\Delta}(t-u)} du.$$

Now we can express a European swaption price as:

Theorem 7.1 *The arbitrage-free price at time $t = 0$ for the above European unit-notional swaption (under the FX Analogy) is given by numerically computing the following one-dimensional integral:*

$$ES_{FX \; Analogy}(\omega, T, K, a, b, c, d) =$$

$$- \omega P_D(0,T) \int_{-\infty}^{\infty} \delta(x) \frac{e^{-\frac{1}{2}(\frac{x-\mu_x}{\sigma_x})^2}}{\sigma_x\sqrt{2\pi}}$$

$$\times \left[\Phi(-\omega h_1(x)) - \sum_{i=a+1}^{b} \lambda_i e^{\kappa_i(x)} \Phi(-\omega h_2(x)) \right] dx, \quad (7.4)$$

where $\omega = 1$ for a payer swaption (and -1 for a receiver swaption);

$$\delta(x) := \sum_{i=a+1}^{b} A_D(T,T_i)e^{-B_D(T,T_i)x} + \sum_{i=c+1}^{d} \tau_i K A_D(T,T_i)e^{-B_D(T,T_i)x};$$

$$h_1(x) := \frac{\bar{y}(x) - \mu_y}{\sigma_y\sqrt{1-\rho_{xy}^2}} - \frac{\rho_{xy}(x-\mu_x)}{\sigma_x\sqrt{1-\rho_{xy}^2}};$$

$$h_2(x) := h_1(x) + \alpha_i \sigma_y\sqrt{1-\rho_{xy}^2};$$

$$\alpha_i := -(-B_{f_\Delta}(T,T_{i-1}) + B_{f_\Delta}(T,T_i));$$

$$\lambda_i(x) := \frac{1}{\delta(x)} A_D(T,T_i)e^{-B_D(T,T_i)x} \frac{A_{f_\Delta}(T,T_{i-1})}{A_{f_\Delta}(T,T_i)};$$

$$\kappa_i(x) := -\alpha_i \left[\mu_y - \frac{1}{2}(1-\rho_{xy}^2)\sigma_y^2\alpha_i + \rho_{xy}\sigma_y\frac{x-\mu_x}{\sigma_x} \right];$$

$\bar{y} = \bar{y}(x)$ *is the unique solution of:*

$$\sum_{i=a+1}^{b} A_D(T,T_i)e^{-B_D(T,T_i)x}\left(\frac{A_{f_\Delta}(T,T_{i-1})}{A_{f_\Delta}(T,T_i)}e^{(-B_{f_\Delta}(T,T_{i-1})+B_{f_\Delta}(T,T_i))\bar{y}}-1\right)$$

$$= \sum_{i=c+1}^{d} \tau_i K A_D(T,T_i)e^{-B_D(T,T_i)x};$$

and

$$\mu_x := -M_x^T(0,T);$$

$$\mu_y := -M_y^T(0,T);$$

$$\sigma_x := \sigma_D\sqrt{\frac{1-e^{-2a_D T}}{2a_D}};$$

$$\sigma_y := \sigma_{f_\Delta}\sqrt{\frac{1-e^{-2a_f T}}{2a_{f_\Delta}}};$$

$$\rho_{xy} := \frac{\rho\sigma_D\sigma_{f_\Delta}}{(a_D+a_f)\sigma_x\sigma_y}\left[1-e^{-(a_D+a_{f_\Delta})T}\right];$$

and

$$A_*(T,T_i) = \frac{P_*(0,T_i)}{P_*(0,T)}\exp\left[\frac{1}{2}(V(T,T_i,a_*,\sigma_*)\right.$$

$$\left. - V(0,T_i,a_*,\sigma_*)+V(0,T,a_*,\sigma_*))\right]$$

$$B_*(T,T_i) = \frac{1-e^{-a_*(T_i-T)}}{a_*}$$

$$V(T,T_i,a_*,\sigma_*) = \frac{\sigma_*^2}{a_*^2}\left((T_i-T)+\frac{2}{a_*}e^{-a_*(T_i-T)}-\frac{1}{2a_*}e^{-2a_*(T_i-T)}-\frac{3}{2a_*}\right),$$

where $*$ is either f_Δ or D.

Proof We manipulate Equation 7.3 of **ES** above into the same form as for Theorem 4.2.3 [Brigo and Mercurio (2006)] and provide an appropriate new definition of $\bar{y}$ to finish the proof.

The $[]^+$ part of Equation 7.3 of **ES** is of the form:

$$\sum_{i=1}^{n} U_i e^{-V_i x}(F_i e^{-G_i y}-1) - \sum_{j=1}^{m} M_j e^{N_j x}.$$

Expanding:

$$\sum_{i=1}^{n} U_i e^{-V_i x} F_i e^{-G_i y} - \sum_{i=1}^{n} U_i e^{-V_i x} - \sum_{i=j}^{m} M_j e^{N_j x}.$$

Now if we multiply and divide by the two negative terms we obtain:

$$-\left(\sum_{k=1}^{n} U_k e^{-V_k x} + \sum_{j=1}^{m} M_j e^{N_j x}\right)\left(1 - \sum_{i=1}^{n} \frac{U_i e^{-V_i x} \times F_i e^{-G_i y}}{\sum\limits_{k=1}^{n} U_k e^{-V_k x} + \sum\limits_{j=1}^{m} M_j e^{N_j x}}\right).$$

Now define $\bar{y} = \bar{y}(x)$ as the unique solution of:

$$\sum_{i} U_i e^{-V_i x}(F_i e^{-G_i \bar{y}} - 1) = \sum_{j} M_j e^{N_j x}.$$

So if we freeze x we have the same form as Theorem 4.2.3 of [Brigo and Mercurio (2006)], and the rest of the proof is immediate.

□

As an example, we calibrated to EONIA, EURIBOR swaps and EURIBOR swaptions using data as of February 8, 2010 – see Table 7.1.

Swaption calibration with the G1++/G1++ model is similar to that displayed in [Brigo *et al.* (2009)] using a G2++ model, which also uses post-crisis data: see Figure 7.2. The correlation found by the fitting procedure is very high and negative, meaning that as the discounting short rate goes down the forwarding short rate goes up. Given that the data are from September 2010, this indicates that the market was pricing in high basis spreads if the interest rates were low and vice versa. This appears quite reasonable as a picture of government intervention to add liquidity in times of stress and vice versa.

7.2.1.8 Comments

We provide pseudo-analytic pricing for swaptions in a discounting/fixing multi-curve Gaussian short-rate setup. Each different tenor

Table 7.1 Calibration parameters as of February 8, 2010

a_D	σ_D	a_{f_Δ}	σ_{f_Δ}	ρ
1.0	0.4	0.1	0.0105	-0.95

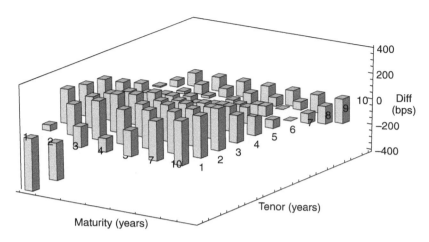

Figure 7.2 Swaption calibration for G1++/G1++ model, errors in bps.

fixing Δ gives rise to a different libor curve f_Δ. Semi-analytic swaption pricing for general affine short-rate models is possible by combining simulation up to maturity with analytic bond formulae at swaption maturity. Pricing of other standard instruments, e.g. caps, are simplifications of the swaption formulae provided. Structurally, the pseudo-analytic calculations are very similar to G2++ pseudo-analytic swaption pricing in [Brigo and Mercurio (2006)]. This means that the current calculations could be directly extended to a G1++/G2++ setup or G2++/G2++ setup once EONIA swaptions, that are currently not available, become liquid. This work extends [Kijima *et al.* (2009)], who also worked in the short-rate setting but did not provide pseudo-analytic swaption pricing.

The post-crisis world with significant basis spreads between tenors produces a fundamental change in short-rate models apart from having separate discounting and libor f_Δ curves. Each LIBOR curve can only provide fixings (floating coupons) for the tenor Δ from which it was constructed. Creating a coupon for a different tenor Δ_{other} will not reproduce market-expected fixings for the other tenor. This is because the other tenor represents a different level of risk. This is inherent in the post-crisis market: LIBOR curves multiply whether in short-rate or forward-rate models. Thus the new post-crisis world causes fundamental changes to short-rate modeling: fixings curves can produce floating coupons for any date but only for the tenor Δ associated with the LIBOR curve f_Δ.

There is still a significant lack of data in the market in early 2012. EONIA/OIS swaptions are missing, for example. We calibrated our model jointly to give EONIA and EURIBOR volatility, however it is not possible to explicitly test our identification with current market data. If we make some assumptions then we can construct rules-of-thumb to address this; see later on swaption volatility approximations. Also, 6M volatility data does not give full information about 3M volatility. Although futures options are liquid and can help, the long end of the volatility curve is simply missing for non-standard tenors. Without this data, pricing options on non-standard tenor fixings (e.g. 3M EURIBOR, 12M USD LIBOR) is problematic.

The Gaussian framework is convenient analytically but, as is well known, permits negative rates. In this context it also permits negative basis spreads depending on the strength of the correlation between the driving processes, their relative volatilities, and the strength of their respective mean reversions. It is possible to obtain analytic results with factor-correlated CIR processes where the correlation is done at the process level (not at the level of the driving Brownian motions, which remain independent). However, this does not give rise to constant instantaneous correlations and is left for future work.

7.2.1.9 Data

In Table 7.2, Table 7.3, and Table 7.4 we provide the data used in the model (as of February 8, 2010). Note that the 6M money market instrument is typically a few basis points away from the 6M EURIBOR fixing, and the money market instrument changes throughout the day. Thus the swap rates given are one particular snapshot. (We ignore fixing lags in this section, conventionally 2 business days for EUR.)

7.2.2 Discount + spread

We use essentially the same setup as in the previous section in terms of notation, context, etc. However, we now define, instead of a second short rate for an alternate currency, a spread. Thus we have (with a little repetition for clarity) for the discounting short rate $r_D(t)$ under the riskless bank-account numeraire for D:

$$r_D(t) = x(t) + \varphi_D(t), \quad r_D(0) = r_{D,0}$$
$$dx(t) = -a_D x(t)dt + \sigma_D dW_1(t). \tag{7.5}$$

We also use a one-factor model for the libor curve spread, i.e. to fit the market-expected fixings, and we label this spread $s_{f_\Delta}(t)$ under the same

Table 7.2 EURIBOR and Swap rates (February 8, 2010)

EURIBOR & Swap Rates	
Tenor	Rate (%)
6M	0.97
2Y	1.586
3Y	1.952
4Y	2.264
5Y	2.532
6Y	2.761
7Y	2.959
8Y	3.122
9Y	3.254
10Y	3.366
12Y	3.546
15Y	3.708
20Y	3.798

Table 7.3 EONIA yield rates (February 8, 2010)

EONIA Yields	
Tenor (Years in Act360)	Rate (%)
0.505556	0.45573
1.01389	0.66794
1.52222	0.85542
2.03333	1.05402
3.05278	1.44287
4.06389	1.78273
5.07778	2.08370
6.09167	2.34107
7.10833	2.56461
8.12778	2.75217
9.13889	2.90716
10.15000	3.04098
11.16670	3.15866
12.18060	3.25962
15.2250	3.46469
20.3000	3.57937

riskless bank-account numeraire for D:

$$s_{f_\Delta}(t) = y(t) + \varphi_{f_\Delta}(t), \quad s_{f_\Delta}(0) = s_{f_\Delta,0}$$
$$dy(t) = -a_{f_\Delta}y(t)dt + \sigma_{f_\Delta}dW_2(t), \tag{7.6}$$

Table 7.4 EUR swaption volatilities (February 8, 2010)

					Swaption Implied Volatilities (maturity x tenor)					
	1Y	2Y	3Y	4Y	5Y	6Y	7Y	8Y	9Y	10Y
1Y	51.1	39.2	33.7	30.2	27.6	26.2	25.1	24.4	23.8	23.3
2Y	37.3	30.4	27.5	25.7	24.2	23.3	22.7	22.2	21.8	21.4
3Y	28.8	24.8	23.1	22.	21.1	20.7	20.4	20.2	20.	19.8
4Y	24.1	21.4	20.3	19.6	19.1	19.	18.9	18.8	18.8	18.8
5Y	21.	19.1	18.4	18.	17.7	17.7	17.6	17.6	17.7	17.7
7Y	19.	17.8	17.3	17.1	16.9	16.9	16.8	17.	17.1	17.2
10Y	17.1	16.5	16.3	16.1	16.	16.1	16.1	16.3	16.4	16.6

where $(W_1(t), W_2(t))$ is a two-dimensional Brownian motion with instantaneous correlation ρ. N.B. We do not need a Δ-tenor-level risk bank-account numeraire for f_Δ; it is just a spread in the same numeraire. This is a useful conceptual simplification. We have no need of a quality-exchange rate (the X of the FX Analogy). However, if such bonds exist then we also have (and we use this in our mapping from f_Δ-quality curve to f_Δ-quality fixings):

$$r_{f_\Delta}(t) = r_D(t) + s_{f_\Delta}(t)$$
$$= x(t) + \varphi_D(t) + y(t) + \varphi_{f_\Delta}(t)$$
$$= x(t) + y(t) + \varphi'_{f_\Delta}(t)$$
$$\varphi'_{f_\Delta}(t) := \varphi_D(t) + \varphi_{f_\Delta}(t).$$

It may appear that we have a G2++ model at this point with one extra φ function, however this is not the case. Only one of the stochastic variables will be used for discounting for standard exchange-cleared and collateralized trades, x. Of course, bonds (which by definition cannot be collateralized) of the f_Δ-quality would use $e^{-\int r_{f_\Delta}}$ for discounting. We stress that in the Spread Method we do not usually assume that any f_Δ-quality bonds exist – the f_Δ-quality curve is only used as a quoting mechanism for f_Δ-quality fixings. Thus there are no exchange rate considerations or requirements, which is in contrast to the [Kijima *et al.* (2009)] setup.

7.2.2.1 *Swaption pricing*

Since we are in a spread context we have a mix of one and two-factor models, and one of the factors in the two-factor model is common. We call the two-factor one+one-factor for clarity. For a European swaption strike K and maturity T we have, for any mix of one-factor and one+one-factor affine short-rate model (i.e. bond prices available as $A()e^{B()}$):

$\text{ES}_{\text{Spread}}[\omega, T, K, a, b, c, d]$

$$= P_D(0,T)\,\mathbb{E}^T\left\{\left[\omega\left(\sum_{i=a+1}^{b}\tau_i^{\text{fix}}P_D(T,T_i)L_i(T)\right.\right.\right.$$

$$\left.\left.\left.-\sum_{i=c+1}^{d}\tau_i K P_D(T,T_i)\right)\right]^+\right\}$$

$$= P_D(0,T)\,\mathbb{E}^T\left\{\left[\omega\left(\sum_{i=a+1}^{b}P_D(T,T_i)\left(\frac{P_{f_\Delta}(T,T_{i-1})}{P_{f_\Delta}(T,T_i)}-1\right)\right.\right.\right.$$

$$\left.\left.\left.-\sum_{i=c+1}^{d}\tau_i K P_D(T,T_i)\right)\right]^+\right\}$$

$$= P_D(0,T)\int_{\mathbb{R}^2}\left\{\left[\omega\left(\sum_{i=a+1}^{b}A_D(T,T_i)e^{-B_D(T,T_i)x}\right.\right.\right.$$

$$\left.\times\left(\frac{A_{f_\Delta}(T,T_{i-1})}{A_{f_\Delta}(T,T_i)}e^{q_i(x,y)}-1\right)\right. \tag{7.7}$$

$$\left.\left.\left.-\sum_{i=c+1}^{d}\tau_i K A_D(T,T_i)e^{-B_D(T,T_i)x}\right)\right]^+\right\}f(x,y)dxdy,$$

where $A_*, B_*, C_*, \,*=D, f_\Delta$ are the affine factors for the riskless resp. f_Δ-quality bond prices in their respective units of account, and

$$q_i(x,y) = (-B_{f_\Delta}(T,T_{i-1})+B_{f_\Delta}(T,T_i))y + (-C_{f_\Delta}(T,T_{i-1})+C_{f_\Delta}(T,T_i))x.$$

Conceptually, it is important to realize that f_Δ bonds do not need to exist in the Spread setup, they are simply an artificial construct mapping from the f_Δ-curve to f_Δ-LIBOR fixings. In [Kijima *et al.* (2009)] actual bonds of different qualities do exist but this is not required.

Note that up to this point the equations apply to any one-factor and one+one-factor affine short-rate models. However, to go further analytically we require the joint distribution of x and y under the T-forward measure, i.e. $f(x,y)$ above. This is available for Gaussian models but not for CIR-type specifications.

These formulae could be applied in a CIR-type specification by combining simulation up to T with the affine bond formulae used above.

Alternatively, we could make the assumption that the spread factor was independent of the discount factor. Judging from historical data this is reasonable. However, market-implied calibrations do not necessarily have any connection with historical observations, so this reasoning is suspect. Making the assumption simply for analytic tractability is reasonable (although not required for the Gaussian case).

The development from this point is quite similar to the FX Analogy case. We need Equations (7.5) and (7.6) in the T-forward measure, and these are identical. Since they are identical, so are their explicit solutions.

Now we can express a European swaption price in a similar way as before under the FX Analogy. Where the meaning of a symbol is different with the Spread method it is noted with the superscript S.

Theorem 7.2 *The arbitrage-free price at time $t = 0$ for the above European unit-notional swaption (under the Spread method) is given by numerically computing the following one-dimensional integral:*

$$\text{ES}_{\text{Spread}}(\omega, T, K, a, b, c, d) = -\omega P_D(0, T) \int_{-\infty}^{\infty} \delta(x) \frac{e^{-\frac{1}{2}(\frac{x-\mu_x}{\sigma_x})^2}}{\sigma_x \sqrt{2\pi}}$$
$$\left[\Phi(-\omega h_1(x)) - \sum_{i=a+1}^{b} \lambda_i^S e^{\kappa_i^S(x)} \Phi(-\omega h_2^S(x)) \right] dx,$$

where $\omega = 1$ for a payer swaption (and -1 for a receiver swaption);

$\delta(x) := \text{same};$

$h_1(x) := \text{same};$

$h_2^S(x) := \text{uses } \alpha_i^S;$

$\alpha_i^S := -(-B_{f_\Delta}(T, T_{i-1}) + B_{f_\Delta}(T, T_i));$

$\lambda_i^S(x) := \frac{1}{\delta(x)} A_D(T, T_i) e^{-B_D(T,T_i)x} \frac{A_{f_\Delta}(T, T_{i-1})}{A_{f_\Delta}(T, T_i)} e^{(-C_{f_\Delta}(T,T_{i-1})+C_{f_\Delta}(T,T_i))x};$

$\kappa_i^S(x) := \text{uses } \alpha_i^S;$

$q_i(x, y) := (-B_{f_\Delta}(T, T_{i-1}) + B_{f_\Delta}(T, T_i))y + (-C_{f_\Delta}(T, T_{i-1}) + C_{f_\Delta}(T, T_i))x;$

where $\bar{y} = \bar{y}(x)$ is the unique solution of:

$$\sum_{i=a+1}^{b} A_D(T, T_i) e^{-B_D(T,T_i)x} \times \left(\frac{A_{f_\Delta}(T, T_{i-1})}{A_{f_\Delta}(T, T_i)} q_i(x,y) - 1 \right) =$$

$$\sum_{i=c+1}^{d} \tau_i K A_D(T, T_i) e^{-B_D(T,T_i)x},$$

and

$$\mu_x := -M_x^T(0, T);$$
$$\mu_y := -M_y^T(0, T);$$
$$\sigma_x := \sigma_D \sqrt{\frac{1 - e^{-2a_D T}}{2a_D}};$$
$$\sigma_y := \sigma_{f_\Delta} \sqrt{\frac{1 - e^{-2a_f T}}{2a_{f_\Delta}}};$$
$$\rho_{xy} := \frac{\rho \sigma_D \sigma_{f_\Delta}}{(a_D + a_f) \sigma_x \sigma_y} \left[1 - e^{-(a_D + a_{f_\Delta})T} \right];$$

and

$$A_*(T, T_i) = \frac{P_*(0, T_i)}{P_*(0, T)} \exp\left[\frac{1}{2}(V_*(T, T_i, a_*, \sigma_*) \right.$$
$$\left. - V_*(0, T_i, a_*, \sigma_*) + V_*(0, T, a_*, \sigma_*)) \right],$$

$$B_*(T, T_i) = \frac{1 - e^{-a_*(T_i - T)}}{a_*},$$

$$C_{f_\Delta}(T, T_i) = B_D(T, T_i),$$

$$V_D(T, T_i, a_D, \sigma_D) = \frac{\sigma_D^2}{a_D^2} \left((T_i - T) + \frac{2}{a_D} e^{-a_*(T_i - T)} \right.$$
$$\left. - \frac{1}{2a_D} e^{-2a_*(T_i - T)} - \frac{3}{2a_D} \right),$$

$$V_{f_\Delta}(T, T_i, a_D, a_{f_\Delta}, \sigma_D, \sigma_{f_\Delta}) = \frac{\sigma_D^2}{a_D^2}\left[T_i - T + \frac{2}{a_D}e^{-a_D(T_i-T)}\right.$$

$$\left. - \frac{1}{2a_D}e^{-2a_D(T_i-T)} - \frac{3}{2a_D}\right]$$

$$+ \frac{\sigma_{f_\Delta}^2}{a_{f_\Delta}^2}\left[T_i - T + \frac{2}{a_{f_\Delta}}e^{-a_{f_\Delta}(T_i-T)}\right.$$

$$\left. - \frac{1}{2a_{f_\Delta}}e^{-2a_{f_\Delta}(T_i-T)} - \frac{3}{2a_{f_\Delta}}\right]$$

$$+ \rho\frac{\sigma_D\sigma_{f_\Delta}}{a_D a_{f_\Delta}}\left[T_i - T + \frac{e^{-a_D(T_i-T)}-1}{a_D}\right.$$

$$+ \frac{e^{-a_{f_\Delta}(T_i-T)}-1}{a_{f_\Delta}}$$

$$\left. + \frac{e^{-(a_D+a_{f_\Delta})(T_i-T)}-1}{a_D+a_{f_\Delta}}\right],$$

where $*$ is either f_Δ or D.

Proof As in the FX Analogy, we manipulate Equation 7.7 of **ES** above into the same form as for Theorem 4.2.3 [Brigo and Mercurio (2006)] and provide an appropriate new definition of $\bar{y}$ to finish the proof.

The $[]^+$ part of Equation 7.7 of **ES** is of the form:

$$\sum_{i=1}^{n} U_i e^{-V_i x}(F_i e^{-G_i y - H_i x} - 1) - \sum_{j=1}^{m} M_j e^{N_j x}.$$

Expanding:

$$\sum_{i=1}^{n} U_i e^{-V_i x} F_i e^{-G_i y - H_i x} - \sum_{i=1}^{n} U_i e^{-V_i x} - \sum_{i=j}^{m} M_j e^{N_j x}$$

$$= \sum_{i=1}^{n} U_i e^{-V_i x} F_i e^{-G_i y} e^{-H_i x} - \sum_{i=1}^{n} U_i e^{-V_i x} - \sum_{i=j}^{m} M_j e^{N_j x}$$

$$= \sum_{i=1}^{n} U_i e^{-(V_i+H_i)x} F_i e^{-G_i y} - \sum_{i=1}^{n} U_i e^{-V_i x} - \sum_{i=j}^{m} M_j e^{N_j x}.$$

Now, if we multiply and divide by the two negative terms we obtain:

$$-\left(\sum_{k=1}^{n} U_k e^{-V_k x} + \sum_{j=1}^{m} M_j e^{N_j x}\right)$$

$$\times\left(1 - \sum_{i=1}^{n} \frac{U_i e^{-(V_i+H_i)x}}{\sum_{k=1}^{n} U_k e^{-V_k x} + \sum_{j=1}^{m} M_j e^{N_j x}} F_i e^{-G_i y}\right).$$

Now define $\bar{y} = \bar{y}(x)$ as the unique solution of:

$$\sum_{i=1}^{n} U_i e^{-V_i x}(F_i e^{-G_i \bar{y} - H_i x} - 1) = \sum_{j=1}^{m} M_j e^{N_j x}.$$

So if we freeze x we have the same form as Theorem 4.2.3 of [Brigo and Mercurio (2006)], and the rest of the proof is immediate.

$\square$

Readers should be aware that we have made use of several results in chapter 4 of [Brigo and Mercurio (2006)], for example to obtain V_*. This chapter should be considered a multi-curve extension for that chapter.

Since we have not increased the number of underlying factors we do not expect ATM pricing to be significantly better. In any case, there is the issue of the volatility smile.

7.2.3 Extensions for smiles

Short-rate smiles are difficult to obtain in general, the closest related approach is perhaps a Markov Functional approach. However, there is a trivial method, the Uncertain Parameter Model (UPM), to obtain short-rate smiles that has been used both conventionally [Brigo and Mercurio (2006)], and in the multi-curve setup [Pallavicini and Tarenghi (2010)].

In the UPM model at time zero we have a set of possible parameters and we assign a probability to each. The probabilities, of course, sum to unity. At one instant after time zero the actual parameter is revealed. The UMP is not a mixture model because in mixture models the mixture is still present at all future times. [Pallavicini and Tarenghi (2010)] in the multi-curve setting created a Spread-type short-rate setup via assumptions on volatility, i.e. they used the HJM mechanism to generate appropriate short-rate models. They found that they could match smiles with only a very small number of possible parameter values (i.e. two or three). This is consistent with mixture models that have found good smile matching with small numbers of elements [Brigo and Mercurio (2006), Kenyon (2008)].

We might expect UPM models to be bad for hedging because they collapse to two independent scenarios immediately after time zero. Whether or not this happens in practice is something for empirical analysis. We would encourage readers to experiment.

Note that there is no need for the set of possible parameters to be finite. Indeed, Variance–Gamma style models with subordinated time can be viewed as UPM with uncountably infinite parameter sets [Cont and Tankov (2003)].

7.3 Tenor forward rate

There are three main approaches with different advantages and disadvantages depending on what instruments are of interest; we compare and contrast them in Table 7.5. The FRA-for-LIBOR approximation is best on reset days, because, by definition, a FRA is paid on the reset date using the LIBOR quantity discounted using LIBOR itself back to the reset date. LIBOR is paid, in a swap, on the pay date and so is discounted completely using the discount curve.

As with short-rate approaches, we have both an FX Analogy and non-FX methods available. The FX Analogy is perhaps more intellectually pleasing in its consistency with FX pricing and multiple qualities of investments, but there is the possibility of negative basis spreads.

The Discount + Forward approach of [Mercurio (2009)] is simple for some instruments, e.g. caps, but since it permits negative bases is not really competitive today given that the Discount + Spread approach is available. We do not cover this method.

Table 7.5 Strengths and weaknesses of multi-curve approaches

Method	Strengths	Weaknesses
FX Analogy	consistency	• quanto terms • negative basis spread possible
Discount + Forward	simple prices	negative basis spread possible
Discount + Spread	reflects market practice approximating LIBORs as FRAs	• FRA and LIBOR rate only coincide on reset dates • loses pricing simplicity • requires volatilities and/or distributions that may be difficult to obtain

The strongest approach is a Discount + Spread method [Mercurio (2010)]. The main assumption it requires for simplicity is independence between the spread and the discount. Market experience over the next year or two will tell whether this is viable.

Mathematically speaking, the trade-off is between quanto terms and the FRA-LIBOR basis. [Mercurio (2010)] has shown that the FRA-wrong-measure basis is small, and he (and we) does not include it in the equations. [Bianchetti (2010)] has shown that the quanto terms are often small, but does include them in the equations. Thus, whilst it appears that the FX Analogy is more complex, this is mathematically not the case. The main difference comes in dynamics, i.e. the fact that if you do not do Discount+Spread then you can get negative basis spreads.

A major problem, as noted in the short-rate section, is the lack of market data for many volatilities – mostly those to do with discounting. To date, authors have simply fitted these new models to market data and declared victory. Readers should consider whether this is equivalent to successful hedging.

7.3.1 FX analogy

The FX Analogy is shown in Figure 7.3. The result of moving from one unit of foreign currency (top right corner), 1_f to domestic currency (bottom left corner) should be the same for both paths, to avoid arbitrage. Note that it is important to keep track of the units as with conventional currencies (where it is more obvious, e.g. 1 EUR $\neq$ 1 USD). Thus for no arbitrage we have:

$$c_d(t) = x_{fd}(t)1_f$$
$$P_d(t,T)X_{fd}(t,T)1_f = x_{fd}(t)P_f(t,T)1_f,$$

where the final quantities of money are always domestic. The top line uses c_d to emphasize that the final quantity is domestic; obviously numerically $c_d(t) = x_{fd}(t)$.

The arguments for the existence of different currencies were covered in Section 7.2, and previously in Chapter 4. We just remind readers that both the FX Analogy and the Spread Method are approximations to dealing with the full complexity of balance sheets, funding, collateral currencies, etc.

We start from FX rates, but what we actually need for pricing are quanto adjustments. We mostly observe the uncollateralized fixing and pay in collateralized currency.

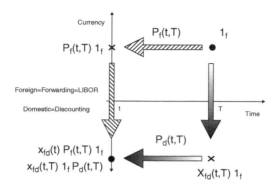

Figure 7.3 FX Analogy. The result of moving from one unit of foreign currency, 1_f (top right corner), to domestic currency (bottom left corner) should be the same for both paths (hatched vs shaded) to avoid arbitrage. Spot FX rate is $x_{fd}(t)$ and forward FX rate is $X_{fd}(t,T)$. Domestic and foreign zero coupon bonds, aka discount factors, are $P_*(t,T)$ where $* = f,d$.

Some definitions:

- $P_x(t,T)$, the discount factor in currency x, observed at t.
- $P_x(t;S,T)$, the forward discount factor in currency x from S to T.
- $F_x(t;S,T)$, the simply compounded forward rate in currency x from S to T.

We have:

$$P_x(t;S,T) = \frac{P_x(t,T)}{P_x(t,S)} = \frac{1}{1 + F_x(t;S,T)\tau^x_{T_1,T_2}}.$$

That is, under the FX Analogy we still believe:

$$P_x(t,T_2) = P_x(t,T_1)P_x(t;T_1,T_2),$$

where x is the currency in question, i.e. d,f where we have not specified which foreign tenor Δ we are considering for simplicity. We also believe that we cannot mix currencies without FX rates, i.e.:

$$P_d(t,T_2) \neq P_d(t,T_1)P_f(t;T_1,T_2) = P_d(t,T_1)\frac{1}{1 + F_f(t;T_1,T_2)\tau^f_{T_1,T_2}}.$$

In fact, the equation makes no sense because we are trying (effectively) to equate EUR and USD in the same equation without any FX rates. What does make sense is to add another FX rate, called by [Bianchetti (2010)] a Basis Adjustment. Note that this is neither the spot FX rate $x_{fd}(t)$, nor the forward FX rate $X_{fd}(t,T)$, but is instead a *basis* (or *tenor*, or *term*) FX rate $X_{fd}(t,T_1,T_2)$, i.e.:

$$P_f(t,T_1,T_2) = \frac{1}{1 + F_d(t;T_1,T_2)X_{df}(t,T_1,T_2)\tau_{T_1,T_2}}$$

$$F_f(t;T_1,T_2) = F_d(t;T_1,T_2)X_{df}(t,T_1,T_2)$$

$$X_{df}(t,T_1,T_2) = \frac{F_f(t;T_1,T_2)}{F_d(t;T_1,T_2)}.$$

We omit the f,d for the tenors δ because they are always the same. To keep track of which sort of FX rate is being used, it suffices to count the number of indices.

[Bianchetti (2010)] points out that the effect of the adjustment can be captured by either a multiplicative term as above, i.e. like an FX rate, or by an additive term, i.e. like a spread. However, it is a spread acting in the place of an FX rate. Thus, whilst it can do the job in terms of numerical equivalence, it makes it hard to see how the units are being changed from d to f or vice versa. Because of this inconsistency on units we do not include the spread version of FX in this section, but rather keep the spread and FX ideas separate. An additive view is inconsistent with an FX interpretation and the changes of measure that are required for pricing, as we now see.

7.3.1.1   FRA

Consider a forward rate agreement, since this is the discounted domestic value of a foreign observation paid as-is; it is actually a quanto. Formally:

$$\mathbf{FRA}(t,T_1,T_2,K) = P_d(t,T_2)\tau_{T_1,T_2}\left(\mathbb{E}_d^{T_2}[F_f(T_1;T_1,T_2)] - K\right)$$

$$= P_d(t,T_2)\tau_{T_1,T_2}\left(\mathbb{E}_d^{T_2}[L_f(T_1,T_2)] - K\right).$$

This also provides our definition of the LIBOR rate $L_f(T_1,T_2)$. We take the expectation of the foreign forward in the domestic measure. In order to get the expectation of the foreign amount in the domestic measure we need the drift (or generally the SDE) of the foreign amount in the domestic measure. What follows are standard FX assumptions and computations.

We assume log-normal dynamics:

$$dF_f(t;T_1,T_2) = \sigma_F(t)F_f(t;T_1,T_2)dW_f^{T_2}(t), \qquad t \le T_1$$

under the foreign probability space $(\Omega, \mathcal{F}_f, \mathbf{Q}_f^{T_2})$. Now the forward exchange rate must be a martingale under the domestic T_2-forward measure because it represents a tradable asset (one unit of forward foreign turned into domestic), and we assume log-normal dynamics for it as well (now in the domestic measure):

$$dX_{fd}(t, T_2) = \sigma_X(t)X_{fd}(t, T_2)dZ_d^{T_2}, \qquad t \leq T_2,$$

where the subscript on the Brownian motions W, Z indicates their currency. The instantaneous correlation is:

$$dW_f^{T_2}(t)dZ_d^{T_2}(t) = \rho_{FX}(t)dt.$$

Using standard change of numeraire methods we have

$$\frac{dF_f(t; T_1, T_2)}{F_f(t; T_1, T_2)} = \mu_F(t)dt + \sigma_F(t)dW_f^{T_2}(t), \qquad t \leq T_1, \qquad \text{under } \mathbf{Q}_d^{T_2}$$

$$\mu_F(t) = -\sigma_F(t)\sigma_X(t)\rho_{FX}(t).$$

Hence:

$$\mathbb{E}_d^{T_2}[F_f(T_1; T_1, T_2)| \mathcal{F}_d(t)] = F_f(t; , T_1, T_2)QA_{fd}(t, T_1, T_2; \sigma_F, \sigma_X, \rho_{FX})$$

$$QA_{fd}(t, T_1, T_2; \sigma_F, \sigma_X, \rho_{FX}) = \exp\left(-\int_t^{T_1} \sigma_F(u)\sigma_X(u)\rho_{FX}(u)du\right),$$

where we use QA for the quanto adjustment.

7.3.1.2 Swaps

Swaps can be dealt with as similar to strips of FRAs. This is technically not quite correct because a FRA pays at reset date using the forward rate to discount the future payments back. We ignore this distinction here. Note that we use D now for the domestic currency as we need d for an index.

$$\mathbf{IRS}[t, K, a, b, c, d] = \sum_{i=a+1}^{b} \tau_i^{flt}P_D(t, T_i)L_i(T) - \sum_{i=c+1}^{d} \tau_i^{fix}KP_D(t, U_i)$$

$$= \sum_{i=a+1}^{b} \tau_i^{\text{flt}} P_D(t, T_i) \mathbb{E}_d^{T_2}[F_f(T_{i-1}; T_{i-1}, T_i) | \mathcal{F}_d(t)]$$

$$- \sum_{i=c+1}^{d} \tau_i^{\text{fix}} K P_D(t, U_i)$$

$$= \sum_{i=a+1}^{b} \tau_i^{\text{flt}} P_D(t, T_i) F_f(t;, T_{i-1}, T_i) QA_{fd}(t, T_{i-1}, T_i; \sigma_F, \sigma_X, \rho_{FX})$$

$$- \sum_{i=c+1}^{d} \tau_i^{\text{fix}} K P_D(t, U_i),$$

where τ^{fix} and τ^{flt} are the year fractions for the fixed and floating coupons respectively. The fixed coupons generally pay on different (at least fewer) dates than the floating coupons, so we use U_i for the those dates.

Fair swap rates are:

$$S[t, a, b, c, d]$$

$$= \frac{\sum_{i=a+1}^{b} \tau_i^{\text{flt}} P_D(t, T_i) F_f(t;, T_{i-1}, T_i) QA_{fd}(t, T_{i-1}, T_i; \sigma_F, \sigma_X, \rho_{FX})}{\sum_{i=c+1}^{d} \tau_i^{\text{fix}} P_D(t, U_i)}$$

$$= \frac{\sum_{i=a+1}^{b} \tau_i^{\text{flt}} P_D(t, T_i) L_i(t)}{\sum_{i=c+1}^{d} \tau_i^{\text{fix}} P_D(t, U_i)}.$$

Now we can rewrite the IRS for off-market swaps in terms of on-market swaps:

$$\textbf{IRS}[t, K, a, b, c, d] = (S[t, a, b, c, d] - K) \sum_{i=c+1}^{d} \tau_i^{\text{fix}} P_D(t, U_i).$$

Discounting has a major effect on pricing.

7.3.1.3 *Caps/floors*

These are direct in that we can apply the same reasoning as Black used originally, i.e. in the (domestic) T-forward measure we assume a log-normal distribution for the observable. This now must include the drift from the measure change. The price of a cap/floor-let is:

$$\mathbf{cf}(t;S,T,K;\omega) = P_d(t,T)\mathbb{E}_d^T[\max(0,\omega(L_f(S,T)-K))]\tau_{ST}$$
$$= P_d(t,T)\tau_{ST}Bl(F_f(t;S,T)QA_{fd}(t,T,\sigma_F,\sigma_X,\rho_{FX}),$$
$$K,\mu_f,\sigma_F,\omega)),$$

where $\omega = \pm 1$ for caplets and floorlets respectively. The Black formula is adapted for the drift, i.e.:

$$Bl(F,K,\mu,\sigma,\omega) = \omega\left(F\Phi(\omega d_+) - K\Phi(\omega d_-)\right),$$
$$d_\pm = \frac{\log(F/K)+\mu(t,T)\pm\frac{1}{2}\sigma^2(t,T)}{\sigma(t,T)},$$
$$\mu(t,T) = \int_t^T \mu(u)du, \qquad \sigma^2(t,T) = \int_t^T \sigma^2(u).$$

7.3.1.4 Swaptions

We are working under our usual assumptions, i.e. fully collateralized and hedged. This means that the swaps referenced in swaptions are standard market swaps, i.e. foreign-floating-domestic-discount. [Bianchetti (2010)] instead calculates swaptions for swaps that are foreign-floating-foreign-discounting. This is not market practice, thus we use standard methods to develop swaption pricing for swaptions referencing foreign-floating-domestic-discount swaps.

First note that both legs of a swap are tradable instruments by definition. Now if we use the annuity numeraire C_D^{cd} (i.e. the fixed leg) and the corresponding swap measure then the swap rate for the foreign-floating-domestic-discount swap is a martingale. If we take the swap rate to have log-normal dynamics then we are back to the usual Black formula for a European swaption:

$$\mathbf{ES}(t,K;a,b,c,d) = C_D^{cd}Bl(K,\mathbf{S}[t,a,b,c,d],\sigma_{abcd},\omega).$$

The key question to ask at this point is: "where is at-the-money?" ATM is given by the appropriate foreign-floating-domestic-discount swap rate.

We can observe that the standard methods of decomposing the swap rate into forwards still work. For example, fair swap rates are:

$$\mathbf{S}[t,a,b,c,d] = \frac{\sum_{i=a+1}^{b} \tau_i^{\text{flt}} P_D(t,T_i) L_i(t)}{\sum_{i=c+1}^{d} \tau_i^{\text{fix}} P_D(t,U_i)}$$

$$= \sum_{i=a+1}^{b} \omega_i(t) L_i(t)$$

$$= \sum_{i=a+1}^{b} \omega_i(t) F_f(t;,T_1,T_2) QA_{fd}(t,T_1,T_2;\sigma_F,\sigma_X,\rho_{FX}),$$

where we write $\omega_i(t)$ for the fraction involving only domestic discount factors. Practically, we would now take the usual freezing-the-forwards approximation of $\omega_i(t) \approx \omega_i(0)$.

7.3.2 Discount + spread

Here we follow [Mercurio (2010)]. We assume a riskless discount curve, i.e. we are in our standard setup: fully-collateralized; fully-hedged; single-currency. Usually this discount curve will be OIS EONIA in the Euro area and OIS Fed Funds in the USA.

7.3.2.1 FRA

We define a FRA rate $\mathbf{FRA}(t;T_1,T_2)$ as the fixed rate such that the swap has zero value at time t. Note that this is not the market definition of a FRA, which actually pays one period earlier using the LIBOR reset (then known) as its discount factor. However, the convexity correction for this is very small [Mercurio (2010)]. Using the present definition, under the T_2-forward measure $\mathbf{Q}_d^{T_2}$ we have:

$$\mathbf{FRA}(t;T_1,T_2) = \mathbb{E}_D^{T_2}[L(T_1,T_2)|\mathcal{F}(t)]$$

$$\neq \frac{1}{\tau_{T_1,T_2}} \left(\frac{P_D(t,T_1)}{P_D(t,t_2)} - 1 \right) = \mathbb{E}_D^{T_2}[L_D(T_1,T_2)|\mathcal{F}(t)],$$

where $L(T_1,T_2)$ is the term-LIBOR fixing at T_1 for payment at T_2, whereas $L_D(T_1,T_2)$ is the fixing from the discount curve. Observe that unlike in the FX Analogy we have only one measure to deal with, i.e. $L()$ is in its natural measure already. Note that $\mathbf{FRA}(t;T_1,T_2)$ is a martingale under $\mathbf{Q}_D^{T_2}$ because it is already an expectation under that measure.

We use a shorthand for the FRA rate as:

$$L_2(t) = \mathbf{FRA}(t;T_1,T_2).$$

We define the discount-forward and spread part S_k of it as expected:

$$L_k(T_{k-1}) = F_k(T_{k-1}) + S_k(T_{k-1}),$$

where $F_k(T_{k-1}) = L_D(T_{k-1}, T_k)$.

Effectively we have removed the need for two currencies by including the drift (quanto adjustment) within the "Libor" rate $L_*(t)$. However, the FRA and actual LIBOR rates mostly coincide only on reset dates. There is a basis on the reset dates because FRAs are paid on the reset date using the discount of the LIBOR rate, whereas LIBOR is paid (exchanged in the swap) on the pay date. Thus the LIBOR rate is discounted with the discount curve rather than the LIBOR curve that the FRA uses.

7.3.2.2 Swaps

Swaps are similar to strips of FRAs, so we can write:

$$
\begin{aligned}
\mathbf{IRS}[t, K, a, b, c, d] &= \sum_{i=a+1}^{b} \tau_i^{\text{flt}} P_D(t, T_i) \, \mathbb{E}_D^{T_i}[L(T_{i-1}, T_i)| \mathcal{F}(t)] \\
&\quad - \sum_{i=c+1}^{d} \tau_i^{\text{fix}} K P_D(t, U_i) \\
&= \sum_{i=a+1}^{b} \tau_i^{\text{flt}} P_D(t, T_i) L_i(t) - \sum_{i=c+1}^{d} \tau_i^{\text{fix}} K P_D(t, U_i),
\end{aligned}
$$

where $L_i(t) = \mathbb{E}_D^{T_i}[L(T_{i-1}, T_i)| \mathcal{F}(t)]$. Fair swap rates are:

$$
S[t, a, b, c, d] = \frac{\sum_{i=a+1}^{b} \tau_i^{\text{flt}} P_D(t, T_i) L_i(t)}{\sum_{i=c+1}^{d} \tau_i^{\text{fix}} P_D(t, U_i)}.
$$

The fixed coupons generally pay on different (at least fewer) dates than the floating coupons so we use U_i for the those dates. Now we can rewrite the IRS for off-market swaps in terms of on-market swaps:

$$
\mathbf{IRS}[t, K, a, b, c, d] = \left(S[t, a, b, c, d] - K \right) \sum_{i=c+1}^{d} \tau_i^{\text{fix}} P_D(t, U_i).
$$

Thus it is evident that the choice of discounting has a major effect on pricing.

At this point it appears that we have done nothing but redefine the symbol L_i. In fact this is exactly what we have done and accepted the side effects mentioned above. Further complexities, and the utility of the approach, only become visible when we consider options or dynamics.

7.3.2.3 Caps/floors

A cap or floor is just a strip of caplets or floorlets, so we consider one member.

$$\mathbf{cf}(t; T_{i-1}, T_i, K; \omega) = P_D(t, T_i)\, \mathbb{E}_D^{T_i}[\max(0, \omega(L(T_{i-1}, T_i) - K))]\tau_{T_{i-1}T_i}$$

$$= P_D(t, T_i)\, \mathbb{E}_D^{T_i}[\max(0, \omega(L_i(T_{i-1}) - K))]\tau_{T_{i-1}T_i}.$$

If we assume log-normal dynamics for $L_i(T_{i-1})$ – ignoring for the moment the division into Discount+Spread – then we get a Black-type formula for the cap/floorlet price:

$$\mathbf{cf}(t; T_{i-1}, T_i, K; \omega) = P_D(t, T_i)\tau_{T_{i-1}T_i}Bl(K, L_i(t), \sigma_i, \omega),$$

where we have assumed:

$$dL_i(t) = \sigma(t)L_i(t)dW_i(t), \qquad t \le T_{i-1}$$

so

$$\sigma_i^2 = \int_t^{T_{i-1}} \sigma^2(u)du.$$

Thus if we are only interested in interpolating between different caplet strikes we could extend this assuming, for example, SABR dynamics on LIBOR.

However, getting back to our original assumptions, we have, from the definition of a caplet:

$$\mathbf{Caplet}(t; T_{i-1}, T_i, K) = P_D(t, T_i)\tau_{T_{i-1}T_i} \int_{-\infty}^{\infty} (l - K)^+ g(l)dl,$$

where $g(l)$ is the density of LIBOR. We have assumed that the discount-forward and spread are independent, so $g(l)$ is the convolution of these two distributions. We can use this independence further, i.e.

$$\mathbf{Caplet}(t; T_{i-1}, T_i, K) = P_D(t, T_i)\tau_{T_{i-1}T_i}$$

$$\times \mathbb{E}_D^{T_i}\left[\left(F_i(T_{i-1}) + S_i(T_{i-1}) - K\right)^+ | \mathcal{F}(t) \right]$$

$$= P_D(t, T_i)\tau_{T_{i-1}T_i}$$

$$\times \int_{-\infty}^{\infty}\int_{-\infty}^{\infty} (f + s - K)^+ h_S(s)\, h_F(f)ds\, df,$$

where h_S, h_F are the densities of the spread and discount-forward respectively. Now we have a pseudo-analytic expression for the caplet in terms of either discount-forward caplets, or spread caplets:

$$\textbf{Caplet}(t; T_{i-1}, T_i, K) = \int_{-\infty}^{\infty} \textbf{Caplet}^S(t; T_{i-1}, T_i, K - f) \, h_F(f) df$$

$$= \int_{-\infty}^{\infty} \textbf{Caplet}^F(t; T_{i-1}, T_i, K - s) \, h_S(s) ds,$$

where:

$$\textbf{Caplet}^*(t; T_{i-1}, T_i, K) = P_D(t, T_i) \tau_{T_{i-1} T_i} \mathbb{E}_D^{T_i}[(*(T_{i-1}) - \kappa)^+ | \mathcal{F}(t)]$$

$$= P_D(t, T_i) \tau_{T_{i-1} T_i} \int_{-\infty}^{\infty} (x - K)^+ h_*(x) dx$$

and $* = F, S$.

7.3.2.4 Swaptions

Swaption pricing is equally simple because the new swap rate is a martingale under the new discount Annuity numeraire, i.e. the discount swap measure. This is because for the new swap rate we have only changed a term in the numerator, and that term combines to make a tradable (just as in the standard case). The discount Annuity C_D^{cd} is:

$$C_D^{cd} = \sum_{i=c+1}^{d} \tau_i^{\text{fix}} P_D(t, U_i).$$

Each leg of a swap is a tradable asset and the numerator is one of those legs: $\sum_{i=a+1}^{b} \tau_i^{\text{flt}} P_D(t, T_i) L_i(t)$.

As in the previous section – if we forget about decomposing – if we take the swap rate to have log-normal dynamics then we can price a swaption:

$$\textbf{ES}(t, K; a, b, c, d) = C_D^{cd} Bl(K, \mathbf{S}[t, a, b, c, d], \sigma_{abcd}, \omega),$$

and the Black formula is exactly as in the previous section.

However, getting back to our original assumption that we have discount+spread, then still under the swap measure $\mathbf{Q}_D^{cd}$ we have, for a payer European swaption:

$$\textbf{ES}(t, K; a, b, c, d) = \sum_{j=c+1}^{d} P_D(t, S_j) \mathbb{E}_D^{c,d} [(\mathbf{S}(T_a, a, b, c, d) - K)^+ | \mathcal{F}(t)].$$

Fair swap rates are:

$$S[t, a, b, c, d] = \frac{\sum_{i=a+1}^{b} \tau_i^{\text{flt}} P_D(t, T_i) L_i(t)}{\sum_{i=c+1}^{d} \tau_i^{\text{fix}} P_D(t, U_i)}$$

$$= \sum_{i=a+1}^{b} \omega_i(t) L_i(t)$$

$$= \sum_{i=a+1}^{b} \omega_i(t) F_i(t) + \sum_{i=a+1}^{b} \omega_i(t) S_i(t).$$

By definition the swap rate is a martingale under its associated swap measure. Now this swap measure is the discount-forward swap measure, so $\sum_{i=a+1}^{b} \omega_i(t) F_i(t)$ as the discount-forward discount-swap rate is also a martingale. Now the difference of two martingales is also a martingale, so the sum of spreads $\sum \omega_i(t) S_i(t)$ expression is also a martingale under Q_D^{cd}. Notice that this last statement is not obvious *a priori* because the weights include $P_D(t, -)$ terms, i.e. discount terms.

The usual way forward in LMMs, which we use here, is to freeze the forwards that are used in the weights, i.e. use $\omega_i(t) \approx \omega_i(0)$. If we now define:

$$\tilde{F}(t) := \sum_{i=a+1}^{b} \omega_i(0) F_i(t)$$

$$\tilde{S}(t) := \sum_{i=a+1}^{b} \omega_i(t) S_i(t),$$

we have:

$$\mathbf{ES}(t, K; a, b, c, d) = \sum_{j=c+1}^{d} P_D(t, S_j) \, \mathbb{E}_D^{c,d} \left[(\tilde{F}(t) + \tilde{S}(t) - K)^+ | \mathcal{F}(t) \right],$$

which (up to an external sum) has the same form as our expression for a caplet above. It can be solved exactly as before since we have frozen the forwards ensuring the independence of the two variables related to the discount-forwards and the spreads.

[Mercurio (2010)] suggests a simple model for the spreads: $S_i(t) = S_i(0) M^S(t)$, $i = a+1, ..., b$. Since these are independent of the discount factors there will be no drift change for any of the spreads when moved to swap measure. Now $M^S(t)$ can be chosen as with any desired smile-producing dynamics, e.g. SABR.

7.4 Volatilities

So far we have developed formulae for pricing non-linear products. However, there has been no mention of what volatilities to use, and the market until very recently did not quote any non-standard cap or swaption volatilities; these could only be determined by calling up a market maker and asking for a price. In this chapter, we want to describe a method of deriving volatilities that have to be fed into the pricing model for a non-standard tenor product from standard tenor volatilities that are quoted in the market.

7.4.1 Cap and floor volatilities for non-standard tenors

In the cap market, cap volatilities are usually quoted for caps with the tenor of a standard floater on the underlying index. In the Euro market, this is six months. However, the short maturity quotes of cap volatilities refer to caps starting in three months and having three periods with a three-month tenor. In order to reconcile this with the 6 months quotations for the caps maturing later, we need an algorithm to produce 6-month volatilities out of 3-month volatilities. Another application for such an algorithm is to compute the volatilities of caps with a non-natural tenor, e.g. twelve months. The method shown here closely follows the one in [Brigo and Mercurio (2006)], with some more details regarding the period lengths. The reader should not be blinded by the indices here; these are needed to keep track of the correct periods. The mathematics behind the formulas is actually very basic.

Assume we are given three points in time, $T_1 < T_2 < T_3$. The day count fractions between times T_i and T_j will be denoted $\tau_{i,j}$, and $\tau_{0,i}$ is the day count fraction from time 0 to T_i. At time $t < T_1$, we have three forward rates $F_{1,2}(t)$, $F_{2,3}(t)$ and $F_{1,3}(t)$. If $P(t,T)$ denotes the price of one currency unit paid at time T as of time t, we know that if the discount and the forward curve are identical, we have

$$F_{1,2}(t) = \frac{1}{\tau_{1,2}} \left(\frac{P(t,T_1)}{P(t,T_2)} - 1 \right), F_{2,3}(t) = \frac{1}{\tau_{2,3}} \left(\frac{P(t,T_2)}{P(t,T_3)} - 1 \right), \text{ and}$$

$$F_{1,3}(t) = \frac{1}{\tau_{1,3}} \left(\frac{P(t,T_1)}{P(t,T_3)} - 1 \right)$$

$$= \frac{1}{\tau_{1,3}} \left(\frac{P(t,T_1)}{P(t,T_2)} \frac{P(t,T_2)}{P(t,T_3)} - 1 \right)$$

$$= \frac{1}{\tau_{1,3}} (\tau_{1,2} F_{1,2}(t) + \tau_{2,3} F_{2,3}(t) + \tau_{1,2} \tau_{2,3} F_{1,2}(t) F_{2,3}(t)).$$

Now if for $F_{1,2}$ and $F_{2,3}$ we assume the dynamics

$$dF_{1,2} = (\ldots)\,dt + \sigma_{1,2}(t)F_{1,2}(t)\,dZ_{1,2}(t),$$
$$dF_{2,3} = (\ldots)\,dt + \sigma_{2,3}(t)F_{2,3}(t)\,dZ_{2,3}(t),$$
$$dZ_{1,2}\,dZ_{2,3} = \rho\,dt,$$

we get the dynamics for $F_{1,3}$ from Ito's Lemma as

$$dF_{1,3} = (\ldots)\,dt + \frac{\sigma_{1,2}(t)}{\tau_{1,3}}(\tau_{1,2}F_{1,2}(t) + \tau_{1,2}\tau_{2,3}F_{1,2}(t)F_{2,3}(t))\,dZ_{1,2}(t)$$

$$+ \frac{\sigma_{2,3}(t)}{\tau_{1,3}}(\tau_{2,3}F_{2,3}(t) + \tau_{1,2}\tau_{2,3}F_{1,2}(t)F_{2,3}(t))\,dZ_{1,3}(t).$$

Taking variance on both sides, we get

$$\sigma_{1,3}^2(t)\tau_{1,3}^2 F_{1,3}^2(t) =$$

$$\sigma_{1,2}^2(t)(\tau_{1,2}F_{1,2}(t) + \tau_{1,2}\tau_{2,3}F_{1,2}(t)F_{2,3}(t))^2$$

$$+ \sigma_{2,3}^2(t)(\tau_{2,3}F_{2,3}(t) + \tau_{1,2}\tau_{2,3}F_{1,2}(t)F_{2,3}(t))^2$$

$$+ 2\rho\sigma_{1,2}(t)\sigma_{2,3}(t)(\tau_{1,2}F_{1,2}(t) + \tau_{1,2}\tau_{2,3}F_{1,2}(t)F_{2,3}(t))(\tau_{2,3}F_{2,3}(t)$$

$$+ \tau_{1,2}\tau_{2,3}F_{1,2}(t)F_{2,3}(t)).$$

If we define

$$u_i := \frac{1}{\tau_{1,3}F_{1,3}(t)}(\tau_{i,i+1}F_{i,i+1}(t) + \tau_{1,2}\tau_{2,3}F_{1,2}(t)F_{2,3}(t)),\ i = 1, 2,$$

we get

$$\sigma_{1,3}^2 = u_1^2(t)\sigma_{1,2}^2(t) + u_2^2(t)\sigma_{2,3}^2(t) + 2\rho\sigma_{1,2}(t)\sigma_{2,3}(t)u_1(t)u_2(t).$$

The usual approximating trick is freezing the forward rates to their value at time 0, so we get an approximation

$$\sigma_a^2 = u_1^2(0)\sigma_{1,2}^2(t) + u_2^2(0)\sigma_{2,3}^2(t) + 2\rho\sigma_{1,2}(t)\sigma_{2,3}(t)u_1(0)u_2(0).$$

For the (T_1, T_3)-caplet, we have for the Black-volatility $v_{1,3}$

$$v_{1,3}^2 \approx \frac{1}{\tau_{0,1}}\int_0^{T_1} \sigma_a^2(t)\,dt =$$

$$\frac{1}{\tau_{0,1}}\left(u_1^2(0)\int_0^{T_1}\sigma_{1,2}^2(t)\,dt + u_2^2(0)\int_0^{T_1}\sigma_{2,3}^2(t)\,dt\right.$$

$$\left. + 2\rho u_1(0)u_2(0)\int_0^{T_1}\sigma_{1,2}(t)\sigma_{2,3}(t)\,dt\right).$$

Now with $v_{1,2}$ the Black volatility of the (T_1, T_2)-caplet, we have

$$\frac{1}{\tau_{0,1}} \int_0^{T_1} \sigma_{1,2}^2(t)\, dt = v_{1,2}^2,$$

but the other two integrals in the sum have to be calculated under another simplifying assumption. The canonical one is that caplet volas are constant in time and identical to the Black volatilities, so

$$\frac{1}{\tau_{0,1}} \int_0^{T_1} \sigma_{2,3}^2(t)\, dt = v_{2,3}^2, \text{ and}$$

$$\frac{1}{\tau_{0,1}} \int_0^{T_1} \sigma_{1,2}^2(t)\sigma_{2,3}^2(t)\, dt = \frac{1}{\tau_{0,1}} \int_0^{T_1} v_{1,2}v_{2,3}\, dt = v_{1,2}v_{2,3}.$$

Here, we assumed that $\tau_{0,1} = \int_0^{T_1} dt$. Thus, we get the approximation

$$v_{1,3}^2 \approx u_1^2(0)v_{1,2}^2 + u_2^2(0)v_{2,3}^2 + 2\rho u_1(0)u_2(0)v_{1,2}v_{2,3}. \tag{7.8}$$

Other more complicated assumptions on the behavior of $\sigma(t)$ usually need more parameters than the quantities the market provides. One can give a strong argument that this formula slightly overestimates the actual volatilities, but we skip this here. For details see [Brigo and Mercurio (2006)], Section 6.20.

As an example, consider the following set of data. We have three times, $t_1 = $ March 29, 2012, $t_2 = $ June 29, 2012, and $t_3 = $ September 28, 2012, each three months apart. This yields in the US market (ACT/360): $\tau_{1,2} = 0.255556, \tau_{2,3} = 0.252778, \tau_{1,3} = 0.513889$. Assume we have forwards $F_{1,2} = 0.46781\%, F_{2,3} = 0.49887\%, F_{1,3} = 0.48389\%$, and caplet volatilities $\sigma_{1,2} = 72\%, \sigma_{2,3} = 73\%$. Then we get for a correlation $\rho = 0$ that $\sigma_{1,3} = 51.39\%$. If $\rho = 1, \sigma_{1,3} = 72.57\%$. There is a strictly monotonic relationship between ρ and $\sigma_{1,3}$, as shown in Figure 7.4.

We can also use Equation (7.8) to derive short tenor caplet volatilities from longer ones, e.g. if we want to know the 3-month caplet volatilities for a longer running cap. Let's assume we know the caplet volatility $\sigma_{1,2}$ for the period (T_1, T_2) (which is three months) and $\sigma_{2,4}$ for the period (T_2, T_4) (six months). This is possible because, as mentioned in the beginning, the volatilities quoted for the shortest caplets are for 3-month tenors. Assuming that $v_{2,3} = (v_{1,2} + v_{3,4})/2$, we have to solve for the positive solution for $v_{3,4}$ in the equation

$$v_{2,4}^2 = \frac{u_1^2}{4}(v_{1,2} + v_{3,4})^2 + u_2^2 v_{3,4}^2 + 2\rho u_1^2 u_2^2 v_{2,3} v_{3,4},$$

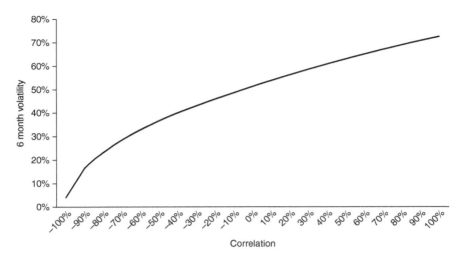

Figure 7.4   6-month caplet volatilities for the period March 29, 2012 to September 28, 2012 as a function of the forward-forward correlation ρ.

or

$$v_{3,4} = \sqrt{\left(\frac{2u_1^2 v_{1,2} + 4\rho u_1 u_2 v_{2,3}}{4u_2^2 + u_1^2}\right)^2 - \left(\frac{u_1^2 v_{1,2}^2}{4u_2^2 + u_1^2} - v_{2,4}^2\right)} - \left(\frac{2u_1^2 v_{1,2} + 4\rho u_1 u_2 v_{2,3}}{4u_2^2 + u_1^2}\right).$$

The method described above is problematic in a multi-curve environment because the longer tenor forwards are calculated from the same interest curve as the short ones. In the example above, one would have to use the basis spread adjusted forward $F_{1,3} = 0.75143\%$ instead of 0.48389%. However, this will reduce the resulting volatilities by about a third, which is far too low.

Only very recently (early 2012) have the market data providers started to present non-standard tenor cap volatilities.

7.4.2 Swaption volatilities for non-standard tenors: first approach

From Equation (5.3) we derived the fact that the fair swap rate is a martingale under the measure associated with the swap rate annuity numeraire $A_T^f := \sum_{i=1}^{n^f(T)} (t_i^f - t_{i-1}^f) d_{t_i^f}^f$. Our first simple approach assumes that two swap rates of tenors k and l are both geometric Brownian motions under this measure. For (hopefully) more clarity we set $k = 3$ and $l = 6$. Furthermore, we make the assumption that the 3/6 basis spread, which is given by $s^6_{T_0,T_1} - s^3_{T_0,T_1}$, remains constant over time. This implies that the two processes are perfectly correlated, so that

$$ds^6_{T_0,T_1}(t) = s^6_{T_0,T_1}(t)\sigma^6_{T_0,T_1}(t)\,dW^{A_{T_0,T_1}}(t)$$

$$ds^3_{T_0,T_1}(t) = s^3_{T_0,T_1}(t)\sigma^3_{T_0,T_1}(t)\,dW^{A_{T_0,T_1}}(t),$$

and the two processes are actually driven by the same Brownian motion.

Now, because $s^6_{T_0,T_1} - s^3_{T_0,T_1}$ is constant, $ds^6_{T_0,T_1} - ds^3_{T_0,T_1} = 0$, i.e.

$$0 = s^6_{T_0,T_1}\sigma(t)^6_{T_0,T_1}(t) - s^3_{T_0,T_1}(t)\sigma^3_{T_0,T_1}(t),$$

from which we imply

$$s^3_{T_0,T_1}(t) = s^6_{T_0,T_1}(t)\frac{\sigma(t)^6_{T_0,T_1}(t)}{\sigma(t)^3_{T_0,T_1}(t)}, \tag{7.9}$$

a formula that was commonly used in front offices for rescaling volatilities. However, since mid 2007, the assumption of a constant spread is absurd, as Figure 7.5 shows.

7.4.3 Swaption volatilities for non-standard tenors: new market approach

The market now follows a different route. First, it must be mentioned that despite the earlier discussions about discounting with an OIS curve, the forward swap rates *for the purpose of computing at the money rates for swaptions* are calculated off a single curve which is built from the proper tenor instruments. That means that 6-month forward swap rates are calculated by discounting with a 6-month curve, which is also used for projecting forwards, and analogously for other tenors. In other words, for the fair forward swap rate at time t for a swap with tenor k starting in t_0 and maturing in $t_n = t'_m$, we have

$$c^k_{t_0,t_n}(t) = \frac{\sum\limits_{j=1}^{m} f^k(t;t'_{j-1},t'_j)\tau_{t'_{j-1},t'_j}d^k_{t'_j}(t)}{\sum\limits_{i=1}^{n} \tau_{t_{i-1},t_i}d^k_{t_i}}, \tag{7.10}$$

with $f^k(t;t'_{j-1},t'_j)$ given by Equation (1.2).

As discussed in Chapter 1, the fair swap rate process is a martingale under the annuity measure, which allows us to price a swaption with

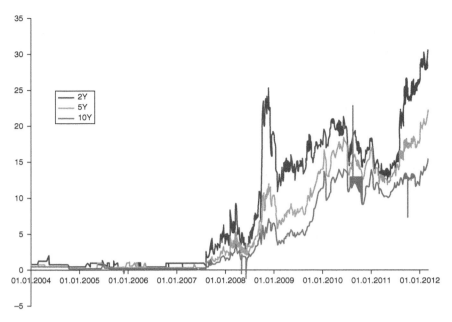

Figure 7.5 The historical 10-year 3/6 basis spreads (Source: Bloomberg).

a given strike if we know its volatility v; see Equation (1.5), where we assumed that the martingale is a geometric Brownian motion. As with other options, the market quotes different volatilities for different strikes. Therefore, swaption volatilities are quoted in cubes, whose dimensions are made up of expiry (or start date of the underlying swap), tenor (or time between start and maturity of the underlying swap), and moneyness (the distance of the strike from the ATM swap rate). Instead of using a log-normal model (i.e. a geometric Brownian motion) for the swap rate process, we might as well use a normal one and assume that the process follows an ordinary Brownian motion. The pricing formula for an option is not very different from the log-normal one. Using the notation from Equation (1.5), this is given by

$$V^k(t) = A^k(t; t_0, t_n)((c^k(t; t_0, t_n) - K)\Phi(e_1) - \phi(e_1)), \qquad (7.11)$$

where ϕ is the standard normal distribution function, and Φ is the cumulative normal distribution function. It is quite clear that to arrive at the same price, the volatility appearing in Equation (7.11) must be different from the one in Equation (1.5), but they can be transformed into each other quite easily.

Note that in deriving Equation (7.11), we have not made any assumptions about the tenor of the underlying swap. The formula really only depends on the annuity factor, the time to expiry, the moneyness $a = c^k(t; t_0, t_n) - K$, and the volatility.

Assumption 7.1 The volatility of the forward swap rate process does not depend on the tenor of the underlying swap.

With this assumption at hand, it is straightforward to compute

$$V^k(t; t_0, t_n, a, \sigma^k(a)) = \frac{A^k(t; t_0, t_n)}{A^l(t; t_0, t_n)} V^l(t; t_0, t_n, a, \sigma^k(a)). \tag{7.12}$$

In other words, the strike K of the k-tenor option has to be transformed into the strike $K + c^k(t; t_0, t_n) - c^l(t; t_0, t_n)$ in the formula for the l-tenor swap in order to keep the moneyness the same. The difference $c^k(t; t_0, t_n) - c^l(t; t_0, t_n)$ is nothing else but the basis swap spread between tenors k and l. We see that this basis spread can indeed be interpreted as the difference between the two fair forward swap rates for the different tenors.

The process to turn standard tenor volatilities into non-standard tenor ones is therefore outlined as follows:

(1) get standard tenor volatilities from the market;
(2) if these are log-normal volatilities, compute prices. Else, continue with (4);
(3) derive normal volatilities for standard tenors from the prices;
(4) use normal volatilities to price non-standard tenor swaptions with Equation (7.11);
(5) derive log-normal volatilities for non-standard tenors from the prices.

Will the next crisis render Assumption 7.1 incorrect?

A note on market conventions: as described above, the standard quotations for European swaptions used to be volatilities based on ATM or the moneyness in percentage points (like $\pm 0.25, \pm 0.5, \pm 1.0$, etc.). Nowadays, contributors also often quote swaption *prices*, which refer to a premium to be paid on the expiry date of the option. That way, the necessity of making any assumptions on the discount curve is eliminated.

8
CVA: Instrument Level

SECOND LORD How mightily sometimes we make us comforts of
our losses!
FIRST LORD And how mightily some other times we drown our gain
in tears!
Shakespeare, *All's Well That Ends Well*.

8.1 Introduction

The acronym CVA stands for Credit Valuation Adjustment; DVA stands
for Debit (or Debt, or Default) Valuation Adjustment; and FVA stands
for Funding Valuation Adjustment. In this chapter we only consider
trade pricing. In the next chapter the effects from the balance sheet
to the trade level and at the balance sheet level itself are discussed.
Thus the Regulatory and Accounting background is in the next chapter,
whereas effects of ISDA language on closeout prices is detailed here.

   If a trade is perfectly collateralized then there is no credit risk:

- *assuming that we consider the trade in isolation* **and**
- *assuming that we don't need to do anything about the price effects of the*
  collateral **and**
- *assuming that it is a trade where perfect collateralization is possible,*

... and thus no CVA and no DVA. If the trade is perfectly hedged then
any requirement for collateral to post will be provided by the hedge.
A perfect hedge for a trade is one that produces exactly the opposite
cash flows under all states of the world. Thus no FVA.

   Note that perfect collateralization only means that the particular
trade in question has no credit risk. Obviously it does not mean
that the firm that owns it has no credit risk. In fact, we shall see in
the next chapter that the precise opposite is possible for trades that
are, in addition, not perfectly hedged (e.g. micro-hedged asset-swap

packages). That is, the presence of collateralized trades can act as a pressure on the survival of the firm because collateralization actualizes losses immediately.

We must consider a portfolio of trades, and potentially a bank's complete inventory, in order to come to conclusions about these adjustments (which are by no means separate). However, individual trading desks and traders need something simpler in order to operate. It is impractical to revalue the entire portfolio of the bank for every trading decision. This chapter describes some simple approximations in current use, as well as the framework for exact solutions.

There is considerable confusion and debate around CVA, DVA, and FVA. This has several causes:

- Regulatory/Capital (Basel III, etc.) and Accounting/Trading (FAS 157, etc.) views serve different purposes but both must be addressed.
- Different scales of activity (desk vs firm) interact so simple views, that are correct when all other factors are held constant, are imprecise in practice.
- Actions change value (think hold-to-maturity vs trade-now).
- Different institutions see genuinely different values.

We will give examples and critiques as well as suggesting reasonable (in the authors' views) practical approaches.

For those coming from the Corporate Finance world, the Modgliani–Millar theorem is now appreciated [Miller (1988)] as an early hedging argument, and is fully consistent with [Piterbarg (2010)] as Modgliani–Millar assume equal borrowing and hedging costs.

It is now standard to include (at least) CVA in the valuation of uncollateralized derivatives. This often requires use of default probabilities and recovery rates that are not directly observed (for example for small to medium-sized counterparties), which has consequences in accounting (and hence in maintenance) terms. Use of internal mappings and models for valuations of illiquid positions means that the valuations are now classified at IFRS (International Financial Reporting Standards) level 3 rather than IFRS level 2, according to IFRS 7 "Financial Instruments: Disclosures", fair value pricing.

8.1.1 Origins

CVA and DVA

Pre-crisis, most banks considered themselves risk free, and this opinion was largely shared by their clients. Thus banks could charge their uncollateralized clients for the risk that the client might default without any symmetric consideration. This was credit valuation adjustment, CVA, from the point of view of the banks, and debit valuation adjustment, DVA, from the point of view of their clients.

Post-crisis bank clients insist that banks can default and thus prices from bank's point of view do now include both CVA and DVA.

FVA

Pre-crisis funding for banks was easy. If a bank bought an asset, say a Euro sovereign bond, it could place it into repo with any number of counterparties and get cash with which to fund its original purchase. The repo price for a Euro sovereign generally had no haircut so there was no need of additional funding. The bank paid the repo rate for the cash, received the bond coupons, and its profit was the difference. Essentially there was no funding cost for the bond, only a profit from the spread between the bond coupon and the repo rate.

Pre-crisis, the capital markets were deep and banks could generally borrow as much as they liked in the short-term markets. Thus if a bank bought an asset that it could not place into repo, it simply funded the purchase by borrowing, say 100M USD at 3-month LIBOR (then the standard) plus some small spread for the bank's risk (a few basis points), for three months. After the three months were up this funding would be rolled by paying back the original 100M, and borrowing a further 100M. The bank would make the difference between borrowing short and lending long.

This went horribly wrong with the crisis. The two main assumptions:

(1) deep capital markets
(2) top-rated assets hold value

both went spectacularly wrong (just remember all those AAA-rated CDO tranches). The capital markets closed and many assets (e.g. Euro sovereign bonds) lost value. Unsecured funding, e.g. for assets that could not be placed into repo, became hugely more expensive compared to pre-crisis. This cost of funding is what FVA aims to capture.

Notice that an institution can take two approaches to a fall in asset value reducing the cash from repo. First, it can simply take the loss onto its books and thus not have a funding cost problem. This risks insolvency if the institution now has insufficient capital to meet regulatory requirements. Secondly, it can look for funding to meet the cash requirements that are not being met from repo. This risks illiquidity if the market refuses to lend cash at any price to the institution. Thus Lehmann fell.

Most banks fail from illiquidity when the markets believe them to be insolvent. A third party, e.g. the ECB or the Fed, can provide liquidity (most banks) but only an equity offering (many banks), a bail-out involving some degree of nationalization (Lloyds, AIG, RBS, UBS, Commerzbank, etc.), can provide solvency.

8.1.2 Closeout

Let the market value of a derivative prior to T be $M(t)$, where any dependence on some underlying S is assumed. On default it is not clear what this should be since the ISDA 2009 master agreement substantially, and explicitly, altered the ISDA 1992 language [ISDA (2009)]. The closeout language now has significant ambiguity, as [Carver (2011)] noted from [Brigo and Morini (2010)], amongst others. The closeout protocol replaces Market Quotation (dealer quotes) with a Close out Amount (DIY calculations), because when Lehman defaulted, market quotations were difficult to obtain for many transactions, especially structured credit. Or, rather, the bid-ask spreads were typically 1%–99%, so practically useless. The relevant text in the new version is:

In determining a Close-out Amount, the Determining Party may consider any relevant information, including, without limitation, one or more of the following types of information:

(i) quotations (either firm or indicative) for replacement transactions supplied by one or more third parties that may take into account the creditworthiness of the Determining Party at the time the quotation is provided and the terms of any relevant documentation, including credit support documentation, between the Determining Party and the third party providing the quotation;

(ii) information consisting of relevant market data in the relevant market supplied by one or more third parties including, without limitation, relevant rates, prices, yields, yield curves, volatilities, spreads, correlations or other relevant market data in the relevant market; or

(iii) information of the types described in clause (i) or (ii) above from internal sources (including any of the Determining Party's Affiliates) if that information is of the same type used by the Determining Party in the regular course of its business for the valuation of similar transactions.

The main point is that, depending on the circumstances, different closeout amounts are possible. There seems to be the intention to use replacement cost and/or the internal valuation of the transaction. At the point where a party defaults it may only be possible to get a collateralized replacement trade, whereas before it may have been uncollateralized. Given gap risk, even collateralized trades will require valuation on default events.

It is quite reasonable to consider both a risk-free replacement on default and a risky replacement on default. The risky replacement can have many different values (if uncollateralized) depending on which other party is willing to enter into the transaction. Indeed, no other party that is still in business will be exactly equivalent to the defaulted party. Let the two parties be a bank b and its counterparty c and their default times be ζ_b and ζ_c as in earlier chapters (where we used τ for year fractions). There are two closeout special cases ($* = b, c$) where $\widehat{V}(t)$ is the risky value of the derivative and $V(t)$ the riskless version:

- $M(\zeta_*) = \widehat{V}(\zeta_*-)$, i.e. closeout using a risky value an instant before default;
- $M(\zeta_*) = V(\zeta_*)$, defined to mean riskless closeout, e.g. replacement with a collateralized instrument.

We can now write the derivative value on default using M, from the point of view of c, as:

$$\widehat{V}(\zeta_b) = M^-(\zeta_b) + R_b M^+(\zeta_b)$$

$$\widehat{V}(\zeta_c) = R_c M^-(\zeta_c) + M^+(\zeta_c).$$

Note that we do not know whether M will be positive or negative, but the $+, -$ superscripts denote max, min with zero and so isolate the two cases.

The definitions above are controversial because for risky closeout we use the value an instant before default, effectively assuming a constant hazard rate model. The ISDA language only explicitly mentions the credit risk of the determining party, thus [Brigo and Morini (2010)] only consider DVA in their valuation. However, implicitly, if the credit risk of one party is included then the trade is *not* collateralized, *hence* the credit risk of *both* parties to the transaction matters.

Now what credit risk should be used for the CVA side of the calculation? This is completely unknown and ambiguous. [Brigo and Morini (2010)]'s choice of zero risk for the CVA side seems optimistic. If we are using a constant hazard rate model then, yes, we can just use a CVA value from an instant before default. However, practically, we do not expect this line of reasoning to be followed. Generally, default is not a complete surprise (except in the case of outright fraud, which is uncommon) so the CDS spread of the going-to-default counterparty the day before default will be very high. Indeed, considering bond prices either side of default, some studies have found little change, i.e. the market had already priced in default. In this case the claim on the defaulting counterparty would be almost zero because the day-before CVA term would be almost the entire value of the trade (if positive).

8.2 Pricing by expectation

Here we consider the risk-neutral expected value of a portfolio under self-default and counterparty risk. We call the two parties the bank b and the counterparty c. We pick the portfolio approach so as to make the value of cash flows up to default visible. This approach, and section, largely follows [Brigo(2011), Brigo and Morini(2010), Pallavicini *et al.* (2011), Brigo and Masetti(2006)], whereas the next section largely follows [Burgard and Kjaer (2011b), Burgard and Kjaer (2011a)]. Given that hedging is not the same as expectation in incomplete markets, *caveat emptor utque venditor*, and read the Critique at the end of the section.

8.2.1 CVA and DVA

In this section we ignore funding costs and assume we can discount at the riskless rate r. Let the riskless discounted portfolio value be $\Pi(t, T)$ and its risky version be $\widehat{\Pi}(t, T)$. The t is the as of date and the portfolio may contain cash flows up to T. Let $\widehat{V}(t, T) = \mathbb{E}[\widehat{\Pi}(t, T) | \mathcal{F}(t)]$, and the riskless version is without hats. We use $D(s, t)$ as the discount factor between s and t. A subscript indicates the point of view so $\widehat{\Pi}_b(t, T) = -\widehat{\Pi}_c(t, T)$.

Unilateral CVA and DVA

Theorem 8.1   UCVA: *When b is riskless and c is risky the value of a portfolio between b and c from b's point of view, with riskless closeout, is:*

$$\widehat{\Pi}_b(t, T) = \mathbb{I}_{\{\zeta_c > T\}} \Pi(t, T)$$
$$+ \mathbb{I}_{\{t < \zeta_c \leq T\}} \left[\Pi(t, \zeta_c) + D(t, \zeta_c)(R_c V_b^+(\zeta_c, T) + V_b^-(\zeta_c, T)) \right]$$

$$\widehat{V}_b(t,T) = \mathbb{E}[\widehat{\Pi}_b(t,T)|\mathcal{F}(t)]$$
$$= \mathbb{I}_{\{\zeta_c>T\}}V_b(t,T) - \mathbb{E}\big[(1-R_c)\mathbb{I}_{\{t<\zeta_c\leq T\}}D(t,\zeta_c)V_b^+(\zeta_c,T)|\mathcal{F}(t)]\big],$$

where superscript $+$ and $-$ indicate signed max and min with zero respectively (not their absolute size), i.e. $f = f^+ + f^-$.

Proof Obvious using the tower property of conditional expectation. □

Hence unilateral CVA, UCVA, from b's point of view is just:

$$\widehat{V}_b = V_b - \text{UCVA}_b$$
$$\text{UCVA}_b = \mathbb{E}\big[(1-R_c)\mathbb{I}_{\{t<\zeta_c\leq T\}}D(t,\zeta_c)V_b^+(\zeta_c,T)|\mathcal{F}(t)\big].$$

The first point to notice is that the counterparty risk adds an option-like term to any portfolio. When considering counterparty, or self, risks in pricing, everything is at least one step more complex. Even a simple fixed-for-floating swap is now dependent on option pricing.

Unilateral DVA, UDVA, from the point of view of c is exactly the inverse of the UCVA term by definition in this setup with no funding costs.

Theorem 8.2   UDVA: *When b is riskless and c is risky the value of a portfolio between b and c from c's point of view, with riskless closeout, is:*

$$\widehat{\Pi}_c(t,T) = \mathbb{I}_{\{\zeta_c>T\}}\Pi(t,T)$$
$$+ \mathbb{I}_{\{t<\zeta_c\leq T\}}\big[\Pi(t,\zeta_c) + D(t,\zeta_c)(V_c^+(\zeta_c,T) + R_cV_c^-(\zeta_c,T))\big]$$
$$\widehat{V}_c(t,T) = \mathbb{E}[\widehat{\Pi}_c(t,T)|\mathcal{F}(t)]$$
$$= \mathbb{I}_{\{\zeta_c>T\}}V_c(t,T) - \mathbb{E}\big[(1-R_c)\mathbb{I}_{\{t<\zeta_c\leq T\}}D(t,\zeta_c)V_c^-(\zeta_c,T)|\mathcal{F}(t)]\big],$$

where superscript $+$ and $-$ indicate signed max and min with zero respectively (not their absolute size), i.e. $f = f^+ + f^-$. Note the changes in subscripts with respect to the previous theorem.

Proof Corollary to previous theorem. □

Hence, unilateral DVA, UDVA, from c's point of view is:

$$\widehat{V}_c = V_c + \text{UDVA}_c$$
$$\text{UDVA}_c = -\mathbb{E}\big[(1-R_c)\mathbb{I}_{\{t<\zeta_c\leq T\}}D(t,\zeta_c)V_c^-(\zeta_c,T)|\mathcal{F}(t)\big]$$
$$= \text{UCVA}_b.$$

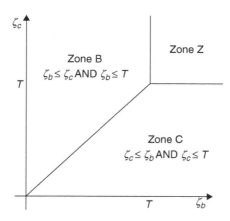

Figure 8.1 Relevant default sequence cases for bilateral CVA and DVA. ζ_b is the default time of b, ζ_c is the default time of c and T is the maturity of the portfolio of interest.

So the situation is exactly symmetric with respect to the two parties, and obviously

$$UDVA_b = UCVA_c = 0,$$

since b has no risk by assumption.

Bilateral CVA and DVA

Bilateral just means that both parties in the transaction, b and c, are risky. Now we need to keep track of which party defaults first and whether this happens before T. These cases are shown in Figure 8.1 and below:

$$B = \{\zeta_b \leq \zeta_c \cap \zeta_b \leq T\}$$
$$C = \{\zeta_c \leq \zeta_b \cap \zeta_c \leq T\}$$
$$Z = \{T < \zeta_b, \zeta_c\},$$

where we do not distinguish the order of default in the last case because the portfolio has matured.

Theorem 8.3   BVA riskless closeout: *When both b and c are risky the value of a portfolio between b and c from b's point of view, with riskless closeout, assuming no contagion and no simultaneous default, is:*

$$\widehat{\Pi}_b(t, T) = \mathbb{I}_{\{Z\}} \Pi(t, T)$$
$$+ \mathbb{I}_{\{C\}} \left[\Pi(t, \zeta_c) + D(t, \zeta_c)(R_c V_b^+(\zeta_c, T) + V_b^-(\zeta_c, T)) \right]$$
$$+ \mathbb{I}_{\{B\}} \left[\Pi(t, \zeta_b) + D(t, \zeta_b)(V_b^+(\zeta_b, T) + R_b V_b^-(\zeta_b, T)) \right]$$

$$\widehat{V}_b(t, T) = \mathbb{E}[\widehat{\Pi}_b(t, T) | \mathcal{F}(t)]$$
$$= \mathbb{I}_{\{Z\}} V_b(t, T)$$
$$- \mathbb{E}\left[(1 - R_c)\mathbb{I}_{\{C\}}D(t, \zeta_c)V_b^+(\zeta_c, T) | \mathcal{F}(t)]\right]$$
$$- \mathbb{E}\left[(1 - R_b)\mathbb{I}_{\{B\}}D(t, \zeta_c)V_b^-(\zeta_b, T) | \mathcal{F}(t)]\right],$$

where superscript + and − indicate signed max and min with zero respectively (not their absolute size), i.e. $f = f^+ + f^-$.

Proof   Obvious using the tower property of conditional expectation.

$\square$

When either party defaults, the contract is closed out so there is no effect of subsequent default by the other party. No contagion means that one party does not cause the other to default within the closeout period. We also assume there is no simultaneous default, for example caused by a third party, e.g. a central clearinghouse or a sovereign.

Hence, bilateral CVA and DVA from b's point of view is:

$$\widehat{V}_b = V_b - \mathrm{CVA}_b + \mathrm{DVA}_b$$
$$\mathrm{CVA}_b = \mathbb{E}\left[(1 - R_c)\mathbb{I}_{\{C\}}D(t, \zeta_c)V_b^+(\zeta_c, T) | \mathcal{F}(t)\right]$$
$$\mathrm{DVA}_b = -\mathbb{E}\left[(1 - R_b)\mathbb{I}_{\{B\}}D(t, \zeta_b)V_b^-(\zeta_b, T) | \mathcal{F}(t)\right],$$

where we have arranged things so that CVA and DVA numbers are always positive. Thus the value of a contract increases when the likelihood of not paying debts increases (so DVA is an additive positive term). Similarly, the value of a contract decreases as the likelihood of receiving positive cash flows decreases (so CVA is a subtractive positive term).

We now turn to the problem of risky closeout. As mentioned above, [Brigo and Morini (2010)] only consider DVA in closeout, although since DVA is considered, by implication, so should *some* CVA. The Theorem below deals with the case where the value of the portfolio an instant before default is used for closeout. This could easily be substituted by DVA only, or some combination. Market practice, and especially ISDA language, is not yet clear.

Theorem 8.4   BVA risky closeout: *When both b and c are risky, the value of a portfolio between b and c from b's point of view, with risky closeout, assuming no contagion and no simultaneous default, is:*

$$\widehat{\Pi}_b(t, T) = \mathbb{I}_{\{Z\}} \Pi(t, T)$$

$$+ \mathbb{I}_{\{C\}} \left[\Pi(t, \zeta_c) + D(t, \zeta_c)(R_c \widehat{V}_b^+(\zeta_c, T) + \widehat{V}_b^-(\zeta_c-, T)) \right]$$

$$+ \mathbb{I}_{\{B\}} \left[\Pi(t, \zeta_b) + D(t, \zeta_b)(\widehat{V}_b^+(\zeta_b, T) + R_b \widehat{V}_b^-(\zeta_b-, T)) \right]$$

$$\widehat{V}_b(t, T) = \mathbb{E}[\widehat{\Pi}_b(t, T) | \mathcal{F}(t)]$$

$$= \mathbb{I}_{\{Z\}} V_b(t, T)$$

$$- \mathbb{E}\left[(1 - R_c)\mathbb{I}_{\{C\}} D(t, \zeta_c) \widehat{V}_b^+(\zeta_c-, T) | \mathcal{F}(t)] \right]$$

$$- \mathbb{E}\left[(1 - R_b)\mathbb{I}_{\{B\}} D(t, \zeta_c) \widehat{V}_b^-(\zeta_b-, T) | \mathcal{F}(t)] \right].$$

Notice that the equations have become recursive. This is also seen in the pricing-by-hedging section below, and in fact leads to simple expressions when closeout is riskless, which we present in that section.

8.2.2 CVA, DVA, and FVA

The expectation framework has been extended to cover funding costs in [Pallavicini *et al.* (2011)]. Funding costs are paid via a hedging argument that whenever the trade is in the money the hedge must have the same value, and this can be obtained by taking positions in funding instruments (and vice versa). Now the funding instruments available for raising cash are simply short-dated cash instruments (effectively short-dated bonds) issued by the bank b. Simplifying, these have a funding cost to b:

$$r_F = r + \lambda_b + l_b,$$

where r is the riskless rate; λ_b the hazard rate of b; and l_b the liquidity cost (aka convenience yield). This is very similar to the approach of [Burgard and Kjaer (2011b), Burgard and Kjaer (2011a)] that we shall see in the next section on pricing by hedging. In fact this subsection is the intersection between the two approaches.

Effectively, [Pallavicini *et al.* (2011)] use a recursive formulation working backwards from maturity, paying hedging/funding costs at each step and allowing for default of either party. Discounting is always with the riskless rate as all other costs are explicit. This is a completely general formulation that, as a consequence of its generality, is only numerical, except for special cases. These special cases give the same results as the next section, although there they are reached by PDE+Feynman–Kac methods.

8.2.3 Critique

This pricing approach for CVA and DVA alone does not start from hedging but from expectation. For complete markets, pricing from hedging or from expectation (under suitable measure and associated numeraire combinations) is identical [Shreve (2004)]. The markets considered here are typically incomplete because hedging instruments, specifically own-bonds, cannot be freely traded as required by hedging strategies. The no-arbitrage bounds for these incomplete markets have not been studied to date (early 2012). Furthermore, whilst the choice of a standard risk-neutral setting means that prices cannot be arbitraged, given that no-arbitrage bounds are typically very large [Cont and Tankov (2003)], any claim to accuracy is dubious.

In short, these prices for CVA and DVA alone are arbitrage free but cannot be reproduced by hedging. Thus, if the historical measure gives prices that are within the no-arbitrage bounds, this is worth considering, in practice, for pricing.

The fully general recursive formulation of the expectation method including FVA presented in [Pallavicini *et al.* (2011)] does not suffer from these weaknesses in theory because it is fully general. This means that it can be run numerically with only the actual hedging/funding instruments available to the institution present. Thus it can, in theory, give prices by hedging. This recursive formulation has an obvious implication: *in general, it is not possible to separate CVA, DVA, and FVA in theory or in practice.*

The situation is not quite as bleak as it may appear. When an instrument value has always the same sign, pricing including CVA, DVA, and FVA is simpler, and the next section gives examples. However, practical pricing methods require realistic hedging/funding instruments. The set used by a bank's treasury is the obvious place to start.

8.3 Pricing by hedging

The classical approach to price a derivative is to construct a replicating portfolio and state that this is the price. Whilst this may be the cost of holding the derivative to maturity for the institution carrying out the replication, it is not clear today that this is the market price [Morini and Prampolini (2011)]. The approach we describe here was first presented by [Burgard and Kjaer (2011b)] and, unlike the hedging-for-P&L-takeout approach in [Fries (2011)], they hedge with contingent instruments – the bank's own bonds. For P&L

takeout, [Fries (2011)] obtains quite different results because he hedges default-contingent cash flows with certain cash flows. We consider that the hedging argument of [Burgard and Kjaer (2011b)] is a useful start and present it here. It could be extended to include the bond-CDS basis which would then link it with the liquidity arguments of [Morini and Prampolini (2011)]. We will comment on practical aspects after the reader has seen the theory.

We build up the theory in steps: first we only consider funding costs, and then we introduce default. This approach has the advantage of making the funding arguments clear.

8.3.1 Feynman–Kac

Since this is central to the classical approach, we remind our readers of the theorem. Note that we use V and $\widehat{V}$ a little differently here as compared with the section on pricing by expectation.

Theorem 8.5 *Let $V(t,x)$ satisfy the PDE:*

$$\partial_t V + \mu(t,x)\partial_x V + \frac{1}{2}\sigma^2(t,x)\partial_{xx} V - r(x,t)V = h(t,x),$$

with terminal condition $V(T,x) = \psi(x,T)$. Then there exists a measure $\mathbf{Q}$ such that W is a standard Brownian Motion under $\mathbf{Q}$ such that:

$$V(t,x) = -\mathbb{E}^{\mathbf{Q}}\left[\int_t^T D_r(t,u)h(u,X(u))du - D_r(t,T)\psi(X(T),T)|\mathcal{F}_t\right]$$

$$\forall t < T,$$

$$dX(t) = \mu(t,X(t))dt + \sigma(t,X(t))dW(t),$$

and

$$D_r(t,u) = e^{-\int_t^u r(X(s),s)ds},$$

provided

$$\int_t^T \mathbb{E}^{\mathbf{Q}}\left[(\sigma(s,X(s))\partial_x V(s,X(s)))^2 | \mathcal{F}_t\right]ds < \infty.$$

This provides, at least formally, a method to turn PDEs into integral equations on expectations of functions of diffusions. See [Oksendal (2002)] for details.

8.3.2 FVA

We want to price a derivative $\widehat{V}(t,S)$ where t is the as-of date and S the underlying asset (say a stock), with $\widehat{V}(T,S) = H(S)$, between a riskless bank b and its riskless counterparty c. Note that we will often drop the explicit dependence on S for simplicity. If they are both riskless why is there a funding cost different from the riskless rate? Empirically we observe a bond-CDS basis (see Section 3.7 on the bond-CDS basis), so there is a cost for cash even after credit has been accounted for. This is key to [Morini and Prampolini (2011)], and a well-known phenomenon in the commodity markets where futures contract prices can only be explained by introducing a convenience yield. Futures contracts have only minimal credit risk because they are exchange traded and marked to market daily. Substantial convenience yields are still observed. Thus we can say that convenience yields have made their way to fixed income markets, or more simply that cash is now another commodity.

We start with a minimal setup

- Stock $S(t)$ where $dS(t)/S(t) = \mu dt + \sigma dW$, and it has dividend yield $\gamma_S(t)$
- Riskless rate r for deposits
- Funding rate r_F for b.

All three are under the historical probability measure. From the Martingale Representation Theorem we know that there is a hedge for the price of any derivative depending only on these inputs. Now we shall construct it.

Since these are the only instruments in the economy, and cash is the same as a riskless bond from the point of view of instruments, the hedging portfolio is:

$$\widehat{V}(t) = \Pi(t) = \delta(t)S(t) + \beta(t).$$

We require the portfolio to be self-financing, i.e.

$$d\widehat{V}(t) = d\Pi(t) = \delta(t)dS(t) + d\beta(t),$$

where $d\beta$ comprises the cash changes. Note that this form implies that changes to the portfolio value are only caused by changes to the stock price. See Exercise 4.10 in [Shreve (2004)] for a derivation.

We have two cases for the cash changes:

$$d\beta = \begin{cases} r(\widehat{V} - \delta(t)S(t))^+ dt + r_F(\widehat{V} - \delta(t)S(t))^- dt + \delta(t)\gamma(t)S(t)dt & \text{No repo} \\ r\widehat{V}^+ dt + r_F\widehat{V}^- dt + \delta(t)(\gamma_S(t) - q_S(t))S(t)dt & \text{With repo} \end{cases}$$

No repo market for shares Hence the cash balance considers the cash left over after share purchase or sale, i.e. share quantitates are inside the $()^+$ and $()^-$ brackets. This is the typical form found in [Shreve (2004)], although without the division into positive and negative funding rates.

With repo Repo market for shares exists, so the cost of purchase can be balanced by cash obtained from the repo market. In this case only a financing yield $q_S(t)$ appears. Note that the repo market usually has little credit risk as shares can be recalled at will (overnight). This follows the reasoning in [Burgard and Kjaer (2011b)].

We know from Ito's Lemma on $\widehat{V}$ that it satisfies:

$$d\widehat{V} = \partial_t \widehat{V} dt + \partial_S \widehat{V} dS + \frac{1}{2}\sigma^2 S^2 \partial_{SS} \widehat{V} dt.$$

Now set

$$\delta(t) = \partial_S \widehat{V}$$

to remove risk from the portfolio. Notice that the hedging strategy for the stock is *symbolically* independent of whether S can be placed into repo or not, but *quantitatively* there will be differences because of differences in $\widehat{V}$.

This gives the PDEs:

$$\partial_t \widehat{V} + \frac{1}{2}\sigma^2 S^2 \partial_{SS} \widehat{V} =$$

$$\begin{cases} r(\widehat{V} - \partial_S \widehat{V} S(t))^+ + r_F(\widehat{V} - \partial_S \widehat{V} S(t))^- + \partial_S \widehat{V} \gamma_S(t) S(t) & \text{No repo} \\ r\widehat{V}^+ + r_F \widehat{V}^- + \partial_S \widehat{V}(\gamma_S(t) - q_S(t)) S(t) & \text{With repo} \end{cases}$$

with terminal condition $\widehat{V}(T, S) = H(S)$.

Alternatively, if we write $r_F = r + s_F$ then we can simplify:

$$\partial_t \widehat{V} + \frac{1}{2}\sigma^2 S^2 \partial_{SS} \widehat{V} - \gamma(t) S(t) \partial_S \widehat{V} - r\widehat{V} =$$

$$\begin{cases} -rS(t)\partial_S \widehat{V} + s_F(\widehat{V} - S(t)\partial_S \widehat{V})^- & \text{No repo} \\ -q_S(t)S(t)\partial_S \widehat{V} + s_F \widehat{V}^- & \text{With repo} \end{cases}$$

In the case that $s_F = 0$ this reduces to the usual Black–Scholes PDE in the no repo case. In the repo case, if we take the financing costs $q_S = r$ we also return to the usual PDE.

We now write $\widehat{V} = V + \widehat{U}$ and apply the Feynman–Kac theorem to the repo case:

$$\widehat{U}(t,S) = -\int_t^T s_F(u)D_r(t,u)\mathbb{E}[((V(u,S(u)) + \widehat{U}(u,S(u)))^-|\mathcal{F}(t)]du,$$

where $D_r(t,u)$ is the discount factor between t and u using r as the instantaneous discount rate.

As a zeroth order approximation, let us assume that $V \gg U$ so we can write:

$$\widehat{U}(t,S) \approx -\int_t^T s_F(u)D_r(t,u)\mathbb{E}[V(u,S(u))^-|\mathcal{F}(t)]du. \tag{8.1}$$

This should be considered no more than an order of magnitude estimate of the funding cost. It is often easier just to price V and $\widehat{V}$ and use the difference, but this is only simple when the derivative always has the same sign (so we cannot easily price swaps exactly).

Depending on the derivative V, we can propose a family of approximations for $\widehat{U}$ guided by the price of $\mathbb{E}[V^-]$ as a function of time to maturity and underlying. For example, in the case of swaps, we would start from swaptions. This is a promising approach because prices are often, but not always, smooth functions of time to maturity and underlying. We leave this for future work.

8.3.3 CVA, DVA, and FVA

We now allow the bank b and the counterparty c to default, and write $\widehat{V}(\zeta_*)$ if $*$ defaults first ($* = b,c$) as a shorthand, i.e.

$$\widehat{V}(\zeta_b) := \widehat{V}(t = \zeta_b) \text{ such that } \zeta_c > \zeta_b \text{ and } \zeta_b \leq T,$$

$$\widehat{V}(\zeta_c) := \widehat{V}(t = \zeta_c) \text{ such that } \zeta_b > \zeta_c \text{ and } \zeta_c \leq T.$$

The value of the derivative on default is called the *closeout amount*. This closeout amount is currently (early 2012) not clear for the reasons given before. We can exactly hedge the value of the derivative (shown in the following section) *provided we know what it is*. The current practical and theoretical ambiguities surrounding closeout are unavoidable sources of pricing error.

Hence we repeat the two special cases for closeout here for convenience ($* = b,c$):

- $M(\zeta_*) = \widehat{V}(\zeta_*-)$, i.e. closeout using a risky value an instant before default;

- $M(\zeta_*) = V(\zeta_*)$, defined to mean riskless closeout, e.g. replacement with a collateralized instrument.

We can now write the derivative value on default using M, from the point of view of c, as:

$$\widehat{V}(\zeta_b) = M^-(\zeta_b) + R_b M^+(\zeta_b),$$

$$\widehat{V}(\zeta_c) = R_c M^-(\zeta_c) + M^+(\zeta_c).$$

Note that we do not know whether M will be positive or negative, but the $+, -$ superscripts denote max, min with zero and so isolate the two cases.

Hedging

The cleanest way to hedge these default risks is to allow the portfolio to trade bonds issued by both participants. The hedging portfolio is now:

$$\widehat{V}(t) = \Pi(t) = \delta(t)S(t) + \alpha_b(t)P_b(t) + \alpha_c(t)P_c(t) + \beta(t),$$

where the bonds can jump, once, to default and under the historical measure are given by:

$$dP_b/P_b = r_b dt - dJ_b,$$

$$dP_c/P_c = r_c dt - dJ_c.$$

The bonds pay 1 at maturity T if they have not defaulted, otherwise zero, and have constant positive yields, r_b, r_c. These zero-recovery bonds are a computational convenience; we could use a fixed recovery rate and will give prices below for such bonds. The J_* are point processes with zero probability of simultaneous default, so hedging will be exact. This means that there is no contagion, so there is zero chance that the default of one party will cause the default of the other party. In the next chapter we analyse a model where contagion is present.

We again require the portfolio to be self-financing, i.e.

$$d\widehat{V}(t) = d\Pi(t) = \delta(t)dS(t) + \alpha_b(t)dP_b(t) + \alpha_c(t)dP_c(t) + d\beta(t). \tag{8.2}$$

There are now two new cash contributions to β from trading in P_*:

$$d\beta = \begin{cases} \left. \begin{array}{l} r(\widehat{V} - \delta(t)S(t) - \alpha_b P_b)^+ dt + r_F(\widehat{V} - \delta(t)S(t) - \alpha_b P_b)^- dt \\ +\delta(t)\gamma(t)S(t)dt \\ -r\alpha_c P_c dt \end{array} \right\} & \text{No } S \text{ repo} \\[2em] \left. \begin{array}{l} r(\widehat{V} - \alpha_b P_b)^+ dt + r_F(\widehat{V} - \alpha_b P_b)^- dt \\ +\delta(t)(\gamma_S(t) - q_S(t))S(t)dt \\ -r\alpha_c P_c dt \end{array} \right\} & \text{With } S \text{ repo} \end{cases}$$

Since positive $\widehat{V}$ value implies long b-risk, the coefficient of P_b, α_b, will be positive (or zero). This means that b will buy back its own bonds, reducing the cash available. A negative $\widehat{V}$ value implies short c-risk, so the coefficient of P_c, α_c, will be negative (or zero).

Why is it not possible to put purchased b-bonds into repo and so only pay financing costs? This is because b-bonds are being bought back from the market by b precisely to reduce b exposure. There must be enough b-bonds outstanding.

Shorting c-bonds requires borrowing them and then selling them. We assume that the cost to borrow them will be the riskless rate r because this is overnight risk to the lender. Repo and overnight rates are usually very close. This is the reverse of the previous paragraph as the objective is now to increase c exposure. There must be enough c-bonds available.

Applying Ito's Lemma to $\widehat{V}$ and taking into account that it is now also a function of jump processes gives:

$$d\widehat{V} = \partial_t \widehat{V} dt + \partial_S \widehat{V} dS + \frac{1}{2}\sigma^2 S^2 \partial_{SS}\widehat{V} dt + (\widehat{V}(\zeta_b) - \widehat{V}(\zeta_b-))dJ_b$$
$$+ (\widehat{V}(\zeta_c) - \widehat{V}(\zeta_c-))dJ_c,$$

because $\widehat{V}$ can only jump once before the derivative contract ends, and this is either because b defaults or because c defaults. The simplified portfolio dynamics, from Equation 8.2, are:

$$d\widehat{V} = \delta(t)dS(t) + \alpha_b(t)P_b(r_b dt - dJ_b) + \alpha_c(t)P_c(r_c dt - dJ_c) + d\beta(t)$$
$$= \delta(t)dS(t) - \alpha_b(t)P_b dJ_b - \alpha_c(t)P_c dJ_c + \alpha_b(t)P_b r_b dt$$
$$+ \alpha_c(t)P_c r_c dt + d\beta(t).$$

Removing all risks, i.e. the dS, dJ_* terms, in the portfolio requires:

$$\delta(t) = \partial_S \widehat{V},$$
$$\alpha_b = -(\widehat{V}(\zeta_b) - \widehat{V}(\zeta_b-))/P_b(\zeta_b-)$$
$$= \frac{\widehat{V}(\zeta_b-) - (M^-(\zeta_b) + R_b M^+(\zeta_b))}{P_b(\zeta_b-)}$$
$$\alpha_c = -(\widehat{V}(\zeta_c) - \widehat{V}(\zeta_c-))/P_c(\zeta_c-)$$
$$= \frac{\widehat{V}(\zeta_c-) - (R_c M^-(\zeta_c) + M^+(\zeta_c))}{P_c(\zeta_c-)}.$$

As before, the hedging strategy is *symbolically* independent of whether S can be placed into repo or not, for all components (δ, α_*), but *quantitatively* there will be differences because of differences in $\widehat{V}$. These differences are precisely the different PDEs that $\widehat{V}$ satisfies:

$$\partial_t \widehat{V} + \frac{1}{2}\sigma^2 S^2 \partial_{SS} \widehat{V} = \alpha_b(t)P_b r_b + \alpha_c(t)P_c r_c + d\beta(t)/dt,$$

where the $\beta(t)/dt$ is just a shorthand to indicate that the dt factors are removed from $d\beta$.

We now focus on the case where S can be repo'd, and write:

$$\lambda_b := r_b - r$$

$$\lambda_c := r_c - r$$

$$s_F := r_F - r$$

$$\mathcal{A}_t <> := \frac{1}{2}\sigma^2 S^2 \partial_{SS} <> +(q_S - \gamma_S)S\partial_S <>,$$

where $\mathcal{A}_t$ is a parabolic differential operator, operating on $<>$. This gives:

$$\partial_t \widehat{V} + \mathcal{A}_t \widehat{V} - r\widehat{V} = (\lambda_b + \lambda_c)\widehat{V} + s_F M^- - \lambda_b(R_b M^+ + M^-) - \lambda_c(R_c M^- + M^+),$$

(8.3)

with terminal condition $\widehat{V}(T,S) = H(S)$. Note that $(M^- + R_b M^+)^- = M^-$. If there were no funding spread and no risk of default, i.e. $s_F = 0$, $\lambda_* = 0$, then the RHS would be identically zero and we would be back to the standard Black–Scholes equation. Previously, for funding only, we had just the second term on the RHS. The other terms relate to default with respect to first the termination of the contract and then to the potential default of the bank and the counterparty.

We now examine a set of cases depending on whether we take $M = \widehat{V}$ or V and whether $s_F = 0$ or not. We will see that we can reproduce many of the direct CVA and DVA results, justifying them on hedging grounds.

Risky closeout, $M = \widehat{V}$

We are interested in the decomposition $\widehat{V} = V + \widehat{U}$, and we have:

$$\partial_t \widehat{V} + \mathcal{A}_t \widehat{V} - r\widehat{V} = s_F \widehat{V}^- + \lambda_b(1 - R_b)\widehat{V}^+ + \lambda_c(1 - R_c)\widehat{V}^-$$

$$\partial_t V + \mathcal{A}_t V - rV = 0,$$

so :

$$\partial_t \widehat{U} + \mathcal{A}_t \widehat{U} - r\widehat{U} = s_F(V + \widehat{U})^- + \lambda_b(1 - R_b)(V + \widehat{U})^+$$

$$+ \lambda_c(1 - R_c)(V + \widehat{U})^-.$$

Recall that V is the standard Black–Scholes solution and is known from the second PDE above. Formally applying the Feynman–Kac Theorem 8.5 above we get:

$$\widehat{U}(t,S) = -\int_t^T s_F(u)D_r(t,u)\mathbb{E}[((V(u,S(u)) + \widehat{U}(u,S(u)))^- | \mathcal{F}(t)]du$$

$$- (1-R_b)\int_t^T \lambda_b D_r(t,u)\mathbb{E}\left[(V(u,S(u)) + \widehat{U}(u,S(u)))^+ | \mathcal{F}(t)\right]du$$

$$- (1-R_c)\int_t^T \lambda_c D_r(t,u)\mathbb{E}\left[(V(u,S(u)) + \widehat{U}(u,S(u)))^- | \mathcal{F}(t)\right]du.$$

We can now look at some standard cases:

1. **b sells bond to c** Here $\widehat{V} = \widehat{V}^+ = P_B$, where we now assume that this bond has non-zero recovery R_b and have indicated this with the uppercase B as the bond subscript. We have:

   $$\partial_t \widehat{V} = (r + (1-R_b)\lambda_b)\widehat{V},$$

   with terminal condition $\widehat{V}(T,S) = 1$. Hence:

   $$\widehat{V}(t) = \exp(-((T-t)(r + (1-R_b)\lambda_b))) = e^{-(T-t)r_F}.$$

   If we had started with a deterministically time-dependent r_F then λ_b would also be a deterministic function of time from its definition and the exponential would simply use the integral of $r_F(t)$ and $\lambda_b(t)$.

2. **b buys bond from c** Now the cash flows are all negative rather than all positive, so $\widehat{V} = \widehat{V}^- = -P_C$, where we consider a c-bond with non-zero recovery R_c, indicated by the capital C on the bond. So:

   $$\partial_t \widehat{V} = (r_F + (1-R_c)\lambda_c)\widehat{V}.$$

   with terminal condition $\widehat{V}(T,S) = -1$. Hence:

   $$\widehat{V}(t) = -\exp(-((T-t)(r_F + (1-R_c)\lambda_c))).$$

   Now if, as is usual, b can place the bond into repo we have:

   $$\widehat{V}(t) = -\exp(-((T-t)(r + (1-R_c)\lambda_c))).$$

   This is a very poor approximation for the bond price in reality because we have ignored the fact that λ_c is stochastic, so the cash from the repo will generally not match the funding requirements over any significant length of time.

3. **No funding spread, single direction cashflows** The s_F term in Equation 8.3 vanishes and the fact that either $\widehat{V} = V^+$ or $\widehat{V} = V^-$

means that we have a linear PDE. Applying the Feynman–Kac theorem in the positive case gives:

$$\widehat{V}(t) = \mathbb{E}\left[D_{r+(1-R_b)\lambda_b}(t,T)H(S(T))|\mathcal{F}(t)\right].$$

Now the CVA/DVA terms (i.e. the $\widehat{U}$ terms) in the respective positive and negative cases are:

$$\widehat{U}(t) = \begin{cases} -V(t)\int_t^T (1-R_b)\lambda_b D_{(1-R_b)\lambda_b}(t,u)du & \widehat{V} \geq 0 \\ -V(t)\int_t^T (1-R_c)\lambda_c D_{(1-R_c)\lambda_c}(t,u)du & \widehat{V} \leq 0 \end{cases}$$

where we split out the riskless part $V(t) = D_r(t,u)\mathbb{E}[V(u,S(u))|\mathcal{F}(t)]$.

4. **No bond-CDS spread, single direction cashflows** Now $s_F = r_F - r = (1-R_b)\lambda_b$. The single direction of the cash flows again gives a linear PDE, and applying Feynman–Kac we have:

$$\widehat{V}(t) = \mathbb{E}[D_{r+k}(t,T)H(S(T))|\mathcal{F}(t)]$$
$$k := (1-R_b)\lambda_b + (1-R_c)\lambda_c,$$

and we get:

$$\widehat{U}(t) = -V(t)\int_t^T k(u)D_k(t,u)du.$$

Single direction cash flows are typical in options. Of course swaps have bi-directional cash flows, and this typically means that possible future values are positive and negative, so the PDEs remain non-linear.

Riskless closeout, $M = V$

The key point here is that the non-Black–Scholes terms and the Black–Scholes terms separate because the Black–Scholes PDE has a zero RHS. Thus, using $\widehat{V} = U + V$, where we omit the hat on the U to indicate that this is the riskless closeout CVA/DVA/FVA term, we now get a linear PDE for U:

$$\partial_t\widehat{V} + \mathcal{A}_t\widehat{V} - r\widehat{V} = s_F V^- + \lambda_b(1-R_b)V^+ \\ + \lambda_c(1-R_c)V^-$$

$$\partial_t(U+V) + \mathcal{A}_t(U+V) - r(U+V) = s_F V^- + \lambda_b(1-R_b)V^+ \\ + \lambda_c(1-R_c)V^-$$

$$\partial_t V + \mathcal{A}_t V - rV = 0,$$

so :

$$\partial_t U + \mathcal{A}_t U - rU = s_F V^- + \lambda_b(1-R_b)V^+$$
$$+ \lambda_c(1-R_c)V^-.$$

Formally applying Feyman–Kac, we get:

$$U(t,S) = -\int_t^T s_F(u)D_k(t,u)\mathbb{E}[V(u,S(u))^-|\mathcal{F}(t)]du$$

$$-(1-R_b)\lambda_b\int_t^T D_k(t,u)\mathbb{E}\left[V(u,S(u))^+|\mathcal{F}(t)\right]du$$

$$-(1-R_c)\lambda_c\int_t^T D_k(t,u)\mathbb{E}\left[V(u,S(u))^-|\mathcal{F}(t)\right]du$$

$$k := r + \lambda_b + \lambda_c.$$

We can calculate the above FVA/DVA/CVA terms by first solving the riskless, zero-funding problem for V and then using that within these integrals.

Now if $s_F = (1-R_b)\lambda_b$ then we get:

$$U(t,S) = -(1-R_b)\lambda_b\int_t^T D_k(t,u)\mathbb{E}[V(u,S(u))|\mathcal{F}(t)]du$$

$$-(1-R_c)\lambda_c\int_t^T D_k(t,u)\mathbb{E}\left[V(u,S(u))^+|\mathcal{F}(t)\right]du.$$

If λ_* were functions of time then they would be inside the integral signs. It is possible to generalise to stochastic functions of time, and then all the terms also go inside the expectation.

8.3.4 Zero funding costs

[Burgard and Kjaer (2011a)] extended their earlier analysis to show that, if b can trade in its own bonds *where these have different recovery rates*, then b can reduce its funding costs to exactly the riskless rate r. The setup is exactly as before, but we include it as another perspective on moving cash from one side of default to another. Banks do normally have bonds of different seniorities and hence with different recovery rates, but see the Critique below.

Setup in the historical measure:

$$dP_1/P_1 = r_1 dt - (1 - R_1)dJ_b$$

$$dP_2/P_2 = r_2 dt - (1 - R_2)dJ_b$$

$$dP_c/P_c = r_c dt - dJ_c$$

$$dS/S = \mu dt + \sigma dW,$$

where bonds 1,2 are issued by b, $0 \leq R_1 < R_2 \leq 1$, and, as previously mentioned, the zero recovery assumption for P_c is simply a computational convenience.

We assume that the stock S can be put into repo for simplicity. From Ito's Lemma we have, exactly as before:

$$d\widehat{V} = \partial_t \widehat{V} dt + \partial_S \widehat{V} dS + \frac{1}{2}\sigma^2 S^2 \partial_{SS}\widehat{V} dt + (\widehat{V}(\zeta_b) - \widehat{V}(\zeta_b-))dJ_b$$
$$+ (\widehat{V}(\zeta_c) - \widehat{V}(\zeta_c-))dJ_c.$$

Choosing the standard hedging portfolio:

$$\widehat{V} = \Pi = \delta S + \sum_{i=1,2} \alpha_i P_i + \alpha_c P_c + \beta.$$

Now, imposing self financing:

$$d\widehat{V} = \delta dS + \sum_{i=1,2} \alpha_i dP_i + \alpha_c dP_c + d\beta$$

$$= \delta(t)dS(t) + \sum_{i=1,2} \alpha_i(t)P_i(r_i dt - (1 - R_i)dJ_b) + \alpha_c(t)P_c(r_c dt - dJ_c)$$

$$+ d\beta(t)$$

$$= \delta(t)dS(t) - \sum_{i=1,2} \alpha_i(t)(1 - R_i)P_i dJ_b - \alpha_c(t)P_c dJ_c +$$

$$\sum_{i=1,2} \alpha_i(t)P_i r_i dt + \alpha_c(t)P_c r_c dt + d\beta(t).$$

And forcing all cash to be raised via own bonds (note that $i = 1, 2$ gives us an extra degree of freedom with respect to dJ_b):

$$\widehat{V} = \sum_{i=1,2} \alpha_i(t)P_i. \tag{8.4}$$

To remove all risk from the portfolio we have:

$$\delta = \partial_S \widehat{V}$$

$$\alpha_c P_c = -(\widehat{V}(\zeta_c) - \widehat{V}(\zeta_c-))$$

$$\sum_{i=1,2} \alpha_i (1 - R_i) P_i = -(\widehat{V}(\zeta_b) - \widehat{V}(\zeta_b-)).$$

So we have the pricing PDE:

$$\partial_t \widehat{V} + \mathcal{A}_t \widehat{V} - r\widehat{V} = \sum_{i=1,2} \alpha_i (r_i - r) P_i + \alpha_c \lambda_c P_c, \tag{8.5}$$

where:

$$\alpha_1 = \frac{R_2 \widehat{V} - M^- - R_b M^+}{R_2 - R_1}$$

$$\alpha_2 = \frac{M^- + R_b M^+ - R_1 \widehat{V}}{R_2 - R_1}.$$

Now if we assume no basis between the bonds and no bond-CDS basis:

$$r_i - r = (1 - R_i)\lambda_b.$$

Then we have a simplification of Equation 8.5 into:

$$\partial_t \widehat{V} + \mathcal{A}_t \widehat{V} - r\widehat{V} = \lambda_b (R_b M^+ + M^-) - \lambda_c (M^+ + R_c M^-).$$

Thus we see that the funding costs have now been reduced to the riskless rate r.

8.3.5 Critique

Hedging with own-bonds of different recovery rate and counterparty bonds, in the theory above, allows perfect replication [Burgard and Kjaer (2011b), Burgard and Kjaer (2011a)] and zero funding spread. This means that prices can be achieved prior to default, which is a direct consequence of hedging with contingent cash flows. In contrast, [Fries (2011)], when hedging with certain cash flows, i.e. riskless bonds, obtains very different results. The key points are:

- Can you trade your own bonds practically as dictated by the hedging requirements?
- Can you trade bonds of different recovery rates freely?
- Can you trade your counterparty's bonds as required?
- Can you put the underlying, here S, into repo? If not, the equations are much less simple (as we demonstrated above).

The model assumes that b can trade freely in its own bonds with specific, fixed, recovery rates. This is clearly a contradiction. Consider for a moment that all outstanding bonds are recovery R_1 and then at a later time *as determined by the derivative portfolio* all outstanding bonds are recovery R_2. Given that the unsecured business of a bank is not driving the recovery rate of the bank alone, this is impossible.

In general, banks cannot trade bonds as dictated by the hedging requirements. Furthermore, it is not to be expected that regulators will allow any entity to freely change its own recovery rate. Although it is well known in the corporate finance literature ([Brealey *et al.* (2010)], Chapters 17 and 18) that taking different types of project does exactly this, systematic alteration of one's own recovery rate is likely to be viewed differently by regulators. Finally, readers should recall that the unsecured derivatives book of a bank is generally not the driver of the entire business, and Basel III is putting serious pressure on this type of business.

In press releases, hedging of DVA appears to consist of CDS trades of baskets of peer banks [Moyer and Burne (2011), Brigo (2011)]. This is a highly inaccurate hedge as demonstrated every time one of these peers defaults. Imagine if Morgan Stanley were to have hedged using CDS on Lehman. The basket argument is that idiosyncratic risk is removed. However, given the practically small number of major banks, and the tiny number of investment banks, this strategy appears limited.

The modeling of this section is important to show what can be achieved in theory, but there are serious inconsistencies in theory when considered from a whole-entity, i.e. firm or balance-sheet, point of view, even without considering any practicalities. The next chapter considers the firm-level view.

8.4 Other perspectives

8.4.1 Conditions for trading

[Morini and Prampolini (2011)] ask when two banks can potentially agree on a price for an asset from a third party, i.e. when can one make a bid that is higher than the other's offer. They consider funding cost as a sum of credit spread and a liquidity spread (the bond-CDS basis). Using simple arguments they show that the credit spread on both sides cancels out because they both benefit from their credit spreads (i.e. no debt repayment). Thus only the liquidity spread is left, and provided the liquidity spread of the buyer is lower than the liquidity spread of the seller then exactly this gap is the room for negotiation.

The implication is that uncollateralized trades on third-party bonds will be made at riskless+liquidity, not riskless+funding (=credit+liquidity).

This is an inventive analysis. However, most traders are charged riskless+funding by their treasury desks so this is unlikely to affect current practice. It is equivalent to a trader saying, "I can bid high because the credit spread is covered if the bank defaults". This is also included in [Morini and Prampolini (2011)] as a counterargument.

8.4.2 P&L takeout

[Fries (2011)] presents liquidation cost and replication cost as alternatives. He also looks at P&L take out value (part of replication cost), which is the question as to how much value can be realized at time zero. The idea is that a trader claims to have a given P&L because of DVA and so his manager asks him for the cash straight away. Clearly, since DVA includes value after default (assuming we go with the simple interpretation, rather than the hedging view of [Burgard and Kjaer (2011b), Burgard and Kjaer (2011a)]) the trader will be unable to produce the cash. This leads Fries to conclude that the correct replication valuation includes only cash that can be realized with certainty (i.e. now).

The critique is obvious along two lines:

- Practically, a bank will accept a price for its own bond issuance that includes the cost that the bank will not repay the debt. This DVA must be accepted or a bank will not issue any bonds. In derivatives, a trader must also accept that her counterparty will want compensation for the probability that her bank will default, otherwise she will not trade competitively.
- Theoretically, Fries's hedging argument hedges an *uncertain* cash flow (an outgoing cash flow) with a certain cash flow (a riskless bond of the opposite sign). This is clearly wrong from a hedge point of view but is correct in Fries's point of view since he wishes to create a certain cash-flow at time zero. From a hedging point of view the correct instrument is a contingent bond, such that the hedge behaves as the outgoing cash-flow in both default and no-default states of the world. That is, paying 1 if the bank has not defaulted, but only the recovery rate otherwise. This contingent replication is examined above based on [Burgard and Kjaer (2011b), Burgard and Kjaer (2011a)].

9
CVA: Firm Level

Credit you give yourself is not worth having.
Irving Thalberg

9.1 Introduction

In the previous chapter we considered CVA, DVA, and FVA from the bottom up, i.e. by focusing on pricing a single instrument or portfolio between a bank b and a counterparty c. We now want to look top down, that is we start from the balance sheet and derive implications for the firm and for pricing individual trades (this especially affects recovery rates). The area is currently in transition as regulatory, accounting, P&L, and tax pressures have not yet reached a new equilibrium after the contrast between the long "new normal" and the wrenching surprise of the financial and sovereign crises.

In order to have a firm-level understanding we introduce an Asset–Bank–Counterparty model to demonstrate the linkages between CVA, DVA, the recovery rate, and collateral. The effect of collateral at the firm level is very different to that for individual trades. When a firm must, net, post collateral and its assets degrade, then it must post more of its assets into its collateral pool. This can become a death spiral because commercial depositors will see that the pool of unpledged assets shrinks. This both puts the bank at greater risk of default, and means that on default the recovery rate will be lower. This can lead commercial customers to flee a bank they perceive to be badly positioned. To the authors' knowledge this is a real phenomenon. Thus, collateralization is not an unmitigated benefit at the firm level. Concretely, assets (minus CVA) can be used to generate recovery rates within a firm's DVA model for liabilities.

Two special firm-level issues are included as they are highly material. Goodwill is a line item on annual reports with values in the billions for at least some large banks. We study the CVA on Good-will and find, in one case calibrated to a large bank, that it is of similar magnitude to the bank's reported DVA. This indicates that the intense work on CVA for the derivatives book can usefully be extended to the rest of the balance sheet. Goodwill is not just an accounting balancing item, although it comes into existence as exactly that. It also has a tax effect and so has concrete effects on future cash flows. Readers should consult appropriate professionals for tax and accounting advice.

The second special issue is bonds on inventory, i.e. accounted at, say, historical cost because they are held to maturity. We point out that this *intention* to hold to maturity will fail if the bank defaults. On default all assets will be priced at fair value, i.e. mark-to-market, as they are sold. Thus, for consistency with derivative accounting, we can value the change in value caused by the change in accounting treatment on default, and include this as an asset valuation adjustment. These two issues, Goodwill and accounting treatment, are only visible at the firm level and we show that they are highly significant.

9.1.1 Regulation and interpretation

Regulations change continuously, especially under pressure of unintended consequences. Here we give a brief appreciation of the current state.

CVA has been present for at least ten years as an adjustment included in the fair value of derivatives. This is reflected in accounting rules, e.g. IAS39 AG73, and capital requirements under Basel II.

A significant new aspect to Basel III is a CVA *risk* capital charge ([BCBS-189 (2011)], pp. 29ff), which is a charge for possible changes in CVA. This is because regulators saw that CVA losses during the crisis were much larger than losses from actual default. One could, of course, have derived the opposite conclusion. That is, since few actual losses occurred from default, maybe CVA was measuring credit risk inaccurately. CVA risk charge calculation in Basel III has been criticized from the beginning; see, for instance, the lengthy discussion on www.risk.net and in Risk Magazine ([Pengelly (2010)]; [Pengelly (2011)]; [Rebonato *et al.* (2010)]; [Pykhtin (2011)]; and many others). We do not deal any further with CVA risk here.

Whilst CVA is a Basel III requirement, DVA is not ([BCBS-189 (2011)], p. 37). It is specifically excluded from capital calculations because profits from DVA cannot be used as a buffer against default.

This CVA loss is calculated without taking into account any offsetting debit valuation adjustments which have been deducted from capital under paragraph 75.

Thus DVA is excluded from capital calculations even though it is a trading reality.

In contrast to capital regulations, some accounting regulations specifically mandate the inclusion of DVA, e.g. FAS 157-3 [FASB (2010)].

> This Statement clarifies that a fair value measurement for a liability reflects its nonperformance risk (the risk that the obligation will not be fulfilled). Because nonperformance risk includes the reporting entity's credit risk, the reporting entity should consider the effect of its credit risk (credit standing) on the fair value of the liability in all periods in which the liability is measured at fair value under other accounting pronouncements, including FASB Statement No. 133, Accounting for Derivative Instruments and Hedging Activities.

This reflects to some extent the fact that DVA is a trading reality. Now that banks have significant CDS spreads they cannot price competitively without including (at least some) DVA.

We give one quote from an Annual Report to demonstrate just how these regulations are interpreted.

> Under SFAS 157, the Company is required to use its own-credit spreads in determining the current value for its derivative liabilities and all other liabilities for which it has elected the fair value option. When Citi's credit spreads widen (deteriorate), Citi recognizes a gain on these liabilities because the value of the liabilities has decreased. When Citi's credit spreads narrow (improve), Citi recognizes a loss on these liabilities because the value of the liabilities has increased.

There appears to be little ambiguity in the US, although there is some debate in the rest of the world.

9.1.2 Reports

The following are a set of typical quotes from annual reports of the recent past.

- **Barclays** *credit spreads improved during 2009, leading to a loss of GBP1,820m (2008: gain GBP1,663m) from the fair value of changes in own credit.*
  2011Q3: Own credit (gain)/charge (2,971)
- **Deutsche Bank** *...taking into account any collateral held, the effect of any master netting agreements, expected loss given default and the credit risk of the Group based on historic default levels of entities of the same credit quality. The impact of this valuation adjustment was that an insignificant gain was recognized for the year ended December 31, 2008. ...an insignificant gain was recognized for the year ended December 31, 2009. ...an insignificant gain was recognized for the year ended December 31, 2010. [p. 241 Annual Report, combined CVA and DVA provisions.] (Annual Reports 2008, 2009 and 2010).*
- **Citi**

In millions of dollars	Pretax revenue	
	2009	2008
Private equity and equity investments	$ **201**	$ (377)
Alt-A mortgages [1][2]	**321**	(737)
Commercial real estate (CRE) positions [1][3]	**68**	270
CVA on Citi debt liabilities under fair value option	**(3,974)**	4,325
CVA on derivatives positions, excluding monoline insurers	**2,204**	(3,292)
Total significant revenue items	**$(1,180)**	$ 189

2011Q3: Third quarter revenues included $1.9 billion of credit valuation adjustment (CVA) reflecting the widening of Citi's credit spreads during the third quarter.

Effects are present in USD, GBP, and EUR – the DB example is a rare exception.

CVA and DVA effects are huge, both in absolute magnitude and in the size of their changes between reporting periods. This was noted by the Basel Committee for Banking Supervision, who introduced new capital requirements for CVA in Basel III (a CVA VaR) as it noted that most losses were CVA driven rather than default driven. This in turn has led to intense interest in CVA hedging, where Basel III provides explicit rules on what is accepted as a hedge and what is not. Basically, CDS and CDS indices are accepted provided that they are sufficiently specific. However, exact matching is difficult since the contingent CDS market is poorly developed.

9.2 Balance sheet

We give an introductory example here of a typical bank balance sheet. Starting at the highest level we see assets, liabilities, and equity. Equity is actually a balancing item so that assets equals liabilities plus equity.

	September 30, 2010	June 30, 2011	September 30, 2011 (1)
Total assets	$ 1,983,280	$ 1,956,626	$ 1,935,992
Total liabilities	$ 1,818,097	$ 1,777,981	$ 1,756,650
Total equity	165,183	178,645	179,342
Total liabilities and equity	$ 1,983,280	$ 1,956,626	$ 1,935,992

(1) Preliminary

- Source: *http://www.citigroup.com/citi/press/2011/111017a.htm*

Moving down one level we see a variety of items within the assets, including Goodwill as a line item. It is typical to see Goodwill, not exceptional.

Assets
Cash and due from banks (including segregated cash and other deposits)
Deposits with banks
Fed funds sold and securities borr'd or purch under agree. to resell
Brokerage receivables
Trading account assets
Investments
    Available-for-sale and non-marketable equity securities
    Held-to-maturity

Total Investments
Loans, net of unearned income
  Consumer
  Corporate

Loans, net of unearned income
Allowance for loan losses
  Total loans, net
Goodwill
Intangible assets (other than MSR's)
Mortgage servicing rights (MSR's)
Other assets
Assets of discontinued operations held for sale

Liabilities also have a wide range of possibilities.

Liabilities

Non-interest-bearing deposits in U.S. offices
Interest-bearing deposits in U.S. offices

   Total U.S. Deposits

Non-interest-bearing deposits in offices outside the U.S.
Interest-bearing deposits in offices outside the U.S.

   Total International Deposits

Total deposits

Fed funds purch and securities loaned or sold under agree. to repurch.
Brokerage payables
Trading account liabilities

Short-term borrowings
Long-term debt
Other liabilities (2)
Liabilities of discontinued operations held for sale

Finally, equity has a rather smaller set of items, but it is essentially a balancing item.

Stockholders' Equity

Preferred Stock
Common Stock
Additional paid-in capital
Retained earnings
Treasury stock
Accumulated other comprehensive income (loss)

9.3 Asset–bank–counterparty model

To deal with firm-level effects we need a model at that level, which we give here. We first give the intuition at the balance sheet level, then discuss effects of own-default on assets and liabilities, then describe the model.

9.3.1 Intuition

The key point is that the recovery rate post-default is derived exactly from the assets available. Hence, the CVA on the assets has a direct effect on the DVA.

- Before Bank default:

$$\boxed{\text{Assets} = \text{Liabilities} + \text{Equity}}$$

  Really:

$$\boxed{\text{Assets} > \text{Liabilities}}$$

- After Bank default:

$$\boxed{\text{Assets } < \text{ Liabilities}}$$

Usually written as:

$$\boxed{\text{Assets } = \text{ Recovery } \times \text{ Liabilities}}$$

Equity is a balancing item reflecting shareholders' claims on the net assets of the company. It is theoretically possible for Assets to exceed Liabilities post-default. We omit this case as not materially likely, at least in the financial industry.

9.3.2 Effect of own-default on assets and liabilities

9.3.2.1 Effect on assets

Direct Genuine change in value, e.g. Goodwill written down on own-default, often to zero.

Revealed Revealed value, e.g. assets move from original cost value (banking book) to mark-to-market (aka fair value, trading book).

Fire-Sale Revealed value, e.g. assets move from mark-to-model to sale price.

None No change: for example, assets already marked-to-market, and which are not sensitive to the own-default event, e.g. collateralized derivatives (with no gap risk).

Contagion For example, supplier owns stock in customer, on default creates problems for customer.

Derived Derived change in value, e.g. derivative written to provide claim on defaulting entity in the event of default (e.g. ratings triggers that act just prior to default).

Here we focus on the first two: Direct and Revealed asset value changes. Note that economically Revealed does nothing. We include Revealed effect as accounting treatment valuation adjustments to reflect post-own-default valuation changes pre-default (whilst holding the asset at original cost up to default).

9.3.2.2 Effect on liabilities

Claims Most claims do not change on default.

Covered bonds Have bankruptcy-remote pool of (over-collateralized) assets that goes into administration, so no change in payment on claims (so far, since 1769), but assets are removed from the pool available to pay creditors. If a bank has too high a proportion of funding from this source then the bank may find it difficult to issue unsecured bonds (i.e. senior unsecured liabilities).

Payments to unsecured creditors are made from asset sales in seniority order (possibly modified by many legalities, etc.). Wind-down may take years, but debt auctions take place soon after the default event to give a precise tradable recovery rate.

Buying back one's own liabilities seems an obvious strategy if they have fallen in value, i.e. as default approaches. However, if liabilities (issued bonds) are trading at a low price, then there is some impediment for the issuer to sell assets and buy back the liabilities locking in a profit. It may be that the bank has no free assets or that they are not sufficiently liquid to sell at short notice, etc.

9.3.3 ABC model

We first introduce the high-level balance sheet, summarized in Table 9.1, and then create a useful abstraction for demonstrations. We will make four demonstrations: base case; including collateral; including Goodwill; and finally including assets on inventory.

Liabilities are with a single Counterparty, and both Assets are also from a single source (which is not the Counterparty). The Issued Bond (IB) is a bond issued by the Bank to the Counterparty.

Unpledged Assets are those not posted as collateral. We assume that the Collateralized Liabilities do not change with Bank or Asset CDS spread changes. Assets (whether or not used for collateral) will change value as their CDS spread changes.

Schematically we have:

$$V = \mathrm{Cap} + G + U \times \mathrm{RB}_{m2m} + \mathrm{RB}_{oc} - \mathrm{MM} - \mathrm{IB}.$$

U is the proportion of the risky assets that are unpledged, i.e. not used for collateral. Pledged assets are modeled through this dependency. Thus U is derived from the ratio of risky assets not pledged to those pledged, at the starting point for comparisons.

Table 9.1 Summary of balance sheet item types

Bank		
Unpledged Assets	Uncollateralized Liabilities	Collateralized
Capital (liquid securities, cash)	Money Market instrument (MM)	Assets
Goodwill	Shareholder's Equity	Liabilities
Asset1 (Risky Bond, mark-to-market = RB_{m2m})	Issued Bond (IB)	
Asset2 (Risky Bond, original cost = RB_{oc})	Depositors	

We have included the Depositors in the Issued Bond, i.e. we are not modeling runs on the bank. Cash (Capital) is accumulated or reduced at each Reporting Date.

Conventionally $V = 0$ (identically) by using a balancing item but, as mentioned, we will omit it to allow changes in V to calculate P&L effects. In general, under $\mathbf{Q}$ (the risk-neutral measure) and using the standard filtration change [Brigo and Mercurio (2006)], $0 \le s < t \le \tilde{T}$ where $\tilde{T}$ is the shortest maturity:

$$V(t) = \mathbb{I}_{\{\zeta_A,\zeta_B,\zeta_C > t\}}\widetilde{\mathbb{E}}[\mathrm{Cap}(t) + G(t) + U(t) \times \mathrm{RB_{m2m}}(t) + \mathrm{RB_{oc}}^{\mathrm{ATA}}(t)$$
$$- \mathrm{MM(t)} - \mathrm{IB(t)} \mid \mathcal{F}(t)] \qquad (9.1)$$
$$P\&L(s,t) = V(t) - V(s).$$

Below, we use the subscript 0 to denote the risk-free value:

- $\zeta_A, \zeta_B, \zeta_C$ are the default times of the Asset, Bank, and Counterparty.
- $\mathrm{Cap}(t)$ is simply observable at t.
- $G(t) = G_0(t) - \mathrm{CVA}(G_0(t))$; no DVA since Goodwill is always positive.
- $\mathrm{RB_{m2m}}(t) = \mathrm{RB_{m2m0}}(t) - \mathrm{CVA}(\mathrm{RB_{m2m0}}(t))$, since this asset is a ZCB (Zero Coupon Bond).
- $U(t)$ is the proportion of $\mathrm{RB_{m2m}}$ not pledged as collateral.
- $\mathrm{RB_{oc}}^{\mathrm{ATA}}(t)$ is the Accounting Treatment Adjusted banking book asset.
- $\mathrm{MM(t)} = \mathrm{MM_0}(t) - \mathrm{DVA}(\mathrm{MM_0}(t))$, only a liability.
- $\mathrm{IB}(t) = \mathrm{IB_0}(t) - \mathrm{DVA}(\mathrm{IB_0}(t))$, only a liability.
- P&L(s,t) is the profit (or loss) at time t relative to time s.

CVA terms on $\mathrm{RB_{m2m}}$ are exogenous; other CVA and DVA terms will be considered below in the specific examples.

9.3.4 Base case: all assets MtM, no collateral, no goodwill

This is a very simple model that can be extended, but the objective here is to show the links between the Asset, Bank, and Counterparty (that holds the Issued Bond).

The asset and liability zero coupon bond NPVs (Net Present Values) for unit notional in Equation 9.1 within the $\widetilde{\mathbb{E}}[.|\mathcal{F}(t)]$ are:

$$\mathrm{RB_{m2m}}(t) = D(t, T_A)\mathbb{I}_{\{\zeta_A > T_A\}} + \mathrm{Rec}_A D(t, \zeta_A)\mathbb{I}_{\{\zeta_A < T_A\}}$$
$$\mathrm{IB}(t) = D(t, T_{\mathrm{IB}})\mathbb{I}_{\{\zeta_B > T_B\}} + \mathrm{Rec}_B(\zeta_B)D(t, \zeta_B)\mathbb{I}_{\{\zeta_B < T_{\mathrm{IB}}\}},$$

assuming no correlation between interest rates and hazard rates.

Indicator functions without curly brackets {.} indicate whether or not the clause is fulfilled, whereas indicators with curly brackets pick out the exact event (time).

$D(u, v)$ is the discount factor between u and v.

Rec_A is exogenous but Rec_B is endogenous and, assuming that it is the senior claim, given by:

$$\text{Rec}_B(\zeta_B) = \min\left(\frac{\text{Cap} + n_{\text{RB}_{\text{m2m}}} U(\zeta_B)\text{RB}_{\text{m2m}}(\zeta_B)}{n_{\text{IB}}}, 1\right)$$

$$\text{RB}_{\text{m2m}}(\zeta_B) = \text{Rec}_A \mathbb{I}_{\{\zeta_A \leq \zeta_B \wedge\ T_B\}} + \text{RB}_{\text{m2m}}(\zeta_B-)\mathbb{I}_{\{\zeta_A > \zeta_B\}},$$

where $n_{\text{RB}_{\text{m2m}}}$, n_{IB} are the notionals of the risky bond and issued bond. $\text{RB}_{\text{m2m}}(\zeta_B-)$ is the value of the risky bond an instant before ζ_B.

We assume that default (or effective default) of the asset can cause default of the Bank, e.g. large exposure to Euro sovereign that defaults or withdraws from the Euro zone and then sets the FX rate to new currency by legislation.

We use the reduced-form approach to price risky assets and liabilities. Using a standard approximation – [Brigo and Mercurio (2006)] (see chapter 4, Equation 4.5) – we calculate an equivalent constant hazard rate for the Bank and the Asset, where we use the assumption that default of the Asset can lead to default of the Bank via contagion:

$$\lambda_B = g\lambda_A + \lambda_b = \frac{\text{CDS}_B}{1 - \text{Rec}_B}, \qquad \lambda_A = \frac{\text{CDS}_A}{1 - \text{Rec}_A}$$

g is the contagion parameter, i.e. the probability that default of A will cause B to default.

$\text{CDS}_A, \text{CDS}_B$ can be related, but since λ_b is independently specified do not need to be.

We have approximated $\text{Rec}_B \approx \text{Rec}_B(t)$, which underestimates the Bank recovery rate in the model but mimics a constant recovery rate on the Asset. This avoids maturity effects from the Asset. We will also approximate $U(\zeta_B) \approx U$ for the same reason.

Here $U = 1$ because there is no collateral, so 100% of assets are unpledged (not posted as collateral). Below, in the collateral section, we describe how to calculate U.

We see that the IB value depends on RB_{m2m} in three ways:

(1) Relation between CDS spreads of Asset and Bank.
(2) Recovery rate of the Bank.
(3) Hazard rate of the Bank depending on recovery rate of Bank and CDS spread of Bank.

Continuing, we observe:

$$\lambda_B = g\lambda_A + \lambda_b = \frac{\text{CDS}_B}{1 - \frac{\text{Cap} + n_{\text{RB}_{\text{m2m}}} U\widetilde{\mathbb{E}}[\text{RB}_{\text{m2m}}(\zeta_B)]}{n_{\text{IB}}}} \tag{9.2}$$

$$= \frac{\text{CDS}_B n_{\text{IB}}}{n_{\text{IB}} - (\text{Cap} + n_{\text{RB}_{\text{m2m}}} U\widetilde{\mathbb{E}}[\text{RB}_{\text{m2m}}(\zeta_B)])},$$

where the expectations are conditional on $\mathcal{F}(t)$.

We have picked a dependence structure for A and B via the contagion g, see Figure 9.1,

- Zone I: b defaults first, and within T, so RB_{m2m}
- Zone II: b defaults within T, but after A: Rec_A
- Zone III: b does not default within T, A does and **may** cause B to default: Rec_A
- Elsewhere: no events within T so no default or recovery on B.

From the zones we see:

$$\widetilde{\mathbb{E}}[\text{RB}_{\text{m2m}}(\zeta_B)|B] = \frac{P[z_I]\text{RB}_{\text{m2m}}{}^{\zeta_{B^-}} + P[z_{II}]\text{Rec}_A + g \times P[z_{III}]\text{Rec}_A}{P[z_I] + P[z_{II}] + g \times P[z_{III}]},$$

where $\text{RB}_{\text{m2m}}{}^{\zeta_{B^-}}$ is the value of the risky bond an instant prior to default.

Now, given the thinning properties of Poisson processes, we have (taking $t = 0$):

$$P[z_I] = \frac{\lambda_b}{\lambda_A + \lambda_b}\left(1 - e^{-(\lambda_A + \lambda_b)T}\right)$$

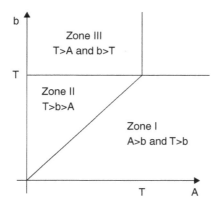

Figure 9.1 Default time combinations for A and B

$$P[z_{II}] = \left(1 - e^{-\lambda_b T}\right) - \frac{\lambda_b}{\lambda_A + \lambda_b}\left(1 - e^{-(\lambda_A + \lambda_b)T}\right)$$

$$P[z_{III}] = e^{-\lambda_b T} - e^{-(\lambda_A + \lambda_b)T},$$

where we have used the approximation(s):

$$\widetilde{\mathbb{E}}[\mathrm{RB_{m2m}}(\zeta_B-)\mathbb{I}_{\{\zeta_A > \zeta_B\}}\,|\,\mathcal{F}(t)] \approx P[\zeta_A > \zeta_B]\mathrm{RB_{m2m}}^{\zeta_B-}$$

$$\mathrm{RB_{m2m}}^{\zeta_B-} = \mathrm{RB_{m2m}}(t).$$

Hence we can calculate Rec_B, and so P&L changes. We do this starting with the setup in Table 9.2. The line plots in Figures 9.2 and 9.3 show

Table 9.2 Setup for base case of ABC model. This has $\mathrm{Cap}/(\mathrm{Cap} + \mathrm{RB_{m2m}}(0)) \approx 8\%$

Base Case: only risk asset at MtM + capital	
r	2%
T	5 years
Cap	0.7
$n_{\mathrm{RB_{m2m}}}$	9
$n_{\mathrm{RB_{oc}}}$	0
n_G	0
n_{IB}	9
CDS $\mathrm{RB_{m2m}}$	200 bps
recovery rate $\mathrm{RB_{m2m}}$	40%
CDS_b	100 bps
contagion	0.5, 0, 1

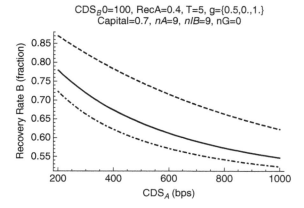

Figure 9.2 Base case = only MtM risky assets, no Collateral, no Goodwill. *nA* is notional of Asset, *nIB* is notional of Issued Bond, RecA is recovery rate of risky Asset. Curves are for constant idiosyncratic Bank hazard rate, i.e. λ_b. Bank recovery rate changes for Asset CDS changes.

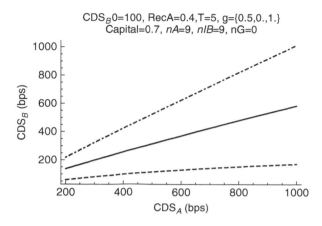

CDS$_B$0=100, RecA=0.4,T=5, g={0.5,0.,1.}
Capital=0.7, nA=9, nIB=9, nG=0

Figure 9.3 Base case = only MtM risky assets, no Collateral, no Goodwill. *nA* is notional of Asset, *nIB* is notional of Issued Bond, RecA is recovery rate of risky Asset. Curves are for constant idiosyncratic Bank hazard rate, i.e. λ_b. Bank CDS changes for changes in Asset CDS changes.

the effects of increasingly bad assets for constant idiosyncratic bank hazard rates. A more comprehensive picture for P&L is shown in Figures 9.4 and 9.5 considering changes in both the bank's CDS spread and asset CDS spreads. Of course, many combinations of bank+asset CDS spreads are simply infeasible and these areas are shaded out.

In Figure 9.2 we see recovery rates in the 55% to 80% range that are somewhat high relative to typical defaults of investment banks. However, they may be more reasonable for large, mainly retail banks. The recovery rates are high simply because the assets are relatively good, there is no loss from Goodwill, no revealed loss from held-to-maturity assets, and no mark-to-model surprises. All of these extras typically happen in real cases for investment banks, where Lehman is the classical recent example.

Figure 9.3 shows changes in bank CDS spread for changing asset CDS spread for different levels of contagion. Obviously, higher contagion makes the Bank riskier, but even with moderate contagion bank CDS spread still increases significantly.

Figures 9.4 and 9.5 compare P&L effects for different levels of contagion: some versus none. There is very little effect once both the bank and asset CDSs have been given.

Figure 9.4 shows that roughly half the CDS combinations are feasible, and of that area perhaps a quarter leads to overall P&L gains as both CDS spreads increase. Clearly the bank's CDS spread has to

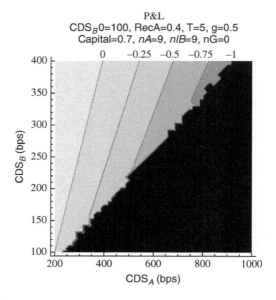

Figure 9.4 Bank P&L. Base case = only MtM risky assets, no Collateral, no Goodwill. Note that P&L only increases in a triangular region in the top left where Bank CDS (cdsB) increases relatively more than Asset CDS (cdsA). Bottom right is unfeasible region.

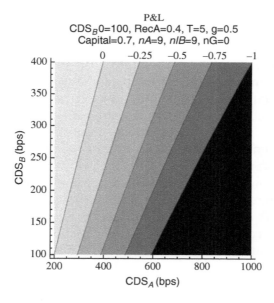

Figure 9.5 Bank P&L. Base case = only MtM risky assets, no Collateral, no Goodwill. Relative changes in P&L are very similar to base case – essentially because we are conditioning on CDS values.

increase faster than its asset's CDS spread for this to occur. Whilst this is technically feasible, intuitively it means that the bank is seen as much more risky and that this is not because of its assets. Possibly a challenge to the business model *without damaging the assets* could lead to this situation. However, recent history consists mostly of examples where banks are under pressure because their assets are deemed weak. Where there has been business model pressure, e.g. Northern Rock's emphasis on capital market funding, this dried up because of doubts about the assets (residential mortgages).

9.3.5 Collateral

A final value of 8.625% was set on bonds of Lehman Brothers today, in an auction intended to cash-settle credit default swap (CDS) trades linked to the toppled dealer.
Risk Magazine, 10 October 2008
In the case of Lehman Brothers, a significant amount of its assets was pledged as collateral and therefore liquidated at distressed prices by counterparties at the time of default. As a result, many of these counterparties joined the pool of unsecured creditors with their balance of unpaid claims.
Financial Stability Review – March 2010, Reserve Bank of Australia

We cover the first of the two mechanisms described in the Financial Stability Review quote: the quantity of assets drawn into collateral assets. We do not deal with their fire-sale pricing or subsequent claims. We shall see that assets drawn into collateral pools are a significant mechanism of actualizing losses and increasing risk of default.

Collateralization removes from the picture precisely those assets that are pledged as collateral. In the same way it removes the liabilities for which those assets are pledged. The DVA paradox arises from the liabilities that are not collateralized (since otherwise the liabilities would not pay only recovery on default). However, changes in asset value pledged as collateral provide a default mechanism for the bank, and reduced recovery. As pledged assets lose value, more assets must be pledged. Legally, collateralized positions must usually be valued at typical-major-market-player level, as per the CSA (Collateral Support Agreement) in place between the two institutions (however, see the discussion on Closeout in the previous chapter). A bank may not use its own lack of creditworthiness (whilst it is still a going concern) in pricing for collateral purposes.

Suppose initially the NPV of unpledged assets is u and the NPV of pledged assets is p. Now if they have a common risk factor which changes so that both assets lose the same fraction f of their value, then the ratio u of unpledged assets available afterwards is:

$$U(f) = \frac{u(1-f) - pf}{u(1-f)}.$$

Thus, as a Bank's assets deteriorate, more must be pledged as collateral, so the recovery on uncollateralized liabilities decreases. This provides a natural negative correlation between institutional CDS spread and recovery rate on default, as has been noted empirically [Cantor *et al.* (2002)].

Figure 9.6 shows the effect of requiring collateral on assets available for paying the recovery rate (if the bank defaults). As the average CDS spread of the assets moves from 200bps to 650bps the available assets drop from 100% to 80%. This calculation assumes that this is the only market change, i.e. that the net collateral position does not change.

The effect of degraded assets on the recovery rate, assuming no other market changes, is shown in Figure 9.7. Here we see clearly the leveraging effect as compared to no assets required for collateral. In the no-collateral case the recovery rate stays relatively high at over 55% even when the average asset CDS reaches 1000bps (10%). In contrast, when there is a significant collateral requirement, here 1:1, then the

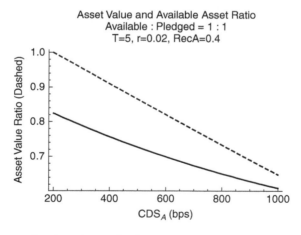

Figure 9.6 Asset value (continuous line) versus asset CDS spread. Also ratio of assets remaining for uncollateralized trades. Dashed line gives the available asset ratio, i.e. the assets remaining after some assets have been used to replenish the assets already used for collateral.

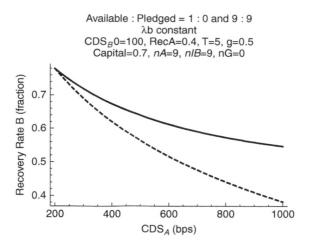

Figure 9.7 Including Collateral, no Goodwill. *nA* is notional of Asset, *nIB* is notional of Issued Bond, RecA is recovery rate of risky Asset. Curves are for constant idiosyncratic Bank hazard rate, i.e. λ_b. Bank recovery rate changes for Asset CDS changes.

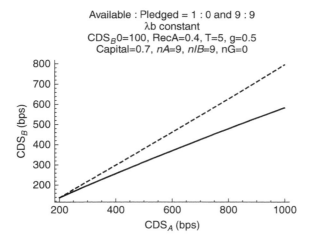

Figure 9.8 Including Collateral, no Goodwill. *nA* is notional of Asset, *nIB* is notional of Issued Bond, RecA is recovery rate of risky Asset. Curves are for constant idiosyncratic Bank hazard rate, i.e. λ_b. Bank CDS changes for changes in Asset CDS changes.

recovery rate drops below 40%. Thus we have a mechanism to generate Lehman-like recovery rates for senior unsecured claims.

Figure 9.8 shows the effect of asset degradation on bank CDS spread for constant idiosyncratic risk, for no collateral (continuous line) and 1:1 collateral (dashed line). The CDS increase is almost linear with a

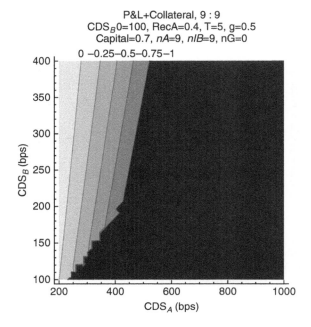

Figure 9.9 Bank P&L. Including Collateral, no Goodwill. Note that P&L increase region is very small, and loss regions are compressed before infeasibility.

factor of roughly 30%. Thus, collateral significantly accelerates a bank's decline.

The P&L picture in Figure 9.9 has major changes with respect to the previous no-collateral case in Figure 9.4. First, we observe that the feasible region is decreased. Simply put, as the assets decrease the bank's CDS spread must increase; there is no room for positive outcomes. Although it is still possible for overall P&L gains (upper left triangle to left of the "0" line) this is much reduced. Overall, the most likely consequence of assets going bad is an overall P&L loss.

9.3.6 Goodwill

We will briefly introduce Goodwill and then see how it affects the ABC model. Goodwill is a controversial and subjective topic in the corporate finance world [Ramanna and Watts (2010)]. However, in as much as it is a line item on a balance sheet, it is a concrete asset. This is not a small asset; values of tens of billions of USD can be found on some banks' balance sheets. Goodwill is listed on financial reports and must be kept up to date. Goodwill typically comes into existence when a company is bought for more than its book value so a balancing term is added to the accounts. This is Goodwill. When a firm defaults, Goodwill is usually reduced to zero – this can also happen when customers lose confidence, or when the firm's brand value is lost.

How real is Goodwill? First, it is a line item on corporate reports and so affects reported accounting P&L. Secondly it has a tax existence, and typically the accounting and tax treatment can differ. The tax treatment can affect future cash flows because Goodwill is typically written down, according to tax law, in a straight line amortization (although it can be linked, in some jurisdictions, to accounting treatment). We remind readers that the authors are not offering accounting or tax advice and that they should consult the relevant experts. The tax writedown on Goodwill generates tax credits that may be used against tax liabilities. Also, deferred tax assets and liabilities are allowed under Basel III against capital (paragraph 69). However, Goodwill itself is not allowable for capital under Basel III (paragraph 67). In short, Goodwill has a variety of aspects that require highly expert judgement with respect to capital, tax, and accounting. We go no further into detail, but illustrate the potential impact of CVA on Goodwill and hence its accounting treatment.

We use a simplified formula for Goodwill, assuming constant interest and hazard rates for analytic tractability. We assume Goodwill amortizes linearly up to maturity T_G; this is the AMORTIZING model from [Kenyon (2010a)].

$$
\begin{aligned}
G(t) &= \mathbb{I}_{\{\zeta_B > t\}} \left(1 - \int_0^{T_G} \frac{T_G - s}{T_G} \lambda_B e^{-s(r + \lambda_B)} ds \right) \\
&= \mathbb{I}_{\{\zeta_B > t\}} \left(1 - \frac{e^{-T_G(r + \lambda_B)} \lambda_B (1 + e^{T_G(r + \lambda_B)}(T_G(r + \lambda_B) - 1))}{T_G(r + \lambda_B)^2} \right).
\end{aligned}
$$

Here we extend the analysis of [Kenyon (2010a)] by putting Goodwill into the context of the rest of the balance sheet, i.e. getting the hazard rate from the balance sheet.

[Kenyon (2010a)] showed that for one case, calibrated to actual balance sheet data and observed CDS spreads, calculated Goodwill effects were roughly the same magnitude as reported DVA effects, but with the opposite sign.

If Goodwill is an extra item then:

- Since Goodwill has zero recovery it has no effect on recovery rates.
- Since Goodwill has zero recovery it has no effect on CDS spreads.

Table 9.3 Base + Collateral + Goodwill setup; Goodwill is modeled as a substitute for some of the risky assets. We include collateral with 1:1 available:pledged asset ratio.

Base+Goodwill Case	
r	2%
T	5 years
Cap	0.7
$n_{RB_{m2m}}$	9
$n_{RB_{oc}}$	0
n_G	1
T_G	20
n_{IB}	9

- It does, however, have an effect on P&L – it is always a loss with increasing Bank hazard rate.

If we were to substitute some Goodwill for assets then, of course, we would see effects – but essentially only from the different asset balance.

We use the setup in Table 9.3. The amortization on Goodwill can be very long, hence we pick 20 years. [Kenyon (2010a)] showed that results could be insensitive to the length of amortization beyond five years.

Figure 9.10 shows the P&L effects of including Goodwill on the balance sheet. It always decreases the P&L as the bank CDS spread increases. Now there is no region where the bank's P&L increases overall as its CDS spread increases. Clearly, other results would be obtained with different parameter settings. This is illustrative in comparison to the other cases considered.

With respect to Goodwill it could be argued that if they are regularly valued then they already include any effects of CDS spread changes (at least for Goodwill). In as much as an Accounting Impairment to Goodwill is recognized, this will be the case. However, Accounting Impairments require a particular standard of evidence [Chen *et al.* (2008)] whereas CDS curves are simply observed day-to-day.

9.3.7 Assets on inventory

We touch on another aspect of self-default here, the consequences for the accounting treatment of the value of bonds on inventory, i.e. *not*

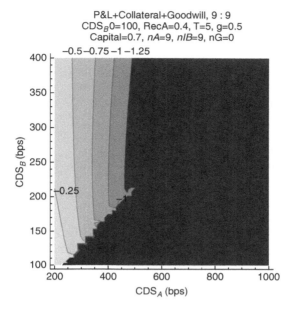

Figure 9.10 Bank P&L. Including Collateral and Goodwill. Now there is no region where P&L increases. Note that the feasible region is larger since the bank can lose more without becoming significantly insolvent, since we added an asset (Goodwill).

held at mark-to-market. This could be called an accounting treatment valuation adjustment.

The argument for holding assets at original cost is that the bank will hold them to maturity. That is, it is a comment on the bank's intentions. Thus, given that banks can default, it is arguably reasonable to price in the effect of the bank defaulting on bank P&L given that this is now normal practice for liabilities in DVA. This is what we carry out next.

We need to price in the value of the risky asset if the bank defaults as it is then priced at mark-to-market. We use the same approach as for the risky asset that is mark-to-market, i.e. we assume that default of the Asset can cause default of the Bank (not implausible with sovereign assets) but that default of the Asset is independent of default of the Bank.

• For a unit notional zero coupon bond we get:

$$
\begin{aligned}
\mathrm{RB}_{\mathrm{oc}}(t) = \mathbb{I}_{\{\zeta_A \wedge \zeta_B > t\}} \widetilde{\mathbb{E}} \big[& \mathbb{I}_{\{\zeta_B > T\}} c + \\
& \mathbb{I}_{\{\zeta_B < T \cap \zeta_A > \zeta_B\}} \mathrm{ZCB}(\zeta_B) + \mathbb{I}_{\{\zeta_A \le \zeta_B < T\}} \mathrm{Rec}_{\mathrm{oc}}(\zeta_A) \big],
\end{aligned}
\tag{9.3}
$$

where ZCB is a risky zero coupon bond.
- Equation 9.3 allows the Asset to be priced at original cost c unless the Bank defaults.
- Given default of the Bank the Asset is either priced as a risky asset, or – if the Asset caused the bank default – at its recovery rate.
- We thus have the same zones as before for outcomes.

Given that B defaults we have the same value as before:

$$\widetilde{\mathbb{E}}[RB_{m2m}(\zeta_B)|B] = \frac{P[z_I]RB_{m2m}{}^{\zeta_{B^-}} + P[z_{II}]Rec_A + g \times P[z_{III}]Rec_A}{P[z_I] + P[z_{II}] + g \times P[z_{III}]}.$$

So now we see:

$$RB_{oc}(t) = \mathbb{I}_{\{\zeta_A \wedge \zeta_B > t\}}\widetilde{\mathbb{E}}\left[\mathbb{I}_{\{\zeta_B > T\}}c + \mathbb{I}_{\{\zeta_B \leq T\}}\widetilde{\mathbb{E}}[RB_{m2m}(\zeta_B)|B] | \mathcal{F}(t)\right]$$

$$RB_{m2m}(t) = \mathbb{I}_{\{\zeta_A \wedge \zeta_B > t\}}\widetilde{\mathbb{E}}\left[\mathbb{I}_{\{\zeta_A \wedge \zeta_B > T\}}df(t,T) + \mathbb{I}_{\{\zeta_A \leq T < \zeta_B\}}Rec_A\right.$$
$$\left. + \mathbb{I}_{\{\zeta_B \leq T\}}\widetilde{\mathbb{E}}[RB_{m2m}(\zeta_B)|B] | \mathcal{F}(t)\right].$$

That is, the difference between Mark-to-Market and Hold-to-Maturity is essentially (assuming that c is marked to market but not credit risk):

$$\widetilde{\mathbb{E}}\left[\mathbb{I}_{\{\zeta_B > T\}}df(t,T) - \left(\mathbb{I}_{\{\zeta_A \wedge \zeta_B > T\}}df(t,T) + \mathbb{I}_{\{\zeta_A \leq T < \zeta_B\}}Rec_A\right)\right].$$

Mark-to-Market takes into account that the asset may default and not lead to bank default, whereas Hold-to-Maturity assumes that the Asset is not affected by (roughly speaking) market or credit risk.

In the current setup we can write:

$$diff \propto \widetilde{\mathbb{E}}\left[\mathbb{I}_{\{\zeta_B > T\}} - \mathbb{I}_{\{\zeta_A \wedge \zeta_B > T\}}\right]df(r, T-t) - \widetilde{\mathbb{E}}[\mathbb{I}_{\{\zeta_A \leq T < \zeta_B\}}Rec_A]$$

$$= (CDF[\lambda_b + g\lambda_A, T-t] - CDF[\lambda_b + \lambda_A, T-t])df(r, T-t)$$

$$- \widetilde{\mathbb{E}}[\mathbb{I}_{\{\zeta_A \leq T < \zeta_B\}}Rec_A]$$

$$= e^{-(r+\lambda_b+g\lambda_A)(T-t)} - e^{-(r+\lambda_b+\lambda_A)(T-t)}$$

$$- (e^{-\lambda_b T}(1 - e^{-(1-g)\lambda_A T})).$$

Thus, Hold-to-Maturity assets pre-Bank-default depend critically on their contagion. More contagious assets become similar to Mark-to-Market. In all cases the CVA effect post-Bank-default is as important as with MtM assets, as is shown in Figure 9.11.

9.3.8 Critique

The models introduced here are simplistic. They show overall themes and effects, but for true application require detailed study either of the firm's own balance sheet or its competitors (or trading partners).

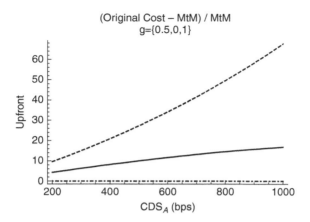

Figure 9.11 Size of accounting treatment valuation adjustment for increasing asset CDS spread for constant idiosyncratic bank risk.

9.4 Final comment

We remind our readers that the authors are neither accounting nor tax experts. However, we expect the consequences of the financial and sovereign crises to continue to traverse the different domains. Having started at the core, i.e. trading and capital, we expect further revisions to capital, accounting and tax practice to reflect new appreciations of reporting and economic realities.

10
Basel III

To every action, there is always opposed an equal reaction.
Isaac Newton's Third Law of Motion

10.1 Introduction

Prior to Basel III, virtually no book on pricing for quants included anything about capital. Of course a bank had capital somewhere, but it
was of little direct significance. This was partly due to a long period
up to 2008 when credit spreads were generally low. Now the banking
industry is changing rapidly to take account of the new reality introduced by the 69 pages of [BCBS-189 (2011)]. This is no minor concern
as some studies have found that banks worldwide may need to raise
€345B in capital versus 2010 levels or cut risk-weighted assets by 17%
(*Financial Times, December 15 2011*).

Cutting risk-weighted assets on this scale means exits from businesses, i.e. some trading desks are closed, others refocused. The biggest
growth areas for quant employment over the period 2010–2012 has
been in counterparty risk and on CVA desks. Five years ago few banks
had dedicated CVA desks, today it would be hard to find any significant
bank without one.

In some ways the growth of CVA desks looks a lot like the growth in
structured credit.

- When did you last come across a rapidly expanding financial area?
- With high take-up of quants on fresh desks?
- Could you really realize all the profits your traders were booking?
- Did you push any practical replication, or complete-market prob-
  lems away for later, provided you could see some price today?

Basel III came into force in January 2013. In the next couple of years the market, and the quants, will reassess what is really required (profitable) and what is not. This is another golden era for quants, with a complexity level equivalent to or even higher than the one in the previous structured credit boom. How will it turn out for banks?

Regulators have the unenviable task of policing the added complexity from Basel III. In theory, Basel III makes banks safer. To ask the obvious, what happens when *all* banks deleverage at the same time? Now where will the activities and assets made more costly by Basel III go? Some activities will just stop, others will move or change. As for the assets, they may go to hedge funds, insurance companies, or asset managers. There may be an initial mismatch between the asset complexity and the skills of the buyers. So some quants will move, too.

This book is about pricing, but capital considerations drive which trades are going to be attractive. Essentially, we are considering profitability here rather than the idealized world of no-arbitrage where there are no profits. No-arbitrage is, of course, still valid, but we must widen our horizon. The same type of considerations previously held true for highly structured products. No-arbitrage might produce a number but the trader's price to a client would include a profit margin. In this sense nothing has changed in trading since markets began back in the fertile crescent.

From a regulator's point of view banks are differentiated by the extent to which they are permitted, by the regulator, to use their own models for risk and capital calculations. Being permitted to use your own models is called having IMM Approval. IMM stands for Internal Model Method. This is not a blanket approval for everything, but is divided into market risk (VaR) and credit risk (exposure). Within each category there are degrees of approval and these can be given by asset class. It is quite possible to have IMM Approval for uncollateralized interest rate trades without having such approval for FX trades. Specific details of the approvals and the process to obtain approval are down to national regulators. In this area the UK regulator (the FSA) is, post-crisis, one of the leaders. The Prudential part of the FSA is being merged into the Bank of England to continue its work from there.

10.2 Summary of basel III

In this section we give a summary of Basel III sourced from [BCBS-189 (2011)] itself. There are only a few sections that we will go into in detail, but it is useful to have the context before proceeding. This is not the only change going on; there are accounting and tax changes in progress as well, e.g. IFRS9, convergence between UK and international regulations, etc., but we will focus here on Basel III.

A. **Stronger global capital framework** Five sections covering capital and risk. Regulators care about whether banks have sufficient capital to buffer them against default. Hence, having more and better capital is good. This is exactly why DVA is not counted towards capital – it does not provide a buffer against default, see Paragraph 75 of [BCBS-189 (2011)] and [BCBS-214 (2011)].

1. **Improved capital base** Most losses in the crisis came out of retained earnings, which is part of the bank's equity base. Hence, Tier 1 capital must be almost all retained earnings and common shares. Increased capital requirements of different qualities have started a series of experiments in the market to create Basel III-compliant capital. Two of the first movers have been Credit Suisse with a CoCo (contingent capital) issuance in 2011, and UBS with a different flavor in 2012. These are, to some extent, leaders because they have additional requirements from their local regulator (FINMA) as they are bigger than the country where they are based.

2. **Enhanced risk coverage** This is the area of most interest for quants, both from pricing and risk aspects. The level of interest can also be gauged by the publication of an FAQ on the topic from Basel III [BCBS-209 (2011)].

   Stressed parameters for counterparty risk This covers VaR and exposure, i.e. both collateralized and uncollateralized trades. See also [BCBS-185 (2010)] and below for backtesting.

   CVA risk Essentially VaR on CVA, but with defined formulae to use – see below. It is not just CVA that has to be included in the cost of a position but also the variability (mark-to-market losses) of that CVA.

   Collateral management and initial margining Large and illiquid (think highly structured) positions must use longer margining periods (i.e. higher capital requirements).

   Central counterparties Significant encouragement to use them, i.e. low risk weightings.

   Wrong-way risk That is, cases where exposure increases with deteriorating counterparty status. Better backtesting of exposure is also included, also described in [BCBS-185 (2010)].

3. **Leverage ratio** One of the notable things of the pre-crisis time was that leverage meant profit. The regulators do not want to see the aftermath of that again. It is designed to do two things: constrain leverage, and safeguard against model risk by taking the models out of the equation.

4. **Counter-cyclical buffers** Just what it says.

5. **Systemic risk and interconnectedness** Systemically important banks have to hold more capital: you know who you are.

B. **Liquidity standard** The first phase of the financial and sovereign crises was a liquidity crunch. The aim is to reduce the risk and scale of future liquidity shocks using two tools which will imply that banks need less external funding. This means that certain business models will no longer be practical (e.g. funding mostly from capital markets).

(1) Liquidity coverage ratio (LCR), thirty-day horizon for a significant, but not worst-case, stress.

(2) Net stable funding ratio (NSFR), with a horizon of one year.

There are a number of further monitoring tools that supervisors are encouraged to use: maturity mismatches; funding concentrations; unencumbered assets; LCR per currency; and market-related feedback, e.g. CDS spreads.

C. **Transition** Things get phased in.
- Counterparty credit risk: January 2013.
- LCR: January 2015.
- NSFR: January 2018.

From a quant point of view there are two interesting areas: first, devising new types of capital like CoCos; and secondly dealing with the enhanced risk coverage, especially stressed parameters and CVA volatility risk.

The reflex of a regulator when faced with a risk is to require capital to buffer the institution that risk. The reflex of a trader faced with a risk is to hedge it, and hence price it. For CVA volatility, Basel III permits this trading reflex to some extent, as we describe below.

We focus on uncollateralized derivatives because they are the most affected by Basel III. Hence we must first describe how things used to be under Basel II.

10.3 Exposure under basel II

We assume that the bank has IMM Approval for the derivatives and asset classes of interest, and we will describe the situation that is broadly consistent with respect to the UK embodiment (BIPRU 13). **Caveat:** check with internal compliance and risk departments for details, this is only an introduction.

If you have exposure to another institution, that means that it may owe you money and then default. That is, you are exposed to potential losses from default. Exposure limitation can be thought of as the opposite of VaR in that it considers the positive part of the value distribution of trades. For these potential losses due to counterparty default, you must have capital so that you do not go bankrupt if some statistically plausible fraction of your counterparties default over some horizon of interest. Trading desks will be charged for this capital usage and have limits with respect to this risk. This may be folded into funding charges or be split out separately.

Exposure is calculated at the netting set level. A netting set is a set of trades for which there is a legally enforceable netting agreement. It is quite possible to have several different netting sets between the same pair of institutions.

For Basel II the horizon of interest for exposure is 12 months, or the longest maturity in the netting set if this is shorter.

- Exposure = $\alpha \times$ Effective EPE.
- Effective EPE is the average of Effective EE over the next 12 months (or shorter if the longest maturity in the netting set is shorter).
- Effective EE at time t is the non-decreasing Expected Exposure (EE) at that time. That is, the Expected Exposure is calculated at all time points out to one year and then "effectivized". This consists of starting from the beginning and then taking the max of the previous and current value as time increases.
- Expected Exposure at time t is the average future exposure at time t considering market risk factors, e.g. changes in interest rates, FX rates, etc. For CDS positions the market risk factors would, of course, include future possible CDS spreads.
- Future exposure at t is the loss that the bank might suffer if the legal entity on the other side of the netting set failed to meet its obligations at t (and afterwards).

Basically, capital requirements depended on the exposure profile out to 12 months. α was defined by the regulator and could be in a small range. Note that there was no life-of-trade (LOT) calculation, and calculation was done with today's parameters.

The market risk factors for the future exposure calculation are explicitly permitted to be calibrated to either historical data, or to market-implied factors. In whatever way these risk factors are calculated, there is a second level of checking called backtesting, that compares forecast exposures with actual exposures as time goes forward. Whenever the forecast exposure and the historical exposure is different by some defined factor, then the bank is required to hold extra capital.

Furthermore, the Basel Committee has now published requirements for backtesting [BCBS-185 (2010)]. Needless to say, to obtain IMM Approval for an asset class, both the instrument pricing validation and the backtesting validation are part of typical approval submission packs.

10.4 Contingent capital (CoCo)

Basel III spends pages 12 through 29 carefully describing what is, and what is not capital of different qualities and eligibility. We refer the interested reader there for details and just mention one design that has appeared in the news since Basel III was announced: CoCos, which are a type of convertible bond with a trigger. These have not been declared eligible for Core Tier 1 under Basel III but are still of interest for other qualities of capital, and are permitted above the minimum level by some national regulators provided that they have high triggers (e.g. 7%) [FINMA-TBTF (2011)].

The idea of contingent capital (CoCo) is simple: the instrument pays a coupon to investors that is high enough to compensate for the fact that if the bank gets into trouble then it doesn't have to pay it, and indeed will never pay it again because the instrument turns into equity. As equity holders the investors will be in line for future dividends, but on default will be among the last creditors in line.

CoCos are controversial because some commentators have opined that as the bank gets close to the conversion trigger they will be sold, producing more downward pressure on the bank. The downward pressure will come from two sources: first, potential dilution as the bonds turn into shares, and secondly simply the fact that all the holders of the CoCos will have the same incentive to act at the same time. Thus this extra capital may be present only when it is not needed.

However, the argument above neglects the fact that CoCos are funding instruments, i.e. they produce cash which can help the bank stay out of trouble in the first place. This effect declines over time as the coupon payments add up, and since they are high they pressure the bank to generate a higher return on capital. Thus they may have predominantly a short to medium-term positive effect. The designers of CoCos seem aware of this fact in that CoCos usually have a call right. In short, they appear useful to get out of a crisis but are not a panacea. Realistically, that is all financial engineering can be expected to do. Staying out of trouble in the longer term is the job description of the bank's management.

From the arguments above it is clear that any pricing model for CoCos is subject to debate. Depending on the factors that the quant includes in the model, a large range of values is possible. This is a clear case of model risk. Until there is some evidence about which way things go in practice, a model will just be the quantification of an opinion on interactions between the market and the bank. These can be useful, but are limited as they cannot predict what the dominant effects will be.

10.5   Stressed parameters for counterparty risk

Prior to the crisis banks could calibrate their risk factors to a wide range of possibilities. These did not, however, have to include a crisis. Thus, if the bank did not include a business cycle within its calibration and, more to the point, have a model that was capable of including all parts of the business cycle, then it might have insufficient capital to meet a crisis. Creating regime-dependent models was significantly more sophistication than most banks were willing to pay for – at least, this is the authors' conjecture. Hence, the regulators have decided to impose something simple and effective: calculate under normal and crisis conditions and take the worst result as your capital requirement.

- Banks must calculate the default risk capital charge under current market conditions and under stressed market conditions and take the worst at a total portfolio level. That is, across all netting sets and all counterparties.
- The stressed calibration must be a single consistent stress for all counterparties.
- If calibration is historical, then three years of data must be used. If not, market-implied parameters must be updated at least quarterly (or more if conditions indicate).
- Stress is defined as a period when the CDS spreads of a representative selection of the bank's counterparties are elevated.

- This does not include the CVA risk capital charge (next section).

Will this recipe produce a good outcome in the next crisis? The problem is that this depends on exactly what the next crisis is. However, it will have done its job well if it prevents a repeat of the previous crisis. Preventing all possible crises, whilst permitting banking to continue as a profitable activity, is too much to ask for.

There is one point to note with respect to this recipe – it will probably only be applied to the previous crisis. This is reasonable in that this crisis was the worst since the Great Depression. However, the crisis was a credit crisis, not an inflation crisis like that of the oil-shocks in the 1970s. Thus the interest rates that will appear in the recipe will not control interest rate induced capital volatility because the interest rates during the crisis were very low compared to historical highs.

10.6 CVA risk capital charge

As if it were not enough to include CVA on derivatives, now Basel III requires that the volatility of the CVA be included as well. By included we mean that there is a capital charge and hence an associated cost. This is an excellent way to disincentivize uncollateralized trading, which is exactly what it was intended to do. It is also a great way to incentivize structures and quants to find ways to cope with it.

The CVA risk capital charge is to cover losses from changes in mark-to-market value of OTC derivatives, i.e. fluctuation in exposure. That is, the charge is most significant for changes in the credit valuation adjustment on uncollateralized derivatives. The motivation is that the Basel Committee noted that 2/3 of the losses were mark-to-market losses, rather than default losses. We have remarked earlier that the committee could easily have drawn the opposite conclusion – since the counterparties did not default and cause actual losses, then why add a risk charge? One answer is that the transaction price for the derivative changed. Just as when interest rates change, prices change, now the fact that credit risk is just another market variable has been acknowledged.

10.6.1 Alternative calculation methods

A bank cannot calculate its CVA risk capital charge using the method that its quants consider to be the best one. Because there is a clear potential conflict of interest between the bank and its regulator (a bank might want to hold as little capital as possible because this makes trading more expensive) there are regulations stating how calculations can be done. A bank can use some of its own methods if it gains approval to do so. This approval process includes submitting the proposed model(s) to the regulator together with reports from the bank's model validation team and details of governance processes.

For the CVA risk capital charge there are two calculation methods:

A. **Advanced CVA risk capital charge** (described below). Here the exposure profiles are calculated using the bank's internal models for which the bank has regulatory approval.
B. **Standardised CVA risk capital charge** This is a simple formula using the discounted exposure at default (EAD) allowing for credit hedges.

In approach B, the EAD is calculated using whatever level of approval the bank has. The approval level is either IMM (internal model method), SM (standardized method), or CEM (current exposure method).

Once a bank has a given level of approval it must use it. Thus the alternative choice lies in the decision of level of approval to seek.

10.6.2 Calculation under IMM

Here we will focus on banks with IMM approval and Specific Interest Rate Risk VaR model approval. This is called the Advanced CVA risk capital charge. Both approvals are required because machinery from both areas is used. The pieces are put into the bank's VaR model for bonds, but only considering changes in credit spreads. This VaR model restriction means that wrong-way risk will not be included in the calculation. Equally, right-way risk will also be excluded.

The following formula must be used as part of the calculation of the charge; it is defined in the Basel III document proscriptively.

$$
\text{CVA} = \text{L}_{\text{GD}} \sum_{i=1}^{T} \max \left(0, \ \exp \left(-\frac{s_{i-1} t_{i-1}}{\text{L}_{\text{GD}}} \right) - \exp \left(-\frac{s_i t_i}{\text{L}_{\text{GD}}} \right) \right)
$$

$$
\times \left(\frac{\text{EE}_{i-1} D_{i-1} + \text{EE}_i D_i}{2} \right) \tag{10.1}
$$

$$
= \text{L}_{\text{GD}} \sum_{i=1}^{T} \max \left(0, \text{default probability in interval } i \right)
$$

$$
\times \left(\text{average exposure in interval } i \right),
$$

where:

- t_i is the ith valuation time, starting with $t_0 = 0$.
- t_T is the longest contractual maturity with the counterparty.
- s_i is the credit spread of counterparty at t_i. If not available then any proxy must be based on rating, industry, and region.
- L_{GD} is a market assessment of loss given default, *not* an internal assessment.
- D_i is the default risk-free discount factor at time t_i, where $D_0 = 1$. That is, a bank cannot use its own funding curve.

How Equation 10.1 is used depends on the bank's VaR engine as follows:

- Full revaluation: use Equation 10.1 as is within the calculation.
- Sensitivities per tenor: use tenor-sections of Equation 10.1.
- Parallel shifts: use 1bps times the CVA from Equation 10.1.
- Second-order: as parallel but with additional second-order terms.

The VaR engine is used twice, not once, in the capital calculation since now stressed VaR is part of capital calculations. Thus the result is the sum of the stressed and non-stressed VaR. For the stressed VaR the stressed EE profiles must be used together with a VaR calibration to the worst one-year period within the three-year stressed period chosen for counterparty risk.

10.6.3 Mitigation

Basel III states explicitly the mitigation that is possible, and states that only what is stated explicitly is permitted. It also states explicitly that certain mitigants are not permitted.

- Only hedges expressly targeted for CVA risk and managed as such may be included in the VaR model used to calculate the CVA capital charge. Just having a convenient CDS somewhere in the bank is not sufficient. The regulation (Paragraph 102) does not state whether dual-use positions are permitted, or what tests would be applied to see whether a given position would be eligible.
- The only eligible hedges, which must be removed from the bank's market risk capital calculation, are:
  - Single-name CDSs.
  - Single-name contingent CDSs.

- Equivalent hedging instruments referencing the counterparty directly.
- Index CDSs where the basis between the counterparty and the index is included in the VaR model. This also applies to the case where a proxy for the counterparty CDS is used (e.g. when there are no CDSs referencing that name). When no spread is available a representative basket of similar names may be used.

- Ineligible hedges are:

- nth to default CDSs are not permitted.
- Tranched structures are not permitted.

Given how the regulation is written it is almost mandatory to have a dedicated CVA desk to manage the hedging. Although the wording may appear highly restrictive, the regulators have given themselves flexibility by stating that "equivalent hedging instruments" are permitted. In addition, contingent CDSs are permitted, and a contingent CDS can have almost anything as its underlying – it is simply credit protection on what it refers to. However, regulators have clearly restricted direct securitization of CVA by making tranched structures ineligible.

Mitigation is a highly active research area that has the potential for competitive advantage. Do not expect people to publish before they have profited. Academics had publish-or-perish; practitioners have profit-then-publish.

The obvious mitigation is to develop other lines of business. From press announcements it seems that most banks have decided that Private Banking, and especially Asian wealth management, is the hottest possibility. At this point it is back to classic business school basics: segmentation, differentiation, and value propositions, all helped along by branding.

10.6.4 Why is the CVA risk capital charge important?

(1) It is a life-of-trade calculation. Previously, only the first 12 months of a trade mattered for capital purposes.
(2) It is expensive, either to deal with or to avoid. Reducing risk-weighted assets on a large scale or raising significant amounts of capital has a concomitant impact on the bottom line, for the institutions and for shareholders.
(3) It is complicated at an institutional level. By bringing together credit hedging and exposure calculations it requires that Risk and Trading have a much more interactive dialogue than ever before.

Credit hedging is bought in the risk-neutral world so it needs risk-neutral EE profiles to work with. However, EE profiles are generated by risk factor processes which must pass historical backtesting. Regulations require that the same profile is used for default risk and for CVA volatility risk.

10.6.5 Consequences

The wording of the CVA risk capital charge suggests, to the authors at least, that it may be difficult to run an active CVA hedge without a dedicated CVA desk. That is, the wording explicitly states that credit hedges specific to CVA must be managed as such.

The Advanced Method explicitly requires the use of CDS spreads. These are often not available for small to medium businesses. Thus proxies (permitted) will be used, taking into account rating, industry, and region of the counterparty. Whilst an external rating will also not usually be available, the bank's credit department will have assigned an internal rating prior to doing business with the counterparty.

Where CDSs are available their use for CVA hedges may widen the market, and potentially create feedback loops. One has already been suggested (by Professor Brigo) in CDS hedging of DVA that could potentially create systemic risk. To understand the mechanism, consider – hypothetically – Morgan Stanley hedging its risk using CDS on Lehman. Morgan Stanley has hedged its spread risk but if Lehman defaults (which it did) then Morgan Stanley would have to pay out large sums exactly when it was weakest. Thus whilst hedging spread risk, DVA hedging might increase the likelihood of systematic failure.

The advanced method explicitly requires the use of market recovery rates. Tradable recovery rates are available from recovery swaps, but – and this is a large but – there are very few, and these are illiquid. The usual recovery rates that are provided with CDS swaps are **not** tradable numbers. They are simply provided for convenience of communication, but have no significance beyond this. We described a potential heuristic solution to this lack of observable recovery rates in our earlier Section 3.2.4 on credit spreads. It is not a panacea, and this is one of the largest practical gaps for calculation since it affects all sizes of counterparty.

10.7 Wrong-way risk

Wrong-way risk is exposure that increases as the risk of default increases. For example, if a bank has an interest rate swap receiving the floating side, and as floating rates increase the probability of the counterparty defaulting increases. Thus the bank is owed more exactly when the counterparty is riskier. The CVA Capital charge cannot capture this effect because the formula treats each part (exposure and default risk) separately. There is a separate section in Basel III dealing with wrong-way risk but, perhaps because of the wide scope of the problem, the section only goes into detail with the most extreme case. The most extreme case is where there is a legal connection between the source and the underlying (e.g. a company selling put options on itself). Basel III supplies principles here, but little detail; this is a practical limitation.

11
Backtesting

DUKE To vouch this is no proof,
without more certain and more overt test
than these thin habits and poor likelihoods
of modern seeming do prefer against him.
Shakespeare, *Othello*

11.1 Introduction

Capital charges for trading desks are calculated from counterparty
exposure profiles per legally enforceable netting set. Exposure is what
the bank can lose if its counterparty defaults. Here we are mostly dealing with uncollateralized trades, as they have much larger exposures
than collateralized trades. Collateralized trades have gap risk (between
collateral transfers) and may have contagion risk, e.g. for a quanto
CDS trade where default of the underlying induces a jump in the FX
rate. However, these effects are generally small compared to the same
uncollateralized trades.

Basel III insists that banks may only use one exposure profile for
both the default charge and the CVA volatility charge. As mentioned
in the previous chapter, the default charge looks at only the first 12
months of trades, whilst the CVA volatility charge uses the entire
life of the trade. This, new, second capital charge may dominate for
longer portfolios. In any case, it will usually be significant. These,
traditionally, *have been* related to fundamentally different concepts:
historical default versus market-implied credit valuation adjustment
(which *must* be calculated using market CDS spreads). Exposure profiles depend on the future development of underlying risk factors
(e.g. discount curves, market-implied swaption volatilities, etc.). Basel
III explicitly permits calibration of RFEs to either historical data, or

market-implied. However these RFEs are calibrated, they must pass *historical* backtesting.

Why would a bank attempt to pass historical backtesting with an RFE calibrated to market-implied data? Precisely because the resulting exposure profiles are being used to calculate the CCDS protection to buy to mitigate the CVA volatility capital charge. These CCDS are, of course, priced using risk-neutral no-arbitrage arguments. This is not to say that all banks will take this approach. Indeed, some will question whether they should calculate exposure based on market-implied calibration if they do not actually fully hedge the credit risk. The standard argument goes like this:

- For: since replication pricing gives prices whether we hedge or not, we should use those prices.
- Against: if our counterparty defaults *whilst we are not credit hedged* then we will face the real-world losses not the market-implied losses.

This is reminiscent of DVA pricing, where different stakeholders need different numbers for their purposes (trading versus capital). The problem of actual default makes the situation less clear-cut than would otherwise be the case.

We expect a consensus to emerge in the next couple of years; in the meanwhile, most decisions will be taken pragmatically. We present a backtesting framework that can be applied to both situations. In our example we will use a historical calibration to a traditional RFE setup found in Risk departments. This may not be familiar to readers coming from a pricing point of view so we show how multiple measures (real-world and market-implied) are combined and can be exploited. At the end of the chapter we show the starting point for a market-implied setup for the same example.

Regulators are measure-indifferent, their concern is capital conservatism – whatever passes historical backtesting is good. In statistical, or econometric terms, historical backtesting is out-of-sample prediction.

Risk Factor Evolution testing is a relatively recent development, in that regulatory guidance from BIS and in Basel III has only appeared in 2010–2011, first in consultative form [BCBS-171 (2010)], then final [BCBS-185 (2010)], and within Basel III later [BCBS-189 (2011)]. The guidance itself acknowledges that the field is still developing. Academic work on distribution testing often uses transformations for greater power [Berkowitz (2001), Hamerle and Plank (2009)]. More work has been done on VaR, where some consistent frameworks have been proposed [Paolella and Steude(2008), Colletaz *et al.*(2011) Colletaz, Hurlin and Perignon, Angelidis and Degiannakis(2007)].

Here we describe an RFE testing framework based on regulatory guidance [BCBS-185 (2010), BCBS-189 (2011)] in that it explicitly includes the significance of different parts of predicted distributions for exposure calculations. Exposure refers both to expected positive exposure (EPE) and potential future exposure (PFE, based on a quantile of value, which is then floored at zero). PFEs are often used as part of the limit setting for trading desks. We test RFE-model-derived distributions against the null hypothesis that the RFE model is correct using a Cramer–von Mises/Anderson–Darling type of approach, with weights derived from the exposure significance of the distribution relative to the underlying portfolio. The RFE testing framework directly includes multiple horizons and multiple tests for a single decision: accept or reject the RFE model at a given confidence level.

Why do we not weight all parts of the distribution equally when testing against a null hypothesis? Surely in some case every part matters? The objective here is not to require a perfect RFE equation, because finance is not physics. With real data involving non-physics-based processes we expect every model to fail at some level of detail. Instead, we focus our testing where the outcome makes the most difference for exposure, given a dynamic synthetic portfolio. As well as focusing on the significant areas of the distributions, we also make the tests discrete, i.e. we test intervals of the distribution relative to the data, not every (empirical) point. Asymptotically, our tests reduce to their continuous counterparts. We show that these tests provide discrimination in real situations.

Since backtesting typically covers many years, the method must create dynamic synthetic portfolios over that timeframe. VaR models have typically used static synthetic portfolios for testing [Angelidis and Degiannakis (2007)] which can be appropriate given their short horizon. However, for EPE and PFE no static synthetic portfolio is appropriate when the underlying changes significantly within the horizon of typical trades. Thus, observed portfolios are the integrated results of previous trading decisions under different market conditions. This is usual in EPE and PFE. Whilst creating dynamic synthetic portfolios may appear challenging, in the experience of the authors it is made tractable by two observations. First, RFE models are used for uncollateralized trades, generally client trades – not trades with hedge funds or investment banks. Secondly, one can expect clients to trade with patterns derived from their business. We include explicit (fake) dynamics for synthetic portfolios. The RFE testing procedure introduced here is for non-path-dependent instruments. We leave path-dependent formulations for future research.

Practically, risk groups must demonstrate that their RFE models are acceptable to their regulators. It is always possible that no model passes the testing framework outlined above, within a given deadline. It is not sufficient to propose using the best-available model when a regulator requires conservatism of exposure estimation, as sometimes suggested [Orhan and Köksal (2012)]. Hence this framework includes a capital-efficient extension: the Splitting Approach. This involves using pairs of RFE models for each risk factor. One member of each RFE pair may be biased high and the other may be biased low. These are fed to underlying trades depending on the direction of the trade. Now the backtesting becomes one-sided rather than two-sided and so is generally much easier to pass at a given confidence level.

The Splitting Approach is preferred to indiscriminate increases of volatility because it is capital efficient: potentially only one of the RFE pair elements will need alteration. Additionally, the Splitting Approach enables asymmetric refinements of RFEs, which is impossible using only changes in volatility. This asymmetry is necessary even in the simple example of a swap with fixed payments on both legs but on different dates. Decreasing yield volatility would increase the value of both legs with no clear directional result for exposure. Note that, since the crisis of 2008–2012, a float leg (with notional exchanges) no longer has unit value, since the discounting and LIBOR curves are different. The Splitting Approach is particularly adapted to current developments in Fixed Income, where it is now standard to have separate discounting and LIBOR curves [Bianchetti (2010), Mercurio (2010), Kenyon (2010b)].

Alternatively, the Splitting Approach can be used to estimate a capital buffer in the event that the aim is not to change the RFE but still to have a conservative setup. By conservative we mean that the bank has sufficient capital.

This RFE backtesting framework is demonstrated by applying it to a commodity (WTI oil) in a traditional tenor-point RFE setup. We also specify how to use the framework with market-implied calibration. Market-implied calibration typically means that a different style of RFE model is used, i.e. one directly inspired by trading (possibly exactly the same model). Hence we show how to use a typical short-rate or forward-rate model with market-implied calibration for historical backtesting.

11.1.1 Regulatory guidance

Backtesting is only part of RFE development, but is a highly significant part. A selection of the points in [BCBS-185 (2010)] is given below:

- Guidance: backtesting EPE models and their risk factors should be done for several horizons separately. The horizons should reflect the period of risk. For uncollateralized trades this will be up to maturity.
- Guidance: all models contributing to EPE must be tested, and the tests should be able to identify which models perform poorly.
- Guidance: forecasts should be initialized on several different dates.
- Guidance: there should be a written policy defining precisely what performance is acceptable, and what is not acceptable. The policy should also state what remediation will take place on unacceptable performance.
- Guidance: more than one risk measure should be used to judge performance.
- Guidance: A representative counterparty portfolio for the purposes of carrying out EPE model backtesting should be defined.
- Guidance: A bank should validate its EPE models out to time horizons commensurate with the maturity of trades.
- Guidance: Backtesting should include an assessment of recent performance.

Except for the last one, these are specifically addressed by the design of the RFE testing methodology presented here. The methodology includes multiple horizons; uses backtesting; starts from a number of historical dates; defines acceptable performance explicitly, as a confidence level; the assessment uses multiple measures weighing different quantiles of the distribution according to their significance; starts from a representative portfolio; horizons are set from trade maturity.

The only Guidance that is problematic is assessment of recent performance. This, by definition, requires the use of relatively little data so it is very hard to fail any such test statistically. This is particularly true after an extended period of turbulence, such as during the financial and sovereign crises of 2008–2012. We do not address this requirement specifically, but it would be worth addressing after any extended period of calm.

11.2 Backtesting framework

The objective of the RFE backtesting methodology is to produce good exposure numbers. The testing methodology design works backwards

Figure 11.1 Framework for RFE backtesting methodology. The objective is good expo-sure numbers; these depend on the portfolio. The value of instruments in the portfolio depends on their underlyings. Thus, the testing framework emphasizes distribution correctness to the degree that it influences exposure.

from this objective, as shown in Figure 11.1. Exposure is due to a port-folio relative to the distribution of the underlyings of the portfolio. This direction is also followed in the Splitting Approach.

This section first considers exposure from two representative instru-ments (a forward and a European option); then it develops dynamics for synthetic portfolios; then a modified-weight Cramer–von Mises-style distribution test is presented; this distribution test is then extended to deal with multiple horizons, and multiple-test corrections are detailed.

Section 11.2.8 details the modifications for the framework required to move to tests of conservatism as opposed to correctness. This section concentrates on the null hypothesis that the proposed model is correct.

For concreteness we develop the RFE testing framework in the context of (non-power) commodities. We specifically exclude power commodities because their forward curves can be arbitrarily jagged (think of electricity where there is no storage, for example Texas or Aus-tralia). Note that we leave aside the many practical details (for example delivery, payment, averaging, and so on) as they are not significant for the exposition.

11.2.1 Notation

For(v, T): price at time v for a Forward contract (e.g. on a stock, or commodity) for payment (and delivery) at time T.

$D(t, T)$: discount factor from t to T.

$C_{BS}(t, F, K, T, \sigma)$: Black–Scholes vanilla Call option price.

$\sigma_M(K, T, F)$: market-impled volatility for strike K given ATM-Forward level F at maturity T.

$\tau_u(v, S)$: tenor point S on modeled curve at time v, as seen from u.

$\mathbb{E}$: expectation under the real-world or historical measure (or some other predicted measure, but not generally the market-implied measure).

$\widetilde{\mathbb{E}}$: expectation under the market-implied measure.

11.2.2 Instrument dependence on distributions

The first step is to calculate which parts of the distribution of the underlying are important. We will put greater weight on the more important parts of the distribution when we test whether or not the historical distribution is the same as the model distribution. Which parts of the distribution are important must be relative to a set of instruments. Here we consider two basic instruments: a forward and a European option.

11.2.2.1 Forward contract

We consider a commodity forward contract on an underlying U, $\text{For}_U(v, T)$, as in Figure 11.2. The expected positive exposure (EE($t = 0$)) on the date the contract is entered is zero for a forward contract. Of course, future exposures will be greater than zero, as well as their expectations.

$$t = 0 \qquad \text{EE} = (\text{For}_U(0, T) - \text{For}_U(0, T))^+ = 0$$
$$t1 = \text{now:} \qquad \text{EE} = (\text{For}_U(t1, T) - \text{For}_U(0, T))^+$$
$$t2 \text{ from } t1: \qquad \text{EE} = \mathbb{E}\left[(\text{For}_U(t2, T) - \text{For}_U(0, T))^+ | \mathcal{F}(t1)\right].$$

These expression are similar to, but not the same as, a call option, $C_{\text{BS}}(t, F, K, T, \sigma)$. The main two differences are: 1) no discounting; 2) we work in the real-world (historical) measure (and expectation $\mathbb{E}$).

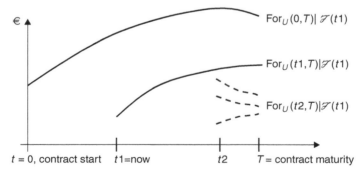

Figure 11.2 Forward curves for different dates on an underlying U, given the information available at $t1$. Observed forward curves (solid lines) are from the past and present, whilst future forward curve examples (dashed lines) are elements from a distribution.

At maturity, the exposure of a long forward contract depends only on the underlying distribution above its fixed rate. At times prior to maturity its exposure is the convolution of the whole distribution at the prior time, with the transition density function to maturity with the call-like weights at maturity. This is similar to a call option; prior to maturity the option depends on the whole distribution, whereas at maturity only the distribution above the strike matters. At the intermediate dates, the call option is not equally dependent on all parts of the distribution but depends more on the parts that contribute more to its value.

It may appear above that we are stating the obvious, however this is key to understanding whether we should pick equal weights in our distribution tests (like Cramer–von Mises) or unequal weights (like Anderson–Darling).

11.2.2.2 *Call option*

$t = 0$ $\qquad$ $EE = \widetilde{\mathbb{E}}[D(0, T)(\mathrm{For}_U(T, T) - K)^+ | \mathcal{F}(0)]$

$\qquad\qquad = C_{\mathrm{BS}}(\mathrm{For}_U(0, T), K, T, \sigma_M(K, T, \mathrm{For}_U(0, T)))$

$t1 = \mathrm{now}$: $\quad EE = \widetilde{\mathbb{E}}[D(t1, T)(\mathrm{For}_U(T, T) - K)^+ | \mathcal{F}(t1)]$

$\qquad\qquad = C_{\mathrm{BS}}(\mathrm{For}_U(t1, T), K, T, \sigma_M(K, T, \mathrm{For}_U(t1, T)))$

$t2$ from $t1$: $\quad EE = \mathbb{E}\left[\widetilde{\mathbb{E}}[D(t2, T)(\mathrm{For}_U(T, T) - K)^+ | \mathcal{F}(t2)] \middle| \mathcal{F}(t1)\right]$

$\qquad\qquad = \mathbb{E}\left[C_{\mathrm{BS}}(\mathrm{For}_U(t2, T), K, T, \sigma_M(K, T, \mathrm{For}_U(t2, T))) \middle| \mathcal{F}(t1)\right].$

The option price uses the (predicted) market-implied volatility σ_M, not any volatility from the real-world RFE. Pricing is done in the risk-neutral measure whereas risk factor evolution is done in the historical measure. Depending on the RFE model used for σ_M it may have different numbers of parameters.

At maturity, the exposure of a long call option depends only on the underlying distribution above its strike. Prior to maturity it depends on the whole of the distribution, as well as the transition density function to maturity weighted with the exposure at maturity. An example is shown in Figure 11.3.

11.2.3 Counterparty exposure setups

There are three main setups for counterparty exposure calculations:

Tenor-points traditional, typical for systems that are not combined with front office pricing.

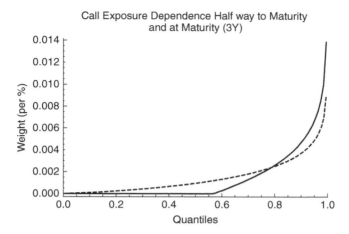

Figure 11.3 Long call option exposure dependence on underlying distribution at maturity (3Y, solid line). Also exposure dependence on underlying distribution half way to maturity (1.5Y, dashed line). Note that the vertical axis means the weight of each 1 percent quantile on the horizontal axis, hence the "per%" in the bracket. Parameters: real-world drift 5%, risk-neutral drift 2%, both volatilities 20%. These parameters are used as in the Call Option section.

Short-rate, aka Markov typical for exposure systems that are combined with CVA calculations. May use market-implied and historical measures simultaneously. Can be fully market-implied.

Forward rate often found in market-implied setups where short-rate approaches are not convenient.

Conceptually, our framework can be directly applied to to all of these setups. We focus on the tenor-points setup as it is widely deployed and may be unfamiliar to those from a pricing background. We later describe how to apply our framework to the short-rate and forward rate setups. Figure 11.4 shows how this works in comparison with forward contracts. Different tenor-points will correspond to the same forward contract over time.

Given a portfolio, we can define a desired prediction horizon T_H. The prediction requirement for each tenor point is then just $T_H - |\tau(t, T)|$, where $|.|$ gives the tenor of the tenor-point (T in the notation used in Figure 11.4 – this notation is not the same as usually used for forward contracts). This is important because it means that longer tenors are not required to predict out as far as shorter tenors.

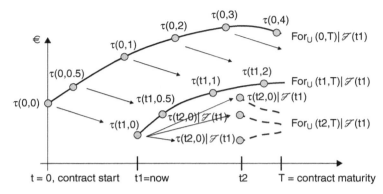

Figure 11.4 Tenor-points, τ(time, tenor), RFE setup, and comparison with forward contracts. Each individual tenor-point can have a separate RFE model, whereas in a short-rate setup the whole curve would be given by one single RFE model (e.g. Hull–White in rates, or Schwartz–Smith in commodities).

11.2.4 Distribution weighting from dynamic synthetic portfolios

Exposure is calculated from instrument prices, thus we need to know which parts of the predicted distribution are important for prices. As an example, consider a vanilla European call option with strike *K*. The price is independent of the distribution below *K*, thus, in this limited example, we should not test the distribution below *K* at all. This is the basis of our test construction: weight the distribution test according to the importance for the outcome metric. In line with Cramer–von Mises-type tests like Anderson–Darling, we use an L_2 metric, rather than the L_∞ metric of Kolmogorov–Smirnov. We use a discrete version of:

$$d = m \int_{x=-\infty}^{x=\infty} (Q_m(x) - Q(x))^2 w(x) dQ(x), \tag{11.1}$$

where *d* is the distance between the two distributions, that is, the test statistic. Cramer–von Mises has $w(x) \equiv 1$, Anderson–Darling has $w(x) = (Q(x)(1 - Q(x)))^{-1}$. *Q* is the theoretical distribution and Q_m the empirical distribution from *m* observations. As an example, note that Anderson–Darling will weight distribution differences symmetrically (too high same as too low), and that differences in the top 1% quantile will be roughly 25 times more important than differences in the center 1% quantile $(1/(0.01 \times 0.99) \text{ vs } 1/(0.5 \times 0.5))$.

As well as using a discrete version of Equation 11.1, we also adapt it to consider multiple horizons simultaneously.

11.2.4.1 *Weight construction*

We consider both EE and PFE.

- EE: Let $q(X,F,i)$ be the contribution of quantile i to the expected exposure (i.e. we are discretizing):

$$q(X,F,i) = \int_{Q^{-1}(F,i/n)}^{Q^{-1}(F,(i+1)/n)} (X(F))^+ dQ(F) \tag{11.2}$$

$$EE = \sum_{i=1}^{n} q(X,F,i),$$

  where:
  $X(F)$ is a derivative depending on F;
  n is the number of quantiles in unity (e.g. 100 for 1% quantiles);
  $Q(F)$ is the distribution of F.
- PFE: this is a quantile of the distribution of the instrument price (not the F distribution), floored at zero. In as much as the two distributions are aligned, this can be similar.

Now we begin to build up the weights used in the distribution tests from the two instrument types we are considering: forwards and vanilla European options (call and put). We are interested in a robust set of weights, which we define to be one that controls the extremes. Thus we focus on dependence of exposure at maturity to the underlying distribution. This simplifies matters as option and forward exposures are then driven by the same computation: realized value of underlying versus fixed rate (or strike).

We need to establish the range of possible dependencies given a range of instrument parameters and market data. We show a range of examples in the Figures referred to below.

- Vanilla put and call options versus market moves: Figure 11.5. This figure shows exposure dependence at contract maturity. The asymmetry of the put and call dependence is largely due to the asymmetry of the payoffs: a call has an unlimited upside.
- Volatility smile dynamics: Figure 11.6. We see changes in the dependence on the mid-lower range of quantiles but no significant changes in the dependence at the highest areas. Note that fixed smiles are just like flat because volatility-at-strike does not

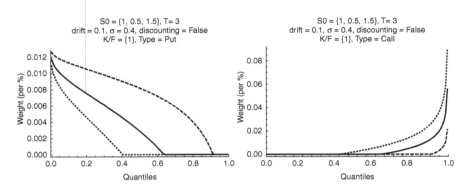

Figure 11.5 Put (LHS) and call (RHS) option dependence on quantiles of underlying distribution against a range of spot moves (none = solid line, down 50% = dashed line, up 50% = dotted lines). Note that the vertical scales of the two graphs are different.

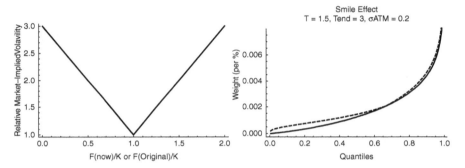

Figure 11.6 Effect of smile dynamics on dependence on quantiles of underlying distribution for call option. LHS gives stylized smile. We consider two extremes of smile dynamics: fixed (aka sticky strike, solid line); floating (aka sticky delta, dotted line). RHS compares fixed smile to floating. Whilst there are some differences in the mid-lower of quantiles, the dependence on high quantiles is not significantly affected.

change. This suggests that we can ignore smile effects when calculating the maximum sensitivity of vanilla options to the underlying distribution.

Having built some intuition on the relation of trades and spot moves to dependence on distribution quantiles, we now need to specify the underlying and the dynamics of the synthetic portfolio. With this information we can then calculate actual weights because we will have the portfolios over time.

11.2.4.2 *Dynamics of synthetic portfolios*

Our objective here is to define the range of trades and markets against which it is reasonable to optimize the RFE test. From Audit

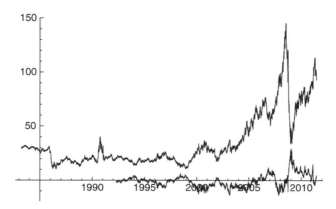

Figure 11.7 Front-month (upper line), and 24th-month versus front-month spread (lower line), WTI oil futures. Note that the spread implies that the 2-year slope of the futures curve can be positive or negative.

requirements all historical portfolios may be available. However, it can be more convenient to use synthetic portfolios together with matching to the current portfolio, and we take this approach here.

Consider Figure 11.7, which shows front-month and 24th-month over front-month spread for WTI futures contract prices. Although the prices change from $10 to $150 over the historical period (1980–2011), depending on the portfolio maximum maturity these moves will be more or less significant. Here significant refers, for example, to the relevant range of Forward/Strike in the case of options. As time goes forward, option strikes in trades already made will not change, but the forward levels will do. By constructing synthetic portfolio dynamics we can identify the correct Forward/Strike ranges for different portfolio maturities.

PFE and EPE deal with uncollateralized trades, thus these are client trades rather than trades with banks or (mostly) hedge funds. We propose here a set of rules for commodities, specifically applied to oil. These rules, if started in the distant past and then applied consistently, should result in a portfolio today that resembles the current one. By distant past we mean longer than the maturity of the longest trade (which is one of the rules itself). If the rules are applied to the whole history of interest they will generate a range of portfolios-vs-markets that we can then use to base our distribution test on.

All institutions have their particular value propositions, and actual portfolios are, of course, proprietary, so the rules presented here should be considered as inspiration rather than definitive.

Rule All trades are placed at-the-money.

Rule Trades are held to maturity.

Parameter Trades are placed at n maturities $= \{m_1, \ldots, m_n\}$.

Parameter Notionals of trades $= \{x_1, \ldots, x_n\}$.

In our examples we pick $m_i = i/12$, $x_i = \pm 1$, describing trades placed uniformly up to maximum maturity. The sign of the notional indicates whether the position is long or short. We consider two extremes: all long and all short.

Note that there is an inconsistency here in our method: we are using observed history to set up limits that we then use in a procedure in which we also use observed history to predict out-of-sample but still within the original history that we used for limits. A fully self-consistent setup would only use the observed history to date to specify the limits. However, this is a weak reuse of data so we accept the small inconsistency.

Figure 11.8 shows synthetic portfolio snapshots 2006–2011, yearly, using the rules and parameters given, with maximum maturity 3 years. Note that ATM (the full lines) can be at a range of positions relative to the bulk of the portfolio.

From Figure 11.8 we can calculate the distribution of Forward/Strike for any given maturity. From this distribution we can then take a desired confidence interval with respect to which we want our distribution tests to be robust. An example is shown in Figure 11.9, where we see that the confidence intervals are quite triangular for a 3Y portfolio.

Figure 11.10 shows the weights, i.e. relative importance of different quantiles, given long and short Forward positions. As demonstrated above, the weights for options would be very similar. Note that the weights are relatively insensitive to underlying volatility, except for the very highest quantiles, and asymmetric. The asymmetry has several causes: the underlying distribution (log-normal) is not symmetric; real-world drift is not usually equal to risk-neutral drift; and most importantly that call options have an unlimited upside, whereas put options have a maximum payoff equal to their strike. Figure 11.11 shows a comparison with Anderson–Darling weights and highlights two differences. First, the Anderson–Darling weights are symmetric, and secondly the Anderson–Darling weights are much higher at the tails.

11.2.5 Hypothesis testing

To decide whether a candidate RFE is acceptable, i.e. cannot be rejected at a given confidence level, we need to go through several steps. First

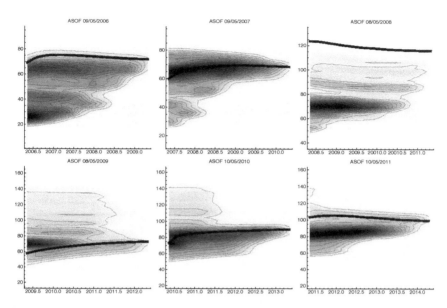

Figure 11.8 Snapshots of implied synthetic portfolios 2006–2011 using the trading rules in the text, for portfolio maximum maturity 3 years. Density plots are for the fixed rates and maturities of contracts which could be options, forwards, or swaps, or a combination. That is, the density is proportional to the number of contracts with the maturity given by the horizontal axis, and the fixed rate given by the vertical axis. The single full (black) line in each plot is ATM for the as of date. The trading rules specify that all trades are placed ATM as of their trade date. The divergence from the ATM curve in the figure is because most trades were placed before the current as of date in each individual plot. For example, the top right plot is for May 8, 2008, when the oil price increased sharply to around 120USD after a longer period between 60USD and 80USD.

we must create data points, i.e. comparisons of predicted distributions versus actual future observations. Then we must create enough data, for example it is often possible to use overlapping predictions. A consequence of this is that appropriate significance levels (p-levels) need to be created to take into account the non-independent nature of the data. Then, typically, we will want to repeat this process, for example for different prediction horizons. Once we have p-values from multiple tests we then use a multiple-test correction to enable a decision on whether the RFE is acceptable.

We first describe the data creation, then the multiple testing procedure.

11.2.5.1 *Overlapping predictions*

Relevant horizons for portfolios depend on the asset class. They also depend on the tenor of the point being considered (longer tenors

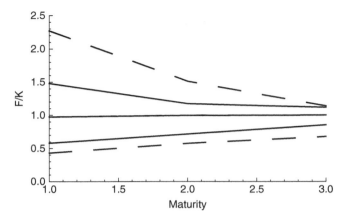

Figure 11.9 {5%, 50%, 95%} (continuous lines) and {1%, 99%} (long dashes) confidence intervals of Forward/Strike for 3Y dynamic synthetic portfolio maturities. Data used for each maturity year is the preceding year, so 3Y point uses maturities 2Y–3Y. Lines are linear interpolations.

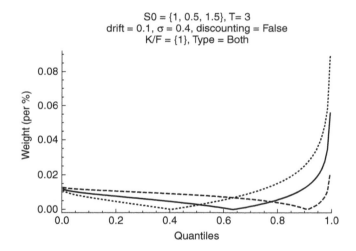

Figure 11.10 Each curve is the combination of a put and a call position with spot moves (flat = solid line, down 50% = dashed line, up 50% = dotted line).

have shorter relevant horizons for a given portfolio maturity). At one extreme is FX where only predicting the spot matters because forward FX is completely specified by the two relevant yield curves. However, the future spot values must still be predicted up to the horizon of the portfolio. This can be of the order of months. At the other extreme, interest rates portfolio horizons can be measured in decades.

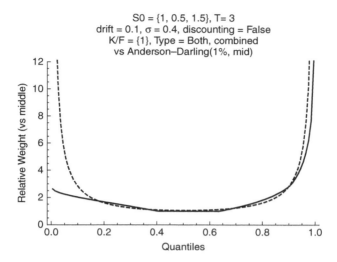

Figure 11.11 Comparison of weights calculated from Figure 11.10 (solid line) with Anderson–Darling weights (dashed line), both calculated for 1% quantiles (note that the vertical axis is truncated for clarity of comparison).

Regulatory advice suggests at least a one-year prediction horizon. In general, the prediction horizon derives from the portfolio. Here we consider commodities with a multi-year horizon.

We face two issues with constructing confidence intervals for overlapping predictions: first, they overlap, and secondly parameters are estimated (not exact). Estimated RFE parameters are used to calculate the quantile to which future observations correspond. Thus testing is independent of the RFE model. Since the parameters are estimates, the quantiles are estimates and not exact. Thus in test building it is important to take into account the noise in the parameter estimates.

We resolve both issues by constructing confidence intervals using simulation. We simulate the process described by the RFE model, then apply the quantile estimators. That is, calibrate the RFE model to the single simulated path, get the out-of-sample predictions, calculate what quantile the actual (future simulated) observation corresponds to. From this single simulated path we obtain one set of quantiles which we then apply our AD-like weights to, i.e. the discrete version of Equation 11.1. This produces a single number as an output which corresponds to a case where the hypothesis that the RFE model is correct is true. Repeating this process many times produces a distribution. Our confidence interval is then just the one-sided confidence level from this distribution.

In the process above the distribution of true values contains estimation noise, and dependence of the overlapping intervals, thus it is appropriate for testing the historical data on. There is a small inconsistency in that the level of estimation noise will depend partly on the parameters used to create the simulated paths. The exact method would be to first estimate RFE parameters from historical data and then create the simulated paths and confidence levels. For simplicity we use approximate parameters to obtain the confidence level since this approximation only affects the level of estimation noise.

11.2.5.2 *Multiple horizons*

On some occasions we may wish to test different horizons separately. In this case no changes to the distance metrics are required. If, on the other hand, we want to test several horizons together we have a combined testing procedure which uses an expanded version of Equation 11.1 as below (but in discrete form):

$$d_i = n \int_{-\infty}^{\infty} (Q_n^i(x) - Q(x))^2 w(x) dQ(x) \tag{11.3}$$

$$d_h = \sum_{i=1}^{i=h} d_i. \tag{11.4}$$

For each horizon i we calculate the difference of the empirical $Q_n^i(x)$ versus the test distribution $Q(x)$ (always uniform) with Equation 11.3 and then sum the differences to obtain an overall metric for the combined horizon h. Thus the overall metric for increasing horizons reflects all the errors up to the last horizon. We obtain the confidence interval for the overall metric d_h as before using simulation.

The discrete form of the weighted L_2 distance metric is as follows:

- Horizons: $H = \{1, \dots, h\}$.
- Ranges: $R = \{1, \dots, r\}$.
- Range widths: $\theta(i)$. Same for all horizons, e.g. $\{1\%, 5\%, 14\%, 30\%, 30\%, 14\%, 5\%, 1\%\}$.
- Cumulative range width: $\Theta(i) = \sum_{j=1}^{i} \theta(i)$, e.g. $\{1\%, 6\%, 20\%, 50\%, 80\%, 94\%, 99\%, 100\%\}$.

Statistic:

$$\text{D-WL2}(H, R) := \sum_{j \in H} \sum_{i \in R} \left(Q_{n,j}(Q_j^{-1}(\Theta(i))) - \Theta(i) \right)^2 \times w_j(\Theta(i)) \times \theta(i).$$

$w_j(y)$ is the weight for quantile y at the jth horizon.
$Q_{n,j}$ gives the empirical quantiles at the jth horizon.
Q_j gives the exact quantiles at the jth horizon.

D-WL2(H,R) is a test statistic that combines multiple horizons, potentially each with separate weights, using discrete ranges. For different horizons the set H is changed. Discrete versions of Cramer-von Mise measures have been developed, but mostly for discrete distributions [Choulakian *et al.* (1994), Steele *et al.* (2005)].

We calculate critical values numerically as described above. This is a limited problem because we always test against the uniform distribution. The discrete form is so that we test more intensively where differences are more important, and less so elsewhere. This complements the weight choices and is driven by the same observations.

11.2.5.3 *Multiple tests for single decision*

We want to decide whether an RFE is acceptable at a given confidence level. Our decision will be based on several tests, typically tests on whether out-of-sample predictions out to different horizons are good, thus we must allow for multiple tests in constructing confidence levels. The most well-known correction is Bonferroni, and we use a uniformly more powerful variant [Holm (1979)]. This works as follows:

- k null hypotheses: RFE is correct with respect to test k;
- Order unadjusted p values: $p_{O(1)}, p_{O(2)}, p_{O(3)}, \ldots, p_{O(k)}$ (small to big);
- Compare with $\alpha/k, \alpha/(k-1), \alpha/(k-2), \ldots, \alpha$;
- Sequentially test hypotheses until the first accept (i.e. null hypothesis not rejected), then accept all subsequent hypotheses.

11.2.6 Example results for WTI oil

To show the methodology in action, we pick WTI oil with a 3Y portfolio horizon. In setting up the backtesting procedure there are first some subjective steps. How long a calibration period? How far back to backtest? Figure 11.12 shows several views of spot (front-month) oil prices in the US from 1950–2011, as typical data discovery views. There are apparent structural breaks in 1973 and 1985 on all plots, which correspond to the start and end of OPEC's most influential period. Thus we may subjectively choose to use data from 1985–present.

We have chosen a 3Y portfolio horizon. Predicting a forward curve using every point on the curve is not necessary for accuracy since the curve points do not behave independently. There are two main data reduction approaches: 1) principal component analysis (PCA);

2) parameterized curve forms (forward curve or short-rate). We will assume that PCA has been used, and that it is sufficient to model only two points on the forward curve. This is equivalent to the statement that the first two PCA components capture all the significant variance, and that the components are a parallel shift and a tilt.

Since the maximum maturity of the portfolio is 3 years, and the forward curve is as described above, we choose to model the spot and 2Y6M tenor points. Although the 2Y6M tenor is not, itself, needed after 6 months of prediction, it is needed to define the long end of the forward curve. We could use a set of tenors, but this is a parsimonious approach. For each tenor we use the prediction horizons in Table 11.1 to test:

We pick a step size of 3M, thus we have one datum in each season, just in case seasonality is significant (although it does not appear to be in Figure 11.12). As mentioned, we do not want to test in isolation: first test horizon 1Y; then 1Y+2Y; then 1Y+2Y+3Y combined. Multiple test corrections are important, of course.

Assuming that we choose the 1% confidence level, we cannot reject the hypothesis that both Spot and the 30M Tenor points are described by Geometric Brownian Motion (GBM). The confidence level refers to how often we would expect to see what we observed: 1% means that we would expect to observe what we saw 99 times in 100.

Table 11.1   Prediction horizons for tenors

Tenor	Predictions		
Spot	1Y	2Y	3Y
2Y6M Tenor	1Y	2Y	3Y

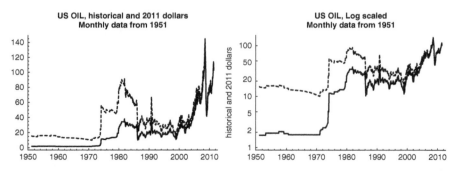

Figure 11.12   Spot (front-month) oil prices in the US, 1951–2011. LHS: Oil prices in historical (continuous line) and in 2011 dollars (dashed line). RHS: Same prices on log scale.

If we had picked the 5% confidence level the GBM hypothesis for the 30M Tenor point would have been rejected. The section on the Splitting Approach covers this situation, but first we mention some diagnostics.

11.2.7 Diagnostics

Whether or not an RFE model passes, it is important to understand why it does, or does not, pass at the desired confidence level.

- Overlapping data is not magic, it is useful but does create a longer data series. This means that whatever we do, for longer horizons tests will have lower discrimination than for shorter horizons, simply because there is less data.
- Remember that we are only testing against a uniform distribution when the samples are independent. This is not the case with overlapping data. The overlaps create correlation between samples, and this changes the test distribution results away from uniform. This is why we create critical values from simulation (using the same parameters as the calibration, or at least testing that the critical values are stable for reasonable ranges of parameter values).
- Figure 11.13 shows the four typical cases of mismatch between empirical distributions and ideal distribution (uniform). At first order, if the volatility is wrong then the effect will be symmetric, whereas if the drift is wrong then we expect an asymmetric effect. If there are regime changes within the testing period then combinations of these effects will be seen.
- More complex models can be harder to diagnose. However, typical simplifications, e.g. changing mean-reversion parameters less often in Hull–White, or Schwartz–Smith type models can facilitate.
- Jumps are ambiguous in backtesting because the horizons used are typically such that these details can be equally well matched with diffusions. However, for combined pricing-and-CVA-and-exposure systems it will be advantageous to keep them in backtesting because they are needed in pricing.

11.2.8 Splitting approach

Regulators require RFE equations to pass backtesting against written statements of the test criteria [BCBS-189 (2011), BCBS-185 (2010)]. It is always possible, as in the example in Section 11.2.6, that an RFE will fail set criteria. It is further possible that there is a deadline by which

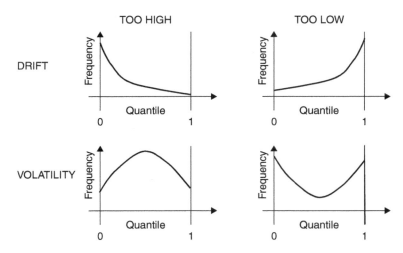

Figure 11.13 Diagnostic signatures of first-order mismatches between calibration and empirical (historical, out-of-sample) observations for an example simple GBM-type model. The ideal outcome, when using independent samples, is a horizontal line (uniform distribution). An ideal outcome means that the calibration predicts the future history exactly in a statistical sense (i.e. gives the same distribution).

RFE must be in place or else the regulator will enact consequences. Typical consequences include capital penalties until the situation is resolved, or moving to a different calculation framework (e.g. Standard Rules) which may be expensive in terms of capital. Thus it is important to have a (potentially more) capital-efficient extension of the RFE development/backtesting framework presented above for RFE models that fail backtesting.

The Splitting Approach introduced here deals with the case where there is one, or several, candidate RFEs that did not pass backtesting and there is a decision to extend these via splitting rather than consider new RFE models. This type of decision is typically driven by deadlines. The previous sections considered what we will call *accurate* RFE; here we develop *conservative* RFE. Conservative means that they will not underestimate exposure.

The idea of the Splitting Approach is that risk factors are split into pairs, where one member of the pair is (now) potentially biased high, and the other member of the pair is (potentially) biased low. We say potentially because it may be that only one member of the pair will need to be biased in order for the RFE-pair to pass the new backtesting. The new backtesting tests that each member of the RFE-pair is flat or

biased in its direction. That is, we require first order stochastic dominance with respect to the test distribution (since we deal with quantiles
this is still the uniform distribution). First-order stochastic dominance
means, in terms of cumulative distributions $F(x)$, $G(x)$:

$$F(x) \leq G(x) \quad \forall x, \tag{11.5}$$

i.e. F dominates G (this is the correct way around). We modify our
D-WL2 test for this as follows, i.e. insisting on a form of expected
dominance.

Statistic:

$$\text{SDD-WL2}(H,R) := \sum_{j \in H} \sum_{i \in R} \left(\max\left(0, Q_{n,i}(Q_i^{-1}(\Theta(i))) - \Theta(i)\right)\right)^2$$

$$\times w_i(\Theta(i)) \times \theta(i). \tag{11.6}$$

Note that this now considers the differences floored at zero because
we want to show that the statistic is no bigger than when the RFE is
accurate. Effectively, we are showing that the statistic is "zero" in a
well-defined sense captured by SDD-WL2. A statistic that accepts the
null hypothesis at a given significance level indicates that $Q_n \leq Q$, i.e.
Q_n dominates Q, according to the definition in Equation 11.6. This definition weights the most important areas for exposure highest, rather
than Equation 11.5 which is a simple $\leq$ on every point. The square on
the max() is to have some comparability with the D-WL2 metric, i.e.
to remain within the L_2 metric framework.

We illustrate the Splitting Approach with a series of examples shown
in Table 11.2. Consider a single fixed payment. If this is to be received
then the exposure is increased as the yield curve (for discounting)
decreases (thus increasing the discount factor). If the payment is to
be made then exposure will be increased as the yield curve increases
(thus decreasing the discount factor). No change in the volatility of the
yield curve would be able to create the necessary asymmetric effect.
Compound instruments are broken down into components and each
component is treated separately. For example, the two legs of a swap
will generally each use different members of each RFE pair (at least for
discounting).

The Splitting Approach cannot handle every trade structure. For
example, consider a windowed knock-in knock-out option, with
sequential windows at the same level. Given that the Splitting
Approach would want to use different volatilities for each window, it is

Table 11.2 Application of the Splitting Approach to different trade types. Note that we distinguish the yield curve (for discounting) and the libor curve (for coupons). We also distinguish the volatility of the underlying RFE from the market-implied volatility used for option pricing since RFE equations are simulated in the historical measure whilst options are priced in the risk-neutral measure. Each leg of a compound structure (e.g. a swap) is treated separately.

Instrument	Curves	Conservative direction vs Payment direction
single fixed payment	yield	opposite
single floating payment	yield	opposite
	LIBOR	same
call option	yield	opposite
	volatility	same
knock-out call	yield	opposite
	σ-underlying	opposite
	σ-market-implied	same

difficult to assess the effect of the earlier volatility biased in one direction on the later volatility biased in the other direction, and hence on the overall effect. Thus, sufficiently structured trades are beyond simple application of the Splitting Approach. However, the methodology is applicable to the majority of vanilla and mildly-structured trades such as those in Table 11.2.

11.3 Short rates, market-implied calibration, historical backtesting

Staying with the commodity example, we choose the no-arbitrage reformulation of [Schwartz and Smith (2000)]'s two-factor mode by [Brigo *et al.* (2008) Brigo, Chourdakis and Bakkar]. The short-rate equivalent in commodities is the spot price $S(t)$ given in the risk-neutral measure by:

$$\log(S(t)) = x(t) + L(t) + \varphi(t)$$
$$dx(t) = -k_x x(t)dt + \phi_x dW_x$$
$$dL(t) = \mu_L dt + \sigma_L dW_L$$
$$dW_x dW_L = \rho dt,$$

where $\varphi(t)$ is a deterministic shift to exactly match the observed futures prices. Since we are dealing with WTI oil, these will generally be monthly contracts. L is the long-term trend, assumed exponential (like a bank account), and $x(t)$ is a mean-reverting component around it. This is a very tractable model.

We can apply our backtesting approach exactly as for the tenor-point situation. That is, the model predicts distributions of future values of tenor points (forward prices, assuming deterministic interest rates) and we can test these predictions. In fact we are in the same situation as before with this model because the predicted Forward rate distributions are log-normal. Thus we can compare observed future forward rates at different tenors with their predicted values given the calibration at the earlier date. Note that the future predicted values will use the *future* φ, not the starting one.

Provided a short-rate model has analytic expressions for expected values and for vanilla options, the backtesting method described above is simple to apply.

Bibliography

Ametrano, F. and Bianchetti, M. (2010). Bootstrapping the Illiquidity: Multiple Yield Curves Construction for Market Coherent Forward Rates Estimation, *MODELING INTEREST RATES, Fabio Mercurio, ed., Risk Books, Incisive Media.*

Angelidis, T. and Degiannakis, S. (2007). Backtesting VaR Models: A Two-Stage Procedure, *The Journal of Risk Model Validation* 1(2).

Bai, J. and Collin-Dufresne, P. (2011). The CDS-Bond Basis during the Financial Crisis of 2007–2009, *SSRN eLibrary*, doi:10.2139/ssrn.1785756.

BCBS-171 (2010). Sound practices for backtesting counterparty credit risk models – consultative document, *Basel Committee for Bank Supervision.*

BCBS-185 (2010). Sound practices for backtesting counterparty credit risk models, *Basel Committee for Bank Supervision.*

BCBS-189 (2011). Basel III: A global regulatory framework for more resilient banks and banking systems, *Basel Committee for Bank Supervision.*

BCBS-209 (2011). Basel III counterparty credit risk – Frequently asked questions, *Basel Committee for Bank Supervision.*

BCBS-214 (2011). Application of own credit risk adjustments to derivatives – consultative document, *Basel Committee for Bank Supervision.*

Berkowitz, J. (2001). Testing Density Forecasts, with Applications to Risk Management, *Journal of Business and Economic Statistics* 19.

Bianchetti, M. (2010). Two Curves, One Price, *Risk Magazine* **August.**

Brealey, R., Myers, S. and Allen, F. (2010). *Principles of Corporate Finance* (McGraw Hill, London).

Brigo, D. (2011). Counterparty Risk FAQ: Credit VaR, PFE, CVA, DVA, Closeout, Netting, Collateral, Re-Hypothecation, WWR, Basel, Funding, CCDS and Margin Lending, *SSRN eLibrary.*

Brigo, D., Chourdakis, K. and Bakkar, I. (2008). Counterparty risk valuation for energy-commodities swaps, *Fitch Solutions.*

Brigo, D. and Masetti, M. (2006). Risk-neutral pricing of counterparty risk, in M. Pykhtin, ed., *Counter-Party Credit Risk Modelling: Risk Management, Pricing and Regulation* (Risk Books, London).

Brigo, D. and Mercurio, F. (2006). *Interest Rate Models: Theory and Practice, 2nd Edition* (Springer, London).

Brigo, D. and Morini, M. (2010). Dangers of Bilateral Counterparty Risk: The Fundamental Impact of Closeout Conventions, *SSRN.*

Brigo, D., Pallavicini, A. and Papatheodorou, V. (2009). Bilateral Counterparty Risk Valuation for Interest-Rate Products: Impact of Volatilities and Correlations, *SSRN eLibrary.*

Burgard, C. and Kjaer, M. (2011a). In the Balance, *Risk Magazine* **November.**

Burgard, C. and Kjaer, M. (2011b). PDE Representations of Options with Bilateral Counterparty Risk and Funding Costs, *Journal of Credit Risk* 7 (3).

Cantor, R., Hamilton, D. and Ou, S. (2002). Default and Recovery Rates of Corporate Bond Issuers, *Moody's Investors Services* **February.**

Carver, L. (2011). Quants call for ISDA to clarify close-out values, *Risk Magazine* **December**.

Chen, C., Lohlbeck, M. and Warfield, T. (2008). Goodwill Valuation Effects of the Initial Adoption of SFAS 142, *Advances in Accounting* **24**, pp. 72–81.

Choudhry, M. (2006). *The Credit Default Swap Basis* (Bloomberg Press, New York).

Choulakian, V., Lockhart, R. and Stephens, M. (1994). Cramér-von Mises Statistics for Discrete Distributions, *Canadian Journal of Statistics* **22 (1)**, pp. 125–137.

Colletaz, G., Hurlin, C. and Perignon, C. (2011). The Risk Map: A New Tool for Backtesting Value-at-Risk Models, *SSRN eLibrary*.

Cont, R. and Tankov, P. (2003). *Financial Modelling with Jump Processes* (Chapman and Hall, London).

Ech-Chatbi, C. (2008). CDS and CDO Pricing with Stochastic Recovery, *SSRN eLibrary*.

Elizalde, A. (2009). *Bond-CDS Basis Handbook* (J.P. Morgan Credit Derivatives Research, J.P. Morgan Securities Ltd).

FASB (2009). *Statement of Financial Accounting Standards No. 133*.

FASB (2010). *Statement of Financial Accounting Standards No. 157 Fair Value Measurements* (FASB, New York).

FINMA-TBTF (2011). Addressing Too Big To FailÓ, The Swiss SIFI Policy.

Fries, C. (2010). Discounting Revisited: Valuation Under Funding, Counterparty Risk and Collateralization, *SSRN eLibrary*.

Fries, C. (2011). Funded Replication: Valuing with Stochastic Funding, *SSRN eLibrary*.

Fujii, M., Shimada, Y. and Takahashi, A. (2010). A Note on Construction of Multiple Swap Curves with and without Collateral, *SSRN eLibrary*.

Gallagher, D. and O'Keeffe, F. (2009). Yield Curve Construction, Eudaemon Consulting Working Paper.

Hamerle, A. and Plank, K. (2009). A Note on the Berkowitz Test with Discrete Distributions, *The Journal of Risk Model Validation* **3 (2)**.

Henrard, M. (2009). The Irony in the Derivatives Discounting Part II: The Crisis, *SSRN eLibrary*.

Höcht, S. and Zagst, R. (2009). Pricing Credit Derivatives under Stochastic Recovery in a Hybrid Model, *Applied Stochastic Models in Business and Industry*.

Holm, S. (1979). A Simple Sequentially Rejective Multiple Test Procedure, *Scandinavian Journal of Statistics* **6 (2)**, pp. 65–70.

Hull, J. (2009). *Options, Futures and Other Derivatives, 7th Edition* (Prentice Hall, New Jersey).

Hull, J., Predescu, M. and White, A. (2004). The Relationship between Credit Default Swap Spreads, Bond Yields, and Credit Rating Announcements, *Journal of Banking and Finance* **28**, pp. 2789–2811.

Hull, J. and White, A. (2004). Valuation of a CDO and and nth to Default CDO Without Monte Carlo Simulation, *Journal of Derivatives* **12 (2)**.

IASB (2010). International Accounting Standard 39 Financial Instruments: Recognition and Measurement.

ISDA (2009). ISDA Close-out Amount Protocol, http://www.isda.org/ isdacloseoutamtprot/isdacloseoutamtprot.html.

Kenyon, C. (2008). Inflation is Normal, *Risk Magazine* **July**.

Kenyon, C. (2010a). Completing CVA and Liquidity: Firm-Level Positions and Collateralized Trades, *SSRN eLibrary*.

Kenyon, C. (2010b). Post-shock Short-rate Pricing. *Risk Magazine* **November**.

Kenyon, C. and Werner, R. (2011). Reassessing recovery rates – floating recoveries, in proceedings: International Conference on Operations Research, Zurich.

Kijima, M., Tanaka, K. and Wong, T. (2009). A Multi-quality Model of Interest Rates, *Quantitative Finance* **9**(2), pp. 133–145.

Lando, D. (2004). *Credit Risk Modeling* (Princeton University Press, Princeton).

Li, Y. (2009). A Dynamic Correlation Modelling Framework with Consistent Stochastic Recovery, *SSRN eLibrary*.

Mercurio, F. (2009). Interest Rates and The Credit Crunch: New Formulas and Market Models, *Bloomberg Portfolio Research Paper No. 2010-01-FRONTIERS*.

Mercurio, F. (2010). A LIBOR Market Model with Stochastic Basis, *SSRN eLibrary*.

Miller, M. (1988). The Modigliani-Miller Propositions after Thirty Years, *The Journal of Economic Perspectives* **2**, pp. 99–120.

Morini, M. and Prampolini, A. (2011). Risky Funding: A Unified Framework for Counterparty and Liquidity Charges, *Risk Magazine* **March**.

Moyer, L. and Burne, K. (2011). Goldman Sachs Hedges Its Way to Less Volatile Earnings, *WSJ* **October 18**.

Oksendal, B. (2002). *Stochastic Differential Equations: An Introduction with Applications* (Springer, London).

Orhan, M. and Köksal, B. (2012). A Comparison of GARCH Models for VAR Estimation, *Expert Systems with Applications* **3**, pp. 3582–3592.

Pallavicini, A., Perini, D. and Brigo, D. (2011). Funding Valuation Adjustment: A Consistent Framework including CVA, DVA, Collateral, Netting Rules and Re-hypothecation, *SSRN eLibrary*.

Pallavicini, A. and Tarenghi, M. (2010). Interest-Rate Modeling with Multiple Yield Curves, *SSRN eLibrary*.

Paolella, M. and Steude, S. (2008). Risk prediction: A DWARF-like Approach, *The Journal of Risk Model Validation* **2**(1).

Pengelly, M. (2010). Basel CVA Changes Criticised, *Risk Magazine* **August**.

Pengelly, M. (2011). Revised CVA Capital Charge Continues to Worry Dealers, *Risk Magazine* **February**.

Piterbarg, V. V. (2010). Funding beyond Discounting: Collateral Agreements and Derivatives Pricing. *Risk Magazine* **February**, pp. 97–102.

Pykhtin, M. (2011). Counterparty Risk Capital and CVA, *Risk Magazine* **August**.

Ramanna, K. and Watts, R. L. (2010). Evidence on the Use of Unverifiable Estimates in Required Goodwill Impairment, *Harvard Business School Accounting & Management Unit Working Paper No. 09-106*.

Rebonato, R., Sherring, M. and Barnes, R. (2010). CVA and the Equivalent Bond, *Risk Magazine* **September**.

Schönbucher (2005). *Credit Derivatives Pricing Models: Models Pricing and Implementation* (Wiley, London).

Schubert, D. (2011). *The Financial Economics of Hedge Accounting of Interest Rate Risk according to IAS 39.*

Schwartz, E. and Smith, J. (2000). Short-Term Variations and Long-Term Dynamics in Commodity Prices, *Management Science* **46**, pp. 893–911.

Shreve, S. (2004). *Stochastic Calculus for Finance II* (Springer, London).

Steele, M., Chaseling, J. and Cameron, H. (2005). Simulated power of the discrete Cramér-von Mises goodness-of-fit tests. *MODSIM*, pp. 1300–1305.

Tuckman, B. and Hom, J.-B. (2003). Consistent Pricing of FX Forwards, Cross-Currency Basis Swaps and Interest Rate Swaps in Several Currencies, Lehman Brothers Report.

Werpachowski, R. (2009). Stochastic Recovery Model Applicable to First-to-Default Basket Pricing, *SSRN eLibrary*.

Whittall, C. (2010). The Price is Wrong, *Risk Magazine*.

Zhou, R. (2008). Bond Implied CDS Spread and CDS-Bond Basis, *SSRN eLibrary*.

Index